Yale Concilium on International and Area Studies

Yale
Russian and East European
Publications

Yale Russian and East European Publications

Yale
Russian and East European
Publications

THE TRAGEDY OF CENTRAL EUROPE

The Tragedy of Central Europe:

Nazi and Soviet Conquest and Aftermath

Revised Edition
With a New Epilogue

BY STEPHEN BORSODY

YALE CONCILIUM ON INTERNATIONAL
AND AREA STUDIES
New Haven
1980

YALE RUSSIAN AND EAST EUROPEAN PUBLICATIONS, NO. 2

The Tragedy of Central Europe originally appeared under the title *The Triumph of Tyranny, The Nazi and Soviet Conquest of Central Europe.*

First published by Jonathan Cape, London, and by the Macmillan Company, New York, 1960.

Published by Collier Books, New York, 1962.

The drawings by Saul Steinberg, cover and frontispiece, are reproduced with the artist's permission.

Distributed by Slavica Publishers, Inc.
P.O. Box 14388, Columbus, Ohio 43214

Library of Congress Card Catalog Number: 80-51032
ISBN: 0-936586-01-X
Typography by Brevis Press
Printed in the United States of America by McNaughton & Gunn, Inc.

In memory of

OSCAR JÁSZI

(1875–1957)

Pioneer of Federalism
in the Age of Nationalism

Contents

Maps of Central Europe

Preface to the New Edition

Soviet territorial conquest in the Second World War radically changed the structure of Europe. Central Europe exists no more; it has been incorporated into Communist Eastern Europe under Soviet hegemony. Europe now consists of two parts only, East and West — a fact sealed by the presence of Russian troops in the heart of Europe. Yet some people still insist on distinguishing between Eastern and Central Europe.[1] They disagree not merely over designations but over interpretations as well. A Communist historian in Hungary today may treat Central Europe as a historically preordained part of Soviet Eastern Europe.[2] But most historians in the West — as well as those in the East who do not follow the Communist party line — would think of such an interpretation as a fantasy. Fact or fantasy, Europe without a Central Europe is a tragedy.

This book is about Central Europe. It is about the conquest of Central Europe by Nazi Germany and by Soviet Russia. It is about the tragedies that led to Europe's East-West division. Originally entitled "The Triumph of Tyranny," it was written during the cold war, well before American revisionist historiography popularized the idea that Soviet territorial and political conquests in Europe were legitimate acts of self-defense in the interest of Russian national security. Condemning the follies of anti-communism of the cold war era should not soften criticism of Soviet policies. I do condemn the irrational anti-communism of the cold war, yet my interpretation of what happened before, during, and after the Second World War differs radically from that of the revisionists.

The main barrier that separates my thinking from that of the revisionists is not their pro-Soviet or my anti-Soviet stance. What separates us is my concern with the freedom of the smaller nations living in the Middle Zone between Germany and Russia. Such concerns are conspicuously absent from the works of the revisionists. Their primary interest is the rivalry among the Great Powers, above all the Soviet-American conflict. This is why, it seems to me, they can so lightly gloss over the subjugation of tens of millions of Europeans and say, as one of the American founders of the revisionist school, D. F. Fleming, did: "Soviet control of East Europe was the price we paid for the years of appeasement of Hitler, and it was not a high price."[3] To Europeans who are actually paying "the price," this sounds exactly like the Western indifference of the 1930s, when Neville Chamberlain, to justify his appeasement policy of Hitler, spoke of "far-away" countries and peoples in Central Europe "of whom we know nothing."[4]

This book has been out of print for nearly a decade. The new edition has *two* epilogues, which is rather unusual. But without disrupting the original design of the book — covering as it did the aftermath of Soviet conquest in an epilogue form — the unusual ending with two epilogues in this updated edition seemed to me unavoidable. Epilogue One, taken over from the original edition, carries the reader through the cold war in the fifties. Epilogue Two, written for the new edition, covers the transition from cold war to détente in the sixties and seventies. Both epilogues are self-contained essays, dealing with two different periods. The rest of the text, apart from a few revisions meant as improvements, is identical with that of the Collier Books edition of 1962. Unchanged also is my desire to serve the cause of reconciliation and peace in Central Europe.

The tragedy I am writing about is not a historical abstraction or a political metaphor. It is reality, past and present, crowded with human suffering, oppression, humiliation, anguish, torture and death. There have been improvements in people's lives in most countries of Eastern Europe since I wrote "The Triumph of Tyranny." Conditions have improved notably in the wake of East-West détente. But despite détente, there have been new tragedies — and new triumphs of tyranny. The most crippling blow was inflicted by the Soviet invasion of 1968 on the people of Czechoslovakia; the wounds of that traumatic experience are still festering. There is no end either to the trauma under which most of the so-called "minority" Hungarians (about one-quarter of all the Hungarians) are living in the countries around Hungary, deprived of their fundamental human right to national equality. For that matter, the tragedy is far from over for any of the peoples living in the Soviet orbit of power. It will not be over until an independent Central Europe is reborn with equal rights for all people, until a just order rises with equal freedom for all nations.

The forces that carried Central Europe to its downfall are my leading themes. Their poignant characteristics are revealed visually in the inimitable Steinberg drawings on the frontispiece and the cover. To me, they symbolize perfectly the causes of the Middle Zone's misfortunes: militarism and imperialism, feeding on narrow-minded nationalism; political trickery and diplomatic cunning, sowing the seeds of disaster; obscurantism and clericalism — not just of the old priestly variety but also of the newer secular kind, perfected by the party bureaucracies of the totalitarian police state. I am grateful to Saul Steinberg for allowing me to reproduce these symbolic figures from a drawing he gave to me many years ago as a personal commentary on the history of Central and Eastern Europe.

In releasing this new edition, it gives me great pleasure to express my heartfelt thanks to our American-born daughter Katherine for her devoted assistance as my thoughtful reader and alert critic. I dedicate this edition to her generation with the wish that their concern for "far-away" peoples may hasten the triumph of democracy over tyranny.

Wellfleet, Massachusetts S.B.
September 1980

From the Preface to the First Edition

The "Age of Tyranny" in the history of the Greek city-states was an era of transition from monarchy — and aristocratic oligarchy — to democracy. The Communist tyranny of the twentieth century, in the history of the Central and Eastern European states, may well prove to be a similar era of transition from monarchy — and capitalistic as well as aristocratic oligarchy — to socialist democracy.

Such an analogy, like every parallel in history, has its obvious limitations. And tyranny, whatever its historical role in an era of transition, is an ugly phenomenon. Its oppressive character is not mitigated by the course of events which ushers it in. "Where there's tyranny, there's tyranny" — to quote the famous poem of the Hungarian poet Gyula Illyés, "A Sentence on Tyranny," written in 1950 under the Stalinist rule of terror. Moreover, to view Communist tyranny exclusively as a revolt against aristocratic privilege and capitalist exploitation would be to miss the most important clue to Central Europe's tragedy. For while social-economic factors were significant in the great upheavals that ultimately led to Communist tyranny in Central Europe, an even more significant factor was imperialistic nationalism. In fact, nationalist conflicts played a far greater role in carrying Central Europe down the road to modern tyranny — first under the Nazis, then under the Communists — than economic oppression or social revolt.[1]

By speaking of both Nazi Germany and Soviet Russia as tyrannies I do not wish to obscure the sharp ideological difference between nazism (a perverted nationalist negation of universal human values) and communism (a lofty ideal in man's long quest for Utopia); but in practice the two tyrannies are similar, in that both rely on brute force, and the Russian nationalist overtone in Soviet communism makes the parallel between the Soviet and Nazi conquest of Central Europe particularly meaningful.

The First World War awakened Western interest in the problems of smaller nations in Central Europe. But the understanding of these problems, almost a *terra incognita* until then, has ever since been hindered by prejudice and propaganda. It was erroneously presumed, above all, that the Western pattern of nation-state was a suitable form of political organization to replace the Habsburg Empire in the Danube Valley. Prejudice against the Empire (well deserved, incidentally, by Habsburg blunders) obscured the fact that the Habsburg realm was not merely a "prison of nations" (as nationalist propaganda quite justifiably called it) but also a unique form of political organism which potentially offered the best possible safeguard of freedom for the smaller nations of Central Europe.

Without, I hope, becoming doctrinaire, I have stressed the disastrous effects of nationalism on the course of Central European history from the Habsburgs to the Soviet Russians. More specifically, I have tried to show the extent to which nation-state policy as such was the underlying cause of the Central European catastrophe. This story is interwoven with the policy of the Great Powers toward the smaller nations of Central and Eastern Europe. Soviet Russia and Nazi Germany, of course, figure prominently here; but so do the Western nations who as free peoples survived the cataclysm of the two world wars of the twentieth century. Moreover, the triumph of tyranny in Central Europe should be a warning to the nations of the free West that they too court disaster by continuing to adhere to the obsolete notions of national sovereignty. And the tragic story of Central Europe also has a lesson to teach the former colonial peoples the world over who are now entering the age of nationalism.

Without extolling federalism as a panacea for all the ills of modern mankind, I believe it is the only conceivable foundation upon which peace can be built in regions, such as Central Europe, where the peoples have paid so dearly for the reckless nationalist policies of their governments. I am using "federalism" as a term opposite to "nationalism." As I understand it, federalism is a truly democratic state of mind, ready to respect the equal freedoms of the individual as well as the equal rights of nations within a broader international community, as opposed to egotistic nationalism, which can be both very demanding of its own "rights" and very forgetful of fairness toward others; and degenerate nationalism, as a destroyer of liberty, is the main theme of this book.[2]

To be a critic of nationalism in the age of nationalism is an unpopular undertaking. I have only to remember my own past state of mind to understand the reactions to this book of any nationalist reader. But to those who may feel hurt, I should like to tender my apologies by saying that I too had to divest myself of strong national biases in order to see events as they are presented in the following pages. I do not, of course, view nationalism merely as an evil force carrying Central Europe down the road to tyranny. Nationalism has been, and still is, an inspiring force in Central and Eastern Europe's struggle for freedom and independence. But, notwithstanding its merits as a source of inspiration in the battles against oppression, nationalism — with its self-centeredness, intolerance, aggressiveness — must be regarded in the long run as an impediment to international peace and social progress.

Every conclusion I have come to with reference to the causes of the tragedy of Central Europe has only served to bring into fuller relief the disastrous consequences of rivalries among the Danubian nations. In my analysis I have paid particular attention to Czechoslovakia and Hungary, both of which have been my homeland. My familiarity with them, however, was not the main reason for devoting particular attention to them. I have done so because the Czechs and the Hungarians played a leading part on opposing sides both at the dissolution of the Austrian Empire and in the era of nation-states following the First World War.

As for terminology, I ought to state that I am using "Middle Zone" as a collective term which refers to the smaller nations of Central and Eastern Europe that are exposed to the pressure of Germany and Russia, the two Great Powers flanking them. This Middle Zone is also flanked, on the south, by Italy — but Italy's impact on the course of Middle Zone history has been only of secondary importance. I borrowed the term from the writings of F. A. Voigt, former editor of the British review *Nineteenth Century and After*. It is the best single expression available, it seems to me, for describing the critical geographical position of the European nations caught in the crossfire of twentieth-century German and Russian imperialism. I am making use of the phrase to stress this critical position and nothing else. Nor do I wish to exclude other terms, such as the now familiar "Eastern Europe," referring to the countries which came under Communist domination after the Second World War, or the time-honored "Central Europe," "Danube Valley," "Southeastern Europe" and "Balkans," which still are meaningful expressions, in both the geographical and the political sense.

On the other hand, I have not availed myself of the term "East-Central

Europe," now widely used by scholars with reference to all the Communist lands in Europe minus Russia — mainly because the two countries upon which this book is focused, Czechoslovakia and Hungary, do not come readily under that description. They belonged, according to the phraseology used before the Second World War, to "Central Europe," and I prefer to keep them there. The West has surrendered so much of Central Europe to the East: why surrender even long-established phraseology? I hope the various phrases will make sense in the context in which they are employed, and will appear neither inconsistent nor confusing to the reader.

The dedication to the memory of Oscar Jászi is in token of my deep gratitude for the inspiration and encouragement he gave me during the last decade of his life. It was my privilege to be his close friend. His federalist teachings have had a great influence on my thinking and his ideas of a Danubian federation have served me as a guiding principle in writing this book.

I am particularly obliged to Dr. Beatrice Shepherd Blane of the History Department at Hunter College, New York [now Mrs. Gordon Silber of Williamsville, New York], for reading the completed manuscript with the care and devotion one would normally give only to one's own work.

The four maps, excellently executed by Mr. D. Baker, graphically show the convulsions which have shaken Central Europe in the twentieth century.

This book was born out of the tempests of recent Central European history. Writing the history of times like these can be almost as trying as life itself in such times. In trials of both sorts my wife has been my faithful companion. I owe her more gratitude than words can tell.

To all those named, as well as to those not named, who in whatever way have assisted me I wish to express my grateful appreciation. I alone, of course, bear responsibility for the views expressed.

Wellfleet, Massachusetts S.B.
September 1, 1959

Introduction: From the Habsburgs to the Soviet Russians

With Austria-Hungary's defeat in the First World War, in the autumn of 1918, the Habsburg Empire fell apart. The force that destroyed the Empire was primarily the nationalism of its peoples. The blunders of the Habsburgs, and of the ruling classes upon whom they relied, precipitated the catastrophe. Defeat in the First World War carried out history's death sentence against the Empire. The great empire of fifty-three million people was broken up into its ethnic components. Parts of the Empire's territory were made into Austria, Hungary and Czechoslovakia, while other parts were incorporated into Poland, Romania, Yugoslavia and Italy.

Although the break-up of the Habsburg state was seen by some as a tragedy, others saw it as a triumph. While the victims and critics of the peace settlement following the First World War spoke disparagingly of Central Europe's "Balkanization," the victorious nation-states which succeeded the Habsburg Empire believed truth and justice had prevailed. There is no doubt that the Habsburgs had failed to create a just order for the peoples of their empire. The Compromise of 1867 had transformed the Empire into an Austro-Hungarian Dual Monarchy, and the political and social structure of the Monarchy was such as to frustrate the various peoples' aspirations for democratic freedoms and to block evolution toward national equality and federalization. This was especially the case in the Hungarian half of the Monarchy, where the Hungarians insisted on transforming, by excessive means of assimilation, their multinational kingdom into a unitary Hungarian nation-state. But the Paris peace settlement after the First World War, though it was supposed to cure the evils and injustices of the past, was itself neither good nor just.

The very program of the nation-state, idolized by the oppressed nationalities who owed their triumph over the Habsburg Empire to the victory of the Western Powers over Germany, was of doubtful value as a foundation for lasting peace in the Danube Valley. This program paid no heed to warnings that only a federal union could safeguard the peace and security of the smaller nations in Central Europe, lodged as they were between a menace from the west by the Germans and from the east by the Russians. Furthermore, the territorial settlement resulting from the partition of the Habsburg Empire grossly violated the very principle of the ethnic nation-state by virtue of which the new order had been created. For by a double standard in the application of this principle the Paris Peace Conference of 1919 gave extensive advantages to the victors and inflicted grave injustices on the vanquished.

The ethnic composition of the post-war nation-states in the Danube Valley duly reflected the distinctions which the Peace Conference made between the rights of the victors and those of the vanquished. The nation-states created or enlarged by the victors included territories which they could claim only partly, or not at all, by virtue of the ethnic principle. Whenever the ethnic principle was insufficient to justify their demands, they claimed other titles, such as economic and military reasons, or ancient historical rights. Thus the German-inhabited frontier lands of historic Bohemia were awarded to Czechoslovakia, multinational Transylvania to Romania, frontier strips of Hungarian ethnic territory to Czechoslovakia, Romania and Yugoslavia; and defeated Austria, Hungary and Bulgaria were cut down in territory, thus losing populations many of whom were ethnically their own people. As a result, Austria, Hungary and Bulgaria (with total populations respectively of 6.5 million, 8 million and 5 million) were ethnically almost homogeneous (respectively 96, 90 and 83 percent), but in Czechoslovakia the three so-called state-making ethnic elements — the Czechs, Slovaks and Ruthenes — together made only 69 percent of the country's total population (13.4 million), the Romanians made only 72 percent of Romania's 16 million, the Serbs, Croats and Slovenes together only 83 percent of Yugoslavia's 11.9 million, and the Poles only 69 percent of resuscitated Poland's 27 million.[1]

The inequities inflicted upon the vanquished seemed merely minor flaws when compared with the freedom and national independence attained by the former oppressed peoples; and the inequity of the post-Habsburg territorial settlement in the Danube Valley seemed particularly negligible, for the triumphal chorus of the three victors, Czechoslovakia, Romania and Yugoslavia, drowned out the protesting voice of one defeated nation, mutilated Hungary. To the Hungarians, however, the consequences of defeat seemed catastrophic. The loss of 71 percent of Hungary's territory and 60 percent of her population included over 3 million ethnic Hungarians (almost one-third of the nation), who were incorporated into Czechoslovakia, Romania and Yugoslavia. This dismemberment of the Hungarian nation by the peacemakers, whose avowed aim it was to unite and free the oppressed nations, was no work of absent-mindedness: rather it was a clear case of a punitive peace. It was the price Hungary paid for her defeat as an ally of Germany, a price which incidentally was relatively greater than that paid by Germany herself. It was also the neighbors' revenge inflicted upon Hungary for her pre-war attempt to transform a multinational historic kingdom into a Hungarian nation-state in which only about half the population was Hungarian.

But the vindictive peace punished not merely Hungary. By ruining Hungary, the geographical center of the Danube Valley, Hungary's neighbors ruined also the prospects of their own peace. Their vindictive policy precipitated the downfall of the Hungarian post-war democratic regime, which was headed by Count Michael Károlyi and which advocated cooperation among the Danubian peoples in the spirit of Professor Oscar Jászi's confederation plans; and the collapse of the Károlyi regime proved in turn disastrous both for Hungary and for all neighbors. A short-lived Communist revolution followed, and then a counterrevolution which under Admiral Nicholas Horthy's regency restored to power the pre-war ruling classes. This regime signed the humiliating Trianon Peace Treaty on June 4, 1920, but did not concede old Hungary's defeat. While extolling historical fraternity among the peoples of the old kingdom, the Horthy regime bent its energies toward restoring Hungarian domination in the Carpathian basin.

Post-war Hungary was an implacable foe of the new order in Central Europe. On the other hand, the chief pillar of the new system was Czechoslovakia. Czechoslovakia served both as a center of alliances concluded under France's leadership for the maintenance of the status quo, and as a center of propaganda on behalf of the new order in Central Europe. The stock of the Czechs, as a democratic nation, stood high in the West. In turn, sympathy for democratic Czechoslovakia strengthened the West's belief that the post-Habsburg settlement in Central Europe was a triumph for democracy, a belief which, unfortunately, has not been borne out by reality.

Czech propaganda had also played a paramount role previously in the crucial period of the new system's creation. It should be noted, however, that the Habsburg system was destroyed primarily by its own shortcomings. The founders of Czechoslovakia, Thomas G. Masaryk and Eduard Beneš, were not as responsible for the destruction of the Habsburg Monarchy as their Austro-Hungarian adversaries charged; indeed their historical role was far greater in convincing the Entente Powers of the viability of the new system. The Czech leaders in exile during the First World War were the chief protagonists of the idea that the nation-states of the liberated Slavic east would serve as a natural counterpoise to Germany. And they also led the campaign against Hungary, denouncing her as an inveterate ally of German imperialism, and advocating her severe punishment.

It was a disaster that Hungary, the *geographical* center of the Danube Valley, did not offer progressive and enlightened leadership; but it was no less a disaster that Czechoslovakia, which became the *real* center of the post-Habsburg settlement in Central Europe, also failed in her role of leadership.

Czechoslovakia was a multinational state. According to the first census, taken in 1921, her ethnic composition was: Czechs, 50.8 percent; Germans, 23.4; Slovaks, 14.7; Hungarians, 5.6; Ruthenes, 3.5; Poles, 0.5 percent. Nationality statistics were unreliable in Central Europe, for as a rule they favored the nations in power conducting the census; but whatever allowance was to be made for the distortion of statistics, one fact stood out clearly: Czechoslovakia's ethnic composition showed a striking resemblance to that of pre-war Hungary. According to the last census, taken in 1910, Hungary's ethnic composition was: Hungarians, 54.5 percent; Romanians, 16.1; Slovaks, 10.7; Germans, 10.4; Ruthenes, 2.5; Serbs, 2.5; Croats, 1.1 percent.

The Hungarian democrats of 1918 had been anxious to transform multinational Hungary into a democratic federation; but their attempt to create this "Eastern Switzerland," in accordance with the plans of Professor Jászi, had failed. No more successful was the program of the Czech democrats, who planned to make Czechoslovakia into "a sort of Switzerland," as Beneš had outlined the future of the new state before the Paris Peace Conference.[2]

Sincere as Beneš's hopes may have been in envisaging Czechoslovakia as "a sort of Switzerland," he was wrong in assuming that Czechoslovakia would be capable of carrying out such a program. In a sense, Czechoslovakia was *too small* for a Central European "Switzerland." In order to build a Central European Federation on the Swiss model a much broader basis would have been needed — the partnership at least of Czechoslovakia, Austria and Hungary. Only a broader combination such as this could have spared Czechoslovakia the insoluble problems of hostile minorities which caused her ruin; only a broader combination such as this could have launched the Danubian nations on the road to federal union. This would have meant of course the partial preservation of the Habsburg Empire — without the Habsburgs — a program which neither Beneš nor anybody else advocated at the Paris Peace Conference. What had been advocated was the creation of national states — the very opposite of a federation of nations. Czechoslovakia herself had in fact been founded as a national state — that is, as a national state of Czechs and Slovaks; and as such she was *too big*.

It was a blessing in disguise that, under the Germanizing influence of the Habsburg rule, the Czechs had lost their feudal nobility. Their good luck, too, had brought more benefits from the industrial revolution to their lands than to any other parts of the Habsburg realm. These two circumstances, coupled with the Hussite tradition of egalitarianism, accounted for the miracle that during the last fifty years or so of old Austria's declining life a young democratic Czech nation was born, full of vitality and energy. But when the Czechs departed from Austria to lead the new Czechoslovakia they carried with them another legacy of the Habsburg past: the virulent nationalism of the Habsburg-dominated peoples. This had been the doom of the Empire, and was to become the doom of the new order of national states in Central Europe.

The nation-state, acclaimed as the fulfilment of President Wilson's celebrated principle of national self-determination, was a doubtful means of safeguarding the peace and security of the small nations wedged between Germany and Russia. In addition, the way in which this program was implemented could only increase the doubtfulness of its value. Its compromises, made for the sake of expediency, failed to solve the national conflicts of the past. Rewards and punishments alike inflated notions of national "rights." Rewards inflated the sense of national justice, and punishments the sense of national injustice. Indeed the new system of nation-states, not unlike the old Habsburg system, carried within itself the seeds of its own destruction. And the nations that hailed their liberation in 1918 from the "tyranny of the Habsburgs" were yet to experience the tyrannies of those who rose to dominate Central Europe largely as the result of the anarchy of national states.

Debates about the liquidation of the Habsburg Empire and the creation of the system of nation-states at one time aroused controversies as heated as the debates of our own days on the Yalta decisions of the Big Three in 1945; and as a matter of fact, the Yalta debates, insofar as they dealt with the Soviet satellites' story, were merely a continuation of a long debate on the state of Central Europe in our stormy twentieth century. The debate began with examinations of the perplexing problems of the Habsburg Empire; it went on, following the collapse of the Empire, with never-ending disputes between the victors and the vanquished of the First World War; after the Munich Conference in 1938 a new series of debates flared up with investigations into the causes of the breakdown of the peace settlement, and then after the Second World War a much longer series followed, with the Yalta conference as the chief subject for argument.

In these debates all sorts of views have been heard, examining the great mistakes of the living and reviving the lingering ghosts of the past. Even the ghosts of the Habsburg past have made their periodic appearance. They appeared, for instance, in the thoughts of Winston Churchill, who, brooding over the unsolved problem and new tragedies of Central Europe, in his meditations on the Second World War, remarked: "This war would never have come unless, under American and modernizing pressure, we had driven the Habsburgs out of Austria and Hungary and the Hohenzollerns out of Germany."[3]

As a result of the Second World War, vast areas once ruled by the Habsburg dynasty fell under the tyranny first of Nazi Germany, and then of Soviet Russia. More experts than at any time before found the dismemberment of the Habsburg Empire to be the principal cause of Central Europe's tragedies, thus acknowledging the failure of the sovereign nation-states of the post-Habsburg era. But the frequent and sometimes wistful remembrance of the Habsburg past included no desire for a Habsburg future. Except for the romantic few who believed in the possibility of Habsburg restoration, these recollections were mainly casual remarks, sometimes nostalgic, sometimes ironic — like the one allegedly made by the late Czech Foreign Minister, Jan Masaryk, in 1946, that "the Czechs had never been so happy as when forming part of the Austro-Hungarian Empire."[4] Actually, most people who remembered the Habsburgs were critical of their rule. Even though appreciation of the advantages which the Habsburg Empire had offered its peoples increased in retrospect, nevertheless censure of Habsburg policy for its grave faults was expressed no less than before. Few people were convinced by the diehard monarchists who on behalf of various vested interests tried to obscure the fatal role that the Habsburgs themselves had played in the dismemberment of their own empire.

Detached students of the Habsburg problem have long concluded that the dismemberment of the Empire was the result of a process of dissolution, precipitated to a large extent by Habsburg blunders.[5] Indeed there is no ground for revising the well-established unfavorable opinion about the Habsburg rule in Central Europe. There is much reason, however, for reconsidering the sympathetic opinions about the sovereign nation-states which succeeded the Habsburgs. For these nation-states have also failed, like the Habsburgs, to create a new stable order of independence in that dangerous Middle Zone of Europe situated between Germany and Russia. They too have failed in their alleged mission as bulwarks of peace and security — notwithstanding the opinions of nationalists who readily lay the blame for Central Europe's tragedy on each other, or on Hitler and Stalin, or on the West's appeasement policy toward Nazi Germany which led to Munich, or on the West's collaboration with Soviet Russia which led to Yalta, but who will not admit that the nation-states purporting to solve Central Europe's problem deserve more than an equal share of the blame.

The old Imperial order before 1914
Petsamo
Murmansk
Archangel
NORWAY
SWEDEN
Christiania
Stockholm
Helsingfors
St. Petersburg
Reval
Baltic Sea
RUSSIAN
EMPIRE
Riga
Moscow
Kovno
DENMARK
GERMAN
EMPIRE
NETH.
BELGIUM
Berlin
Warsaw
Prague
Cracow
FRANCE
R. Danube
AUSTRO-
HUNGARIAN
EMPIRE
Vienna
Budapest
SWITZ-ERLAND
Trieste
Zagreb
RUMANIA
Bucharest
Black Sea
ITALY
Adriatic Sea
Sarajevo
Belgrade
SERBIA
BULGARIA
Sofia
MONTE-NEGRO
ALBANIA
Tirana
Rome
Constantinople
OTTOMAN
EMPIRE
GREECE
Athens
Aegean Sea

Part One: The Tragedy of Nationalism

The Middle Zone
1918–1938
Petsamo
Murmansk
Archangel
NORWAY
SWEDEN
FINLAND
Helsinki
Leningrad
Oslo
Stockholm
Baltic Sea
Tallin
ESTONIA
SOVIET
UNION
Riga
LATVIA
Moscow
DENMARK
LITHUANIA
Kaunas
Danzig
EAST PRUSSIA
Vilna
NETH.
BELGIUM
Berlin
GERMANY
Warsaw
POLAND
Prague
Teschen
CZECHOSLOVAKIA
CARPATHO-RUTHENIA
FRANCE
R. Danube
Vienna
Budapest
N. BUKOVINA
SWITZERLAND
AUSTRIA
HUNGARY
BESSARABIA
TRANSYLVANIA
RUMANIA
Trieste
Belgrade
Bucharest
YUGOSLAVIA
DOBRUDJA
Black Sea
ITALY
Adriatic Sea
BULGARIA
Sofia
Rome
MACEDONIA
Tirana
ALBANIA
Ankara
GREECE
TURKEY
Aegean Sea
Athens

1 The Lost Peace

After the First World War, when the peace treaties were written in Paris, the victorious Western democracies were masters of the European continent. Twenty years later, in September 1938, the Western powers capitulated to Adolf Hitler in Munich, and the Paris peace settlement lay in ruins. The West was defeated.

The crisis began in the moment of victory, and in spite of periodic respites it never really ceased. The war had sharpened the rivalry of the European nations, a morbid rivalry which had been the most significant cause of the war itself; and the peace did nothing to lessen these international hatreds. The treaties, dictated by the victors to the vanquished, transferred war-generated hatreds to the peace organism. The spirit of reconciliation and internationalism that had permeated plans for the League of Nations during the war was not manifest either during the peace negotiations or after. As a result, the League of Nations became more often than not an instrument of power politics and national egotism, while the peace treaties, in their terms and their spirit, challenged the vanquished to combat the gains of the victors.

Winston Churchill, aware in the twenties of being "deeply under the impression of a future catastrophe," coined the maxim "The redress of the grievances of the vanquished should precede the disarmament of the victors."[1] Of this Churchillian statement a critic remarked: "Where and how this should, or could, have been done, fairly or safely, is not stated";[2] and certainly the redress of grievances was an immensely difficult and complicated task. Had it only been tried, even a failure could have been called pardonable; but it was not tried, honestly and sincerely, in all the time that the Western democracies were masters of the European scene.

In the "twenty years' crisis" between the two world wars, Central Europe figured prominently. The causes of the crisis in the areas of the former Habsburg Monarchy were, however, not of local origin only; indeed they branched out far beyond the lands of the Danube Valley.

The roots of this post-war crisis lay in the dissolution of Allied unity. When the United States refused to join the League of Nations, she dealt the first and almost mortal blow to the peace organization. The second blow was Anglo-French rivalry. As a result, post-war Europe was left both without the union with the United States that had won the war for the Western democracies, and without France's union with Britain which, if anything, could have prevented the outbreak of the war itself. Peace in Europe, after the First World War, needed the continuation of both this "Atlantic Community" with the United States and this "Western Union" between the British and French democracies. When the revival of American isolationism frustrated French hopes for transatlantic cooperation, the unity between Britain and France became doubly important. Its lack therefore became doubly disastrous.

The core of the matter between Britain and France was British suspicion that the French were seeking military hegemony over Europe. France's exaggerated search for security, the British believed, so much carried her away as to make her seek domination of the Continent. Antipathy toward French aims not only created a rift with France but also aroused in Britain latent sympathies toward defeated Germany. The British became advocates of the concept expounded in 1919 in John Maynard Keynes' celebrated work *The Economic Consequences of the Peace,* that Europe cannot prosper unless Germany is economically restored. This was the first manifestation of the much quoted wisdom that economic cooperation is imperative between victors and vanquished. But the redress of grievances could not be accomplished by economic means only. Europe's difficulties were basically political in nature. Therefore, without political reconciliation, economic rapprochement was bound to remain sterile. The loans that Britain and the United States, especially the latter, extended profusely to Germany only increased German hatred of the peace settlement. Anglo-American aid, together with subsequent revision of the reparation clauses, was interpreted in Germany as open admission that the Versailles Treaty was not only unenforceable with regard to reparations but also unjust in every respect. The post-war trend, among both allies and former enemies, took the worst possible direction: hatred by the vanquished of the peace settlement increased, mutual understanding between victors and vanquished failed to improve, and relations deteriorated within the innermost circle of the victors.

Italy's deviation helped to weaken the peace front further. Italy did not receive what she had been promised by the secret treaties during the war. Although the peace conference treated Italy's territorial demands generously on the basis of national-ethnic principles, her far-flung ambitions of gaining a foothold in the Balkans and of solving her problem of overpopulation by the familiar mode of colonial expansion in Africa remained unsatisfied. Moreover, with Benito Mussolini's seizure of power in 1922, Italy was not only rebelling against the peace settlement, she was also turning, as the first Great Power inside Europe, against the victors' political system, parliamentary democracy.

More serious than Italy's inimical attitude was the challenge to democracy from the tyranny of the East. The Bolshevik revolution eliminated Russia from the ranks of the victors and cut her from the fabric of European civilization as well. Soviet Russia objected to the European status quo on many scores. She was against the territorial settlement — though for reasons of political exigency she was willing formally to accept her new boundaries, save that she refused to recognize the incorporation of Bessarabia into Romania. She was antagonistic to the victors' balance-of-power policy, which created the cordon sanitaire between Germany and the Soviet Union. But above all, Communist Russia was a sworn enemy of the bourgeois-democratic society of which Europe formed a part.

Thus among the five Great Powers — the United States, Britain, France, Italy and Russia — which in one way or another took part in achieving victory in Europe, only two, France and Britain, maintained a positive and active stand on behalf of the new order, with France taking a rigid, and Britain a somewhat flexible, attitude. Of course, Russia's defection was the less regrettable insofar as her exit from the wartime coalition became a distinct gain at the time of the Paris Peace Conference. The Bolshevik revolution, severing as it did Russia's ties with her Western allies in the last year of the war, considerably simplified the task of the Paris peacemakers, for they were thereby spared the trouble of facing a victorious Russia's demands. Moreover, when Germany was defeated, Eastern Europe found itself in a truly unique historical situation: both Germany and Russia, the two Great Powers flanking the Middle Zone of the smaller nations, lay prostrate. But the peace settlement drawn under these extraordinarily favorable circumstances had two fundamental weaknesses: first, it antagonized Germany and Russia, who were in any case lacking in benevolence toward the small nations, by making the Middle Zone into a "bulwark" against them; second, it failed to create conditions favorable for cooperation among the small nations within the Middle Zone.

The principal cause of dispute within the Middle Zone concerned the new boundaries imposed upon the vanquished countries, Hungary and Bulgaria, by their victorious neighbors, Czechoslovakia, Romania, Yugoslavia and Greece. Then too, territorial issues envenomed relations among the victors, as in the controversy over the Teschen district between Czechoslovakia and Poland, and over Vilna between Poland and Lithuania. (Lithuania, disgruntled over the loss of Vilna, had no diplomatic relations with Poland until 1938!) Conflicts over boundaries also aggravated the problems of national minorities. As a rule, these minorities were irredentist, striving not merely for rights within the states, but for secession from the states they were living in. Moreover, the tensions between the Slavic ethnic groups incorporated under Czech leadership into Czechoslovakia (Czechs, Slovaks and Ruthenes), and under Serbian leadership into Yugoslavia (Serbs, Croats and Slovenes), augmented the instability of the new order.

All these controversies within the Middle Zone were caused primarily by conflicting national aspirations — though of course differences in religion, and in social and economic views, poured oil on the fire of the national rivalries. This was the case, for instance, with the antagonism between the Roman Catholic Croats and the Orthodox Serbs, and with the conflict between the religious Slovaks and the free-thinking Czechs. Another source of conflict was the reactionary spirit of the Hungarian ruling class on the one hand, and the reformist zeal of Czechoslovakia, Yugoslavia and Romania on the other, who were carrying out agrarian and other economic and social reforms with varying degrees of success and sincerity. But the bitter enmity between Hungary and her neighbors — focused as it was on the question of boundaries — was primarily nationalistic; and the reformist zeal of Hungary's neighbors too was strongly colored with nationalist resentment, the dispossession of national rivals often taking precedence over social justice.

During the First World War, exiles from Central and Eastern Europe had assured their Western protectors that the independent nation-states between the Baltic and the Aegean would serve as a solid bastion of peace. But from the beginning these nation-states proved instead to be a source of insecurity; they battled with masses of disloyal citizens, and they were engaged in bitter rivalries among themselves as well as with the Great Powers flanking the Middle Zone. In view of these conditions in the eastern half of Europe, the stabilization of the continent's peace depended all the more upon the unity of the Western nations; yet the obvious weakness of the new order in Central and Eastern Europe did nothing to spur the Western nations to seek unity among themselves and in their policies toward the rest of Europe.

Western disunity was an encouragement to "revisionism," as the movements of discontented nations to change the European status quo came to be known after the First World War. The discontented considered their paramount task to be the raising of doubts about the permanency of the existing order. Meanwhile the contented nations incessantly sought a magic formula for security. To hope that time would heal the wounds of the discontented nations was self-delusion. On the other hand, any rational discussion of the revision of the peace treaties was doomed in advance, due to the agitation of the revisionists and the unwillingness of the status quo defenders to admit even the advisability of any general critical review of the peace settlement. Article Nineteen of the Covenant of the League, which provided the legal basis for "peaceful revision," was invoked from time to time by the vanquished, but its application was persistently rejected by the victors. The intensive propaganda for and against the peace settlements gave vent to much demagogy, which obscured the real conditions of peace. Both defenders and opponents of the status quo exaggerated the significance of the boundary problems — for, important as were the boundary revisions, in certain cases, for smoothing out international frictions, true peace depended much more upon the internal political, economic and spiritual development of the nations dwelling behind the boundaries.

France was the foremost defender of the new Continental order, although in reality she was not entirely happy with it. Victory over Germany did not endow her with a sense of security. As a result of the refusal of the United States to join the League of Nations, the mutual assistance pact (a form of "Atlantic Community") among the United States, Britain and France, which had been stipulated at the peace conference, fell through. Britain proposed to substitute for the three-power agreement a two-power agreement (a kind of British-French "Western Union"); but France, led by Raymond Poincaré, rejected the offer because it did not include a military convention. In 1923, a draft treaty of mutual assistance was proposed, according to which the members of the League were to be under an automatic obligation to render military assistance against an aggressor. The draft treaty was rejected, this time by Britain. In 1924, the so-called Geneva Protocol was signed, which banned aggressive war and defined the aggressor. Britain, however, failed to ratify it. France's reprisals against Germany, such as her insistence on reparation payments and the Ruhr occupation in 1923, were contrary to the Anglo-American point of view advocating European economic reconstruction. And France's so-called cordon sanitaire between Germany and Soviet Russia (a system of alliances between France and the countries of Central and Eastern Europe) made Britain jealous and suspicious of France's ambition to establish military hegemony over the Continent.

France would have felt alone and abandoned, had not the victorious smaller states of Central and Eastern Europe — Poland, Czechoslovakia, Romania and Yugoslavia — shared her obsessive quest for security. But alliances with these four countries, situated in the dangerous Middle Zone between Germany and Russia, were no substitute for the treaties France had hoped to obtain from the United States and Great Britain. France, frustrated and nervous, was not qualified to pursue an enlightened and constructive policy among the smaller nations in Central and Eastern Europe. The boundary changes advocated by the revisionists filled her with rage. Revision for her was tantamount to more insecurity. Had France been given the security she expected from her British and American wartime allies, she might not have become the blind defender of the "follies of the victors" in Central Europe. As it was, French policy, aligned with the defense of the status quo, succeeded only in aggravating the rivalry of nationalistic forces.

Rivalry among the former Habsburg peoples in drawing the new, national boundaries produced a center of European instability in the Danube Valley. Three defeated countries, Austria, Hungary and Bulgaria, were there pitted against three victors, Czechoslovakia, Romania and Yugoslavia. Austria did not raise boundary problems in the usual sense of the term; her feelings were hurt mainly by the ban imposed by the peace treaty on "Anschluss" — that is, union with Germany. A second victim of the peace treaties, Bulgaria, had only minor boundary quarrels, though they were enough to provide an obstacle to peaceful cooperation with her neighbors. The most important single factor contributing to Danubian instability was the hostility between Hungary, dismembered by the Trianon Treaty, and her neighbors who benefited from the dismemberment to such an extent that almost one-third of all the Hungarians living in the Danube Valley were incorporated into Czechoslovakia, Romania and Yugoslavia. These three countries, allied in the so-called Little Entente, stood guard against any revision of the frontiers forced on Hungary.

The pilot-treaty of the Little Entente, signed on August 14, 1920, between Czechoslovakia and Yugoslavia, expressed the firm resolve "to maintain the peace . . . as well as the situation created by the Treaty concluded at Trianon." By the Czechoslovak-Romanian treaty of April 23, 1921, and the Romanian-Yugoslav treaty of June 7, 1921, the encirclement of Hungary was completed; the last of these treaties put Bulgaria, the common enemy of Romania and Yugoslavia, in the same category with Hungary. In addition, the treaties of the Little Entente obligated Hungary's three neighbors to oppose any attempt to bring back the Habsburgs, a clause which lost its opportuneness when ex-King Charles, shortly after two unsuccessful attempts in 1921 to return to his Hungarian throne, died in exile.

The extension of the victors' alliance system to the entire Middle Zone met with less success than the formation of the Little Entente in the Danube Valley. Relations between Czechoslovakia and Poland got off to a bad start immediately after liberation, when in January 1919 a "seven days war" was waged over the Teschen area. The settlement that followed the armed conflict left Poland disgruntled. Although appeals were made to "Slav solidarity" and to common interests, the rift between Poland and Czechoslovakia was not repaired. Prague's repeated efforts to link Poland with the Little Entente met with failure. Poland, however, on March 3, 1921, entered into a treaty of mutual assistance with her other southern neighbor, Romania, to defend their eastern frontiers against Russia. France concluded a similar treaty of defense with Poland, on February 19, 1921, against Germany.

France subscribed to the aims of the Little Entente by signing a treaty of alliance and friendship with Czechoslovakia on January 25, 1924, in order "to concert their action in all matters of foreign policy which may threaten their security or which may tend to subvert the situation created by the Treaties of Peace." A Franco-Romanian treaty of January 10, 1926, and a Franco-Yugoslav treaty of November 11, 1927, completed this network of alliances which was intended to turn the Middle Zone between Germany and Russia into a safety zone, a cordon sanitaire, according to the principles of balance of power.

The greatest weakness of this treaty system was no doubt the link missing between Poland and Czechoslovakia — the link, that is, that would have tied Poland to the Little Entente in the Danube Valley. However, even if the Polish-Czech link had existed, it is doubtful whether the treaty system of the cordon sanitaire could have become a durable instrument of security either for Poland or for the Danubian countries.

Poland's security as an independent country between Germany and Russia — indeed her very "viability," as Jacques Bainville pointed out in his famous book *Les conséquences politiques de la paix,* published in 1920 — depended on a strong Danubian organization.[3] And the Little Entente was no such organization. Hailed by its member-states and its Western sympathizers as a pillar of stability, the Little Entente, despite its temporary success, was not a source of strength in the long run. It may well have been regarded as the natural grouping of the post-Habsburg era since it represented the former oppressed nationalities of the Habsburg Empire. Nevertheless, as an instrument of security and peaceful evolution, the Little Entente could hardly fulfill its role. First of all, it was bound to perpetuate a three-way hostility between Hungary on the one hand, and her neighbors, Czechoslovakia, Yugoslavia and Romania, on the other. Furthermore, since the three Little Entente countries had as their neighbors three Great Powers whom they individually regarded as their principal enemies (Czechoslovakia — Germany; Yugoslavia — Italy; Romania — Soviet Russia), the Little Entente's cooperation was anything but smooth when it came to shaping policies toward these Great Powers. In fact, the Little Entente formed a solid bloc only against Hungary's revisionist aspirations.

Hungary was no less responsible than the Little Entente for the hapless situation in the Danube Valley. For, if the countries of the Little Entente were guilty of imposing on Hungary unduly harsh conditions of peace, Hungary was guilty of undisguised hostility toward the liberated peoples of the former Habsburg Monarchy. Hungary, under Admiral Horthy's counterrevolutionary regime, was ruled by an oligarchy whose past record and revisionist policy could arouse only suspicion and distrust. The rulers of Hungary, arrogant and singularly ignorant of the causes producing revolutionary changes in Central Europe, spoke the insulting language of a feudal past. Their spokesman at the Paris Peace Conference, Count Albert Apponyi, protested against the Trianon Treaty on the ground that it transferred national hegemony to people who stood "on an inferior cultural level." And their propaganda against the treaty was invariably based on the contention of Magyar "cultural superiority." Hungary had a good case in denouncing the injustices of the Trianon Treaty, which forcibly separated one-third of the Hungarians from their mother country; but Hungary's rulers applied inept methods in their attacks on the treaty. As a rule they protested against the total losses of the multinational Hungarian kingdom, which amounted to 71 percent of its territory and 60 percent of its population. The rulers of Trianon Hungary did not even try to conceal their ultimate goal, the restoration of the "thousand-years-old Hungary" of the past, a goal rightfully regarded by Hungary's neighbors as an imperialistic policy directed against their vital interests.

Czechoslovakia, to her credit, showed some willingness, at least once, to reverse her hostile attitude toward Hungary and pave the way for conciliation. At one time, in March 1921, when the Little Entente had not yet grown into a solid bloc encircling Hungary, Eduard Beneš, Czechoslovak Foreign Minister, met with Count Paul Teleki, Prime Minister of Hungary, and Gustav Gratz, Hungarian Foreign Minister, in the Austrian town Bruck an der Leitha. At this meeting Beneš proposed economic cooperation between Hungary and Czechoslovakia as a preliminary to later discussion of territorial issues. The offer was rejected by the Hungarian representatives, who maintained the necessity of a preliminary agreement on territorial questions to precede economic cooperation. During the negotiations, Beneš acknowledged that "the boundaries laid down in the Treaty of Trianon were not the best possible frontiers." He suggested that Hungary would find it more difficult to reach an agreement with the Romanians and the Yugoslavs than with the Czechs. He offered his help in composing Hungary's differences with her neighbors, provided a Czech-Hungarian agreement should be reached. He also urged Hungary to adopt a republican form of government — which, he argued, would make it possible fundamentally to change the relationship between Hungary and the Little Entente countries so as to be able to create a Danubian federation or, as he called it, a "United States of Central Europe."[4]

The rulers of Hungary were certainly most unwise in refusing Beneš's proposals. However, it is doubtful whether any one of the Danubian countries was really ready for a higher form of cooperation, such as was envisaged by Beneš. Their post-war record shows a consistent shying away from the idea of national equality, which was prerequisite to true reconciliation. Jealous and suspicious, infected by the spirit of intolerance, the Danubian states lacked the good will and moderation needed for a federation. The post-war era of nationalism aggravated the antagonisms which had long been frustrating peace among the Danubian peoples. The great nationalist revolution of 1918, which destroyed the Habsburg Monarchy, had also destroyed for a long time to come, the prospects of a Danubian federation.

France sought allies in the Middle Zone in order to counterbalance the power of Germany and Russia. A Danubian federation could have provided exactly the power needed. The old truth that the smaller nations between Germany and Russia should federate both in their own interest and in the interest of Europe remained valid. Failure to produce such a federation had brought the Habsburg Monarchy to its ruin. There was every reason to fear that the heirs to the Habsburgs, the Central European nation-states, would meet the same fate unless they drew the proper conclusions from the Habsburg failure.

The disunity of the Danubian nations was widely deplored, but no progress was made, even theoretically, in clarifying the conditions of unity. The Little Entente held the view that with Hungary's renunciation of its revisionist claims, Danubian federation would become a matter of automatic evolution. Hungarians for their part glorified the territorial unity of their thousand-years-old kingdom, believing its restoration to be the only road to Danubian federation. Moreover, the monarchists, mostly Hungarians, wistfully remembering their special privileges under the former Dual Monarchy, considered the restoration of the Habsburg Empire to be the only possible form of any Danubian federal union. They even praised the old Monarchy as having achieved such a federal union, although in reality the dissolution of the Monarchy had been caused by precisely its failure to transform itself into a federation of its member-nations.

Actually, neither the resuscitation of the Habsburg Monarchy nor the restoration of thousand-years-old Hungary, nor the preservation of the existing nation-states, could ever offer favorable conditions for Danubian unity. The Habsburg, the Hungarian, the Little Entente versions of "federation," though with variations, all tended to perpetuate inequalities and injustices of one kind or another. Only a joint effort which would both acknowledge the equality of all the Danubian nations and also ensure their freedom under democratic institutions could have opened the road to a real federal solution. Unfortunately neither the Danubian nations themselves nor the Great Powers with influence and interest in the Danube Valley were ready for such a fresh start.

The Great Powers are not justified in sitting in judgment over the small nations that failed to establish peaceful cooperation among themselves. Nor of course are the small nations any more justified in blaming the Great Powers exclusively for their troubles. Rivalry, hatred, fear, held the entire continent in their clutches. Nevertheless the failure of cooperation among the smaller nations of Central Europe definitely reflected on the incompetence of the Western Powers too, because they did not make use of their influence and prestige to provide guidance in the right direction. They showed little concern for a true pacification of these smaller nations. They expended far greater energy in their different efforts to make the European peace safe from the wrath of the two giant neighbors of the Middle Zone, Germany and Russia. As a matter of fact, had the Western Powers devoted more attention to the problems of the small nations in the Middle Zone, especially by offering guidance to these nations toward democracy and Danubian federalism, they could have improved considerably the chances of peace with Germany and Russia.

France's alliances with Poland and the Little Entente, which set up the cordon sanitaire in Central and Eastern Europe, were intended to encircle Germany and to keep the Soviet Union contained. But while subscribing to this basic purpose of the French alliances in the Middle Zone, Western diplomacy was also inclined to engage Soviet Russia in Germany's encirclement and to enlist Germany in Soviet Russia's containment. This European "balance of power" could have worked beautifully if Germany and Russia had cooperated in a system which encircled and contained them respectively; but — hardly surprisingly — neither Germany nor Russia filled its appointed role.

The cordon sanitaire, directed against Germany and Russia, had the logical effect of bringing these "two outcasts" closer to each other. Hans von Seeckt, Chief of the Reichswehr from 1920 to 1926, was the first to draw the logical conclusions from the cordon sanitaire. General Seeckt and the chiefs of staff around him, despite their fervent opposition to communism, were quick to realize that with Russian assistance Germany might be able to break up the French encirclement and defeat the Versailles system. Soviet Russia, though absorbed in fomenting revolution in Germany — chosen by Lenin as the center of world revolution — was not slow, either, to embrace the cynical rules of old power politics. While hopes of stirring up a Bolshevik revolution in industrial Germany were dwindling, Soviet Russia stood ready for old-fashioned, nonideological cooperation with the German generals.

Cooperation between reactionary Prussian militarists and Russian Bolshevik revolutionaries started in the early twenties, when, in accordance with secret agreements, Junkers, the great German aircraft builders, began to operate a factory near Moscow. Shells and presumably also guns were manufactured by Krupp in several Russian factories for export to Germany. A tank factory too was established, near Kazan, with training facilities for German officers.[5]

Some of the facts concerning German-Russian cooperation came to the attention of a shocked group of European diplomats gathered at a conference in Genoa in 1922. Britain had been anxious to push the rehabilitation of trade relations, and it was in the spirit of this policy that all European countries, Germany and Russia included, were invited to Genoa. So far as the West was concerned, the conference ended in failure, due mainly to France's uncompromising attitude. Germany and Russia, however, scored a great success when in nearby Rapallo the Soviet People's Commissar for Foreign Affairs, G. V. Chicherin, and the German Minister of Foreign Affairs, Walter Rathenau, signed a separate economic treaty.[6]

The German-Soviet treaty ended the isolation of the "two outcasts" of Europe. It also awakened the West to the unpleasant reality that the cordon sanitaire paved the way to German-Russian rapprochement. Western diplomacy was called upon to find more effective means for keeping Germany and Russia apart. From the point of view of the simple power politics that dominated European diplomacy, the logical course of action lay in taking a more conciliatory attitude toward both Germany and Russia, or one of the two. Western Europe perceived the necessity of reconciliation, but remained indecisive in face of the alternatives. It was a Central European friend of the West, Eduard Beneš, who pondered the alternatives and declared his preference for a rapprochement with Russia.

During the Second World War Beneš liked to remind Western statesmen that it was he who had urged the diplomatic recognition of the Soviet Union immediately after Rapallo. At that time German-Russian rapprochement had hung like the sword of Damocles over the Middle Zone. There was no doubt in Beneš's mind that, in the interest of strengthening the European status quo, the Western Powers would have to cooperate with Russia against Germany.

Beneš had of course always been willing and eager to cooperate with Germany, as with anybody else, on the basis of the status quo. But he was only too well aware that Germany could never become a guarantor of Czechoslovak frontiers. Russia on the other hand was, in his view, despite the Bolshevik revolution, a potential Slav ally in an anti-German European system. Beneš's pro-Russian thinking may be explained also by the fact that Czechoslovakia shared no common frontiers with Russia, and hence — unlike Poland and Romania — had no territorial disputes with her, an almost decisive factor in determining international relations in nationalistic Europe. While Beneš was hoping for a rapprochement between the West and Russia, he took an active part in drafting the Geneva Protocol of 1924. The Protocol was intended to provide collective action under the aegis of the League of Nations against the violator of the territorial status quo. But beyond such paper guarantees Beneš was ahead of everyone else in thinking of the Soviet Union — which was not at that time a member of the League of Nations — as a Great Power, capable of strengthening the real forces of security.

General Seeckt wanted to upset the Versailles system with Russia's help. Eduard Beneš hoped to stabilize the peace settlement by improving the relations between Russia and the West. Britain and France had no such set views on this subject. Although France was preoccupied with security, she could not renew her First World War alliance against Germany with a Bolshevik Russia. In addition to an ideological horror of communism, Paris refused even diplomatic recognition of Soviet Russia because of its repudiation of the debts Tsarist Russia owed France. London's attitude toward the Soviet government was also basically negative. But as one keen observer saw it, British and Soviet politics, for all their ideological conflicts, developed in part along parallel lines. For different reasons, from opposite fringes of Europe, both Britain and Russia sought to counteract the domination of the Continent by a single military power — France.[7] Lloyd George made feeble attempts to improve the relations between Britain and Russia. But when he invited the Russians to the Genoa conference, he was criticized for "coquetting with the Bolsheviks." The failure of Genoa was satisfying to those who wanted to have nothing to do with Soviet Russia. The Russo-German Rapallo Treaty, however, caused concern to everybody, including of course those who were anxious to keep the Russians in quarantine.

The Western Powers were eager to undo Rapallo and neutralize Russo-German cooperation. Strengthening the Middle Zone could have furnished a powerful and logical countermove to Rapallo, but this could have been achieved only by radically changing the policies inside the Middle Zone. Unfortunately, the nations there were all preoccupied with their petty rivalries. Meanwhile France was busy currying favor with those countries in the Middle Zone that had profited from the peace settlement. And Britain's interest was limited to eyeing with suspicion France's maneuvering in that region.

There was some reason to believe, in 1924, that the relationship between the Soviet Union and the West would follow the course favored by

Beneš. For one thing, the political trend in the West took a swing to the Left. In 1924, when the Laborite Ramsay MacDonald became Prime Minister, Britain recognized the Soviet government. Official recognition by the French Socialist government under Edouard Herriot, and by several European states, followed. Interestingly enough, Czechoslovakia was not among the countries that established formal diplomatic relations with the Soviet Union. Although European diplomacy was taking exactly the course Beneš had so favored, nevertheless the delicacy of Czechoslovakia's position — her anxiety to gain sympathy abroad and to build unity at home — cautioned Beneš to go slowly on such a controversial issue as the formal diplomatic recognition of Soviet Russia. However, Czechoslovakia signed two "provisional treaties" with the Russian and Ukrainian Soviet Republics as early as June 1922, shortly after the German-Soviet Rapallo Treaty.

Changes in Soviet policies contributed to easing the tension between East and West. In domestic affairs the Soviet Union returned, with the so-called New Economic Policy (NEP), to a limited form of free enterprise. In foreign policy the Communist International (Comintern) redrafted its strategy for world revolution following the abortive Communist rising in Germany in October 1923. Thereafter, expectation of the collapse of capitalism was relegated to the background, being replaced by the slogan of coexistence between communism and capitalism. Despite this easing up in Communist revolutionary zeal, the rapprochement between the Soviet Union and the West was of very short duration. After a short détente, a new crisis developed, in the autumn of 1924, precipitated by a letter ostensibly written by Gregory Zinoviev, president of the Comintern, to the British Communists, inciting them to revolt. (The authenticity of the letter was denied, however, by the Soviet government.)

In contrast with the failure to improve Russo-Western relations, there was a change for the better between Germany and the West. In the autumn of 1924 France withdrew her troops from the Ruhr. Following this, Gustav Stresemann, Foreign Minister of Germany, repeated his earlier offer of guarantees for Germany's treaty obligations. Aristide Briand, French Foreign Minister, accepted the German offer. Britain favored the move. The result was the Locarno Pact of 1925, which mutually guaranteed the German-French and German-Belgian frontiers. Britain and Italy served as guarantors of the pact, pledging aid to the attacked country in case of treaty violation.

The Locarno Pact underscored Germany's Western orientation and improved her relationship with her former enemies, France and Britain; but it did not guarantee Germany's eastern frontiers, due to Germany's own opposition, as well as to British and Italian reluctance to undertake obligations in regard to the Middle Zone. France, however, signed treaties of mutual assistance with Germany's eastern neighbors, Poland and Czechoslovakia, to assure them against German aggression. And Germany concluded arbitration treaties with Poland and Czechoslovakia as a further assurance that she would not use force against them. In spite of these assurances, the sharp distinction which the Locarno Pact made between Germany's western and eastern frontiers was a sign of the equivocal attitude the Western Powers — especially Britain, but even France, the patron of the status quo in the Middle Zone — were inclined to take toward the security problems of Eastern Europe. It was also a disturbing indication that a rapprochement between the West and Germany might leave the nations of the Middle Zone more exposed to Germany's traditional eastward expansion, the ill-fated *Drang nach Osten.* How far Western disengagement could go in regard to the cordon sanitaire was revealed later — in Munich, in 1938, when Germany was appeased at the expense of Czechoslovakia with fatal consequences for the independence of the entire Middle Zone of small nations; and during the Second World War, when Russia was an ally of the Western Powers against Germany, this disengagement of the West from the Middle Zone produced similar results.

France did not succeed in assuaging the fears of her smaller allies over the Locarno Pact. Only Czechoslovakia, France's most devoted satellite, acclaimed the pact as a means of promoting the continent's general peace. But the true sentiments of France's small allies were voiced by her least enthusiastic satellite, Poland, who was openly critical of the new trend in European politics. Worried Poles gloomily predicted an impending "fifth partition" of Poland and tried to persuade the Western democracies that the Locarno policy did not serve their interests either.

Meanwhile the mutual assistance treaties that France signed with Poland and Czechoslovakia reminded Germany that the danger of encirclement was still the order of the day. Germany reminded the West, too, that the Locarno Pact did not alter her own determination to counteract the threat of encirclement. Almost simultaneously with the Locarno Pact, a new German-Soviet trade treaty was signed. Furthermore, in 1926, the German and Soviet governments concluded in Berlin a non-aggression treaty, the negotiations for which must have run simultaneously with the Locarno conferences.[8] The German General

Staff did not change their attitude toward the Russians either. German military technicians continued, on Russian soil, experiments which under the Versailles Treaty they could not carry out in Germany; in fact they continued "by force of inertia" for some time even after Hitler seized power.[9]

The Locarno Pact was intended to reinforce Russia's containment by luring Germany away from the pro-Soviet course charted in Rapallo. No wonder the Soviet Union did its best to make Locarno unpopular in Germany. "To think that Germany will put up with this state of affairs is to hope for miracles. . . . Locarno, which . . . sanctions the loss by Germany of Silesia, the Corridor and Danzig . . . will share the fate of the old Franco-Prussian treaty, which deprived France of Alsace and Lorraine. . . . Locarno is fraught with a new European war" — such were Stalin's comments on the pact.[10] Meanwhile the Sixth Comintern Congress, in 1928, decided that the era of imperialistic attacks and of preparation for intervention against the Soviet Union must be anticipated. The Communist parties in the capitalistic countries were alerted. The Social Democratic parties were singled out by the Comintern as the archenemies of communism and were labelled "Social Fascists." Communists in Germany, following instructions from Moscow, concentrated their attacks upon the Social Democrats, who were engaged in an evergrowing struggle with Hitler's National Socialists. Stalin thus contributed his share to Hitler's victory in Germany; and the Western democracies, through their failure to follow up the Locarno Pact with a vigorous policy of European cöoperation, contributed their share.

2 *Federalist Failures*

Imperfect as the Locarno Pact was, if ever a favorable opportunity to bring about European reconciliation existed, it was during the Locarno era. The pact was the first step toward better relations between Germany and France, the two former enemy countries, from which European reconciliation had to take its cue. Democracy in Weimar Germany was still at that time strong enough to keep under control the enemies of civilization who on their way "from nationality to bestiality" (in fulfillment of Grillparzer's prophecy) had found their leader in Hitler. Stalin's Russia, the other principal enemy of Western civilization, presented no imminent threat as long as she was isolated behind the cordon sanitaire. Moreover, in 1928 the Soviet government launched its first Five Year Plan, and was anxious to remain in seclusion and preserve the peace of the world during the critical period of Russia's social and economic transformation.

The Spanish philosopher José Ortega y Gasset, a true European, taking the measure of the dangers threatening Western civilization both from within and from without, gave warning in 1929 that to his way of thinking "the building-up of Europe into a great national state is the one enterprise that could counterbalance a victory of the 'five year plan'."[1] A "great European national state," or rather a supranational United States of Europe — for this is what Ortega y Gasset had in mind — could have counterbalanced, of course, not only the Communist threat to Europe, but also the other growing menace of tyranny, Hitler's rise to power.

From Austria, from this cradle and grave of federalist efforts, Count Richard N. Coudenhove-Kalergi had been advocating the idea of "Pan-Europe" since the early twenties. This movement, favoring the creation of a United States of Europe, gained momentum after Locarno and was supported by some of the best European minds. Among the great writers, scientists and artists who endorsed the pan-European movement were Albert Einstein, Sigmund Freud, Thomas Mann, Miguel de Unamuno, José Ortega y Gasset, Bronislav Huberman, Bruno Walter,

Paul Valéry. These men, unfortunately, were not representative of the great masses of people, who were largely influenced by passions of exaggerated nationalism. And the political leaders of Europe, if they supported Coudenhove-Kalergi's movement at all, paid mostly lip-service to European unity, supporting it only as long as it served their special national interests. Thus, status quo supporters who favored the pan-European movement did so with the understanding that it was not a change of frontiers that was needed but their so-called spiritualization. The program of "spiritualization," originated by the Romanian Foreign Minister, Nicolae Titulescu, might have been commendable had it not been merely a shrewd way of circumventing the revision of the Danubian frontiers by elevating the problem above the plane of discussion. The revisionists, on the other hand, if they favored the idea of pan-Europe, did so in the expectation that it would help undo injustices by bringing about frontier revisions.

After Locarno the vanquished began to breathe more freely, but the controversy between supporters and opponents of the peace settlement remained unsolved. In 1926 Germany became a member of the League of Nations and, as a spokesman in Geneva for the rights of German minorities, encouraged the revisionists, who were demanding reconsideration of the status quo according to ethnic principles and rights of self-determination. France and her satellites, on the other hand, solidified the ranks of the anti-revisionists.

In 1927 Italy concluded a treaty of friendship with Hungary, and Mussolini denounced the Trianon Treaty, calling for its revision. At the same time, the British newspaper owner, Lord Rothermere, launched a campaign against the Trianon Treaty. Hungarian revisionist propaganda remained rather ineffective in France, which was a single-minded supporter of the Little Entente; but it attained considerable success in Britain, where Conservative circles lent a sympathetic ear — though a good deal of the favorable response was motivated by British disapproval of French policies in the Danube Valley. The sympathy some British Conservatives retained for Hungary's ruling class also played into the hands of the revisionists; and the information these British sympathizers received about the peace settlement came from conservative Hungarian sources, anxious to persuade the Western Powers that restoration of pre-war Hungary would be the magic cure for the post-war ills of Central Europe.

Hungary's neighbors were irritated enough with what was justifiable in the revisionist demands, namely the return of the territories inhabited by Hungarians; what infuriated them, however, were reckless revisionist claims to be seeking, also, "justice" for pre-war Hungary's non-Hungarian nationalities. The Budapest revisionists asserted that the Slovaks, Ruthenes and Croats were maltreated in the countries of the Little Entente and were disillusioned with the regimes under which they had been kept against their will. Thus Hungary exploited the nationality tensions within the Little Entente countries, while the latter indulged especially in exposing Hungary's reactionary class rule. The two sides had consistently promoted discord in each other by means which they considered best suited for undermining stability.

Encouraged by Lord Rothermere's campaign and by Mussolini's denunciation of the Trianon Treaty, hopes of revision rose high both in Hungary and among the Hungarian minorities in Czechoslovakia, Romania and Yugoslavia. At the same time, the Little Entente grew correspondingly alarmed by this success of Hungarian revisionism. Mass demonstrations organized by the Prague, Bucharest and Belgrade governments of the Little Entente protested against Hungary's revisionist aspirations. In 1929 the three members of the Little Entente reorganized their alliance; their treaty system henceforth was to be automatically renewed at the end of each five-year period.

The propaganda of the revisionists and anti-revisionists was mainly focused on the territorial settlement of the peace treaties. Thus the illusion was spread among both opponents and supporters of the status quo that peace in Europe was essentially a matter either of maintaining or of changing national boundaries. In fact, few territorial changes were needed to satisfy those demands of the revisionists that were justifiable. The kind of "revision" Europe truly needed was a profound change of its political structure. Nationalist rivalries were threatening the peace of Europe as much as were the forces hostile to democracy. International pacification was not simply a matter of redrawing some of the national boundaries; it was above all a matter of democratic governments, social progress, economic prosperity. These conditions of true peace had not been attained under the European system of sovereign nation-states. A League of Nations with supranational powers to guarantee and enforce the rule of democracy throughout Europe could have tackled the intricate problems of international reconciliation. But such a "revision" was out of the question. Europe, alas, was not ready to embrace "democratic internationalism," as advocated by Norman Angell toward the end of the First World War. Attempts at international cooperation for much less ambitious objectives proved failures during the late twenties and early thirties, as Europe approached the crucial point of its post-war history with Hitler's rise to power in Germany.

Plans to extricate Europe from the nationalist deadlock through new forms of international cooperation were not lacking. But the plans, though actually not comprehensive enough, nevertheless proved too ambitious, and failed because of lack of support. The most ambitious plan on a governmental level was launched by France's Aristide Briand in 1929–30. Briand proposed to create a "European Association," or, as it was vaguely interpreted, a United States of Europe. The plan rightly diagnosed that the underlying causes of Europe's ills were of a political nature, and prescribed peaceful arbitration of all international disputes. Some critics felt the plan neglected the economic foundations of international cooperation. Probably the plan did not strike the right balance between economic and political factors; but the real causes of its failure lay elsewhere, and they were summed up twenty years later by another French Foreign Minister, Robert Schuman, who, working for a federated Europe, was trying to save the peace after another world war. Three points emphasized by Schuman may explain the failure of all unity plans, whether continental like Briand's or regional like the Danubian plans:

First, the Briand plan definitely excluded any infringement of national sovereignty. (". . . making it a matter of principle that not a particle of their sovereignty was to be relinquished, the signatories . . . promised to deprive themselves of the chief means of achieving their goal. It was to be accepted in advance that the original organization would be powerless.")

Second, the inferior status of the vanquished was not abolished. ("What hope would there be of common action by France and Germany, when the former clung to her unsatisfied legal rights and the latter clamored for equality and revision of the Treaty? In such an atmosphere there was no possibility of cooperation.")

Third, the time was not ripe for European union. ("The French plan was stillborn because it was ahead of its time, and, even if it had been tried, it would not have worked."[2])

Of course, the policy of federalism was "ahead of its time," not because it was not needed, but because it could not be popular in an age which extolled national egotism. And few politicians had the foresight and courage to perform the unpopular job of stemming popular currents. They preferred drifting along with the old tide of nationalism to charting bold new courses of federalism.

Federalist pioneers were especially and urgently needed in the Danube Valley.

The smaller nations of Danubian Europe, not unlike the French and Germans in the west, were interlocked in rivalries for hegemony. These rivalries were petty affairs in comparison with what was at stake in the rivalry between the two great nations of Europe, Germany and France. What made the rivalry of the small nations especially pernicious, however, was the great number of their conflicting aspirations; crowded into the relatively small area of the middle Danube Valley were more national conflicts than there were in all the rest of Europe. And what made these petty rivalries even more dangerous was the fact that these small nations of Central Europe, in order to bolster themselves against their rivals, were enlisting the support of the Great Powers. The Hungarians thus placed traditional reliance upon Germany, and they also found a new ally in Italy; revisionist policy formed the bond of union between Hungary and these two Great Powers. On the other hand the three Little Entente countries, Hungary's rivals, found their protector in France, with whom they shared a common interest in maintaining the status quo and combating revisionist aspirations. Thus the rivalries of the small nations became intertwined with those of the Great Powers, and the Danubian conflicts, though petty in themselves, became enmeshed in the great conflicts of Europe.

Termination of the rivalry of the Great Powers was no doubt the surest way of making an end to the rivalry between the small nations also; but such a change in the political climate of Europe was as remote as any willingness of the small nations to seize the initiative and compose their differences among themselves.

There was a popular theory circulating, which tried to explain the unhappy Danubian situation by the lack of democracy among the enemies of the peace settlement. This theory, although far from flawless, was not quite without foundation. Even before Hitler seized the leadership of the revisionist camp, the European countries, small and great, which opposed the peace settlement were either poor practitioners or outright enemies of the democratic form of government. Revisionist Hungary as governed by Admiral Horthy was a dictatorship adorned by a facade of parliamentarianism. Hungary's first revisionist friend was Mussolini, the Fascist dictator of Italy. Poland, which refused to cooperate with the anti-revisionist Little Entente, while cultivating a friendship, called "historical," with Hungary, was developing under Marshal Joseph Piłsudski her own brand of dictatorship with parliamentary adornments. Revisionist Bulgaria was another example of democracy's failure; there a coup in 1923 ended Alexander Stambolijski's drastic experiment of a peasant democracy.

On the other hand, in anti-revisionist Yugoslavia too, democratic evolution was arrested by the royal dictatorship of King Alexander. Also in the kingdom of Romania, another anti-revisionist country, the vitality of the reactionary forces curtailed the effectiveness of the post-war democratic reforms. Only Czechoslovakia could equate anti-revisionism with the rule of democracy. Yet, victors or vanquished, reactionaries or democrats, revisionists or anti-revisionists, all the regimes in the Danube Valley had one thing in common: they were strongly nationalistic. Nationalism coupled with democracy was certainly a lesser evil than nationalism coupled with reaction. Nevertheless, a peaceful evolution in the Danube Valley depended as much on the abandonment of the nationalist dogma that viewed the state as a vehicle of power directed against another nation, as on the universal extension of democracy. Only thus, if at all, could the national states of the post-Habsburg era have evolved toward a federal union of the Danubian peoples.

The responsibility of Admiral Horthy's counterrevolutionary Hungary for blocking this evolutionary process was twofold: neither was she a democracy nor was she willing to give up her exaggerated nationalist aspirations to dominate the Carpathian basin. The exiled Hungarian pioneer of Danubian federalism, Oscar Jászi, saw from far-away New York what the rulers of Hungary refused to see from Budapest. In 1924 Jászi wrote: "Only a thoroughgoing democratization of Hungary and loyal intimate relations between this democratized Hungary and the new states, can create such an atmosphere in Central Europe as can cure the gravest evils of the present situation and clear the way for a democratic confederation of all the small nations which are now tormented by the rigid dogma of national sovereignty."[3] Jászi no less clearly saw also the effects of the imperialistic peace forced upon Hungary by her neighbors: "I believed and still believe that a Hungary reorganized on the model of Switzerland, closely united in federal bonds with the neighbor states, would have been a better guarantee of democracy, of economic progress and of peace, than a mutilated Hungary robbed of the means of existence, embittered and pursued by dreams of revanche, and hardening her heart against the surrounding states."[4]

The neighbors of Hungary also shared a twofold responsibility for failure of peaceful evolution in the Danube Valley. First, in a frenzy of nationalism they carved up Hungary well beyond what was permissible according to ethnic principles, thus making themselves rulers over vast Hungarian minorities. Second, they refused to reconsider the harsh terms of the peace. Their favorite way of laying the blame on Hungary for the post-war troubles was to say that the existing controversies could be settled if Hungary had a democratic regime. The practical value of such statements, considering the small chance of replacing the Horthy regime with a democratic government, amounted to almost nothing — although it was fair to assume that a Hungarian democratic regime could have eased the Danubian tensions. More indicative, however, of the true intention of Hungary's neighbors than such vague hints at eventual treaty revision were their efforts to assimilate the Hungarian minorities and to make the territorial settlement irrevocable.

Incidentally, the League of Nations too, as guarantor of the minority protection system, favored a kind of gradual assimilation of the minorities. As Mello-Franco, Brazil's representative on the League Council, said in 1926: "It seems to me obvious that those who conceived this system of protection did not dream of creating within certain states a group of inhabitants who would regard themselves as permanently foreign to the general organization of the country. On the contrary, they wished . . . gradually [to] prepare the way for the conditions necessary for the establishment of a complete national unity."[5] But this was exactly the point of bitter conflict between Hungary and her neighbors. The Hungarians denied their Danubian rivals the right to expand at the expense of the Hungarian nation, by assimilating Hungarian minorities into the Czechoslovak, Romanian and Yugoslav nations.

The extreme difficulties in the way of any reasonable policy between Hungary and her neighbors in this emotionally charged nationalistic atmosphere were recognized and discussed frankly by Thomas G. Masaryk, President of Czechoslovakia, in one of his conversations with Oscar Jászi. Jászi, referring to the "desperate dilemma of some Hungarian progressives between servile submission and secret irredentism," raised the following question: "If you were a Hungarian statesman, what would you do now? What would be the leading ideas of your policy in regard to Hungary proper and the Hungarian minority which had been cut off by the peace treaty?" Masaryk answered that he would try to do two things: "First, I would fight for an honest carrying out of national autonomy for the Hungarians. In the second place, I would advocate the return to Hungary of those territories in the frontier regions where the Magyars constitute a solid, homogeneous majority. . . ." Then he added:

"Of course I do not know how far such a Hungarian statesman would be successful under the prevailing conditions. But he at least would advocate a reasonable program which one day might become reality, instead of the orgies of chauvinism which cannot achieve anything, but only create new inner convulsion and new war. . . ."[6]

T. G. Masaryk, who played such a prominent role in creating the post-Habsburg nationalist order of Central Europe, did much also to tame the "orgies of chauvinism." But in the end, his efforts to control that spirit of nationalism which had been unleashed by the great nationalist revolution of 1918 of which he himself was a leader met with failure.

After the war, Masaryk advocated cooperation of the small nations. "Everywhere the weak, oppressed and exploited unite themselves," he wrote in his book *The New Europe*. But actually his plans, even in theory, did not embrace all the small nations of the Middle Zone but only the victorious ones. The federalist plans he discussed in 1918 with the Romanian statesman Take Ionescu and with Premier Venizelos of Greece envisaged cooperation only among the victor nations — Poland, Czechoslovakia, Romania, Yugoslavia and Greece.[7] The upshot of these plans was, first, a narrow military union among Czechoslovakia, Romania and Yugoslavia — the Little Entente — directed against one of the other small nations, Hungary; and second, the Balkan Pact among Romania, Yugoslavia and Greece, directed against another small nation, Bulgaria.

Common agrarian interests and some vague notions of Slavic solidarity gave birth, in the early twenties, to the International Agrarian Bureau, known also as the "Green International." This International had branches in all the Slav countries of the Middle Zone: Czechoslovakia, Poland, Yugoslavia and Bulgaria. It was criticized at its inception as a "movement of democratic Panslavism, inspired by Czechoslovaks . . . on which Czechoslovakia might rest her policy in Central and Eastern Europe."[8] In fact the center of the movement was the Prague Bureau, and Antonin Švehla, together with Milan Hodža, the two prominent Czechoslovak agrarian politicians, were the guiding and driving spirits of the movement. However, the movement gradually lost its exclusive Slav character. Finnish, Estonian, Latvian, Lithuanian, Romanian, Austrian — and even French, Swiss and Italian — agrarian movements cooperated with the Prague Bureau. Of particular importance were the conferences held in 1930 at which peasant delegates from the Baltic states and from Poland, Hungary, Bulgaria and the Little Entente countries met to discuss the grave problems posed by the agrarian crisis. This so-called "agrarian bloc" tried to coordinate the economic policy of the participating countries, but proved too weak to fulfill its aims.

The economic crisis that rocked Central Europe in 1931 with the bankruptcy of the Austrian Credit-Anstalt (a crisis precipitated, incidentally, by the French withdrawal of the Credit-Anstalt's short-term credits in reprisal for the plan of an Austrian-German customs union) produced new arguments in favor of international cooperation. But efforts to bring about better relations among rivals by economic rapprochement remained unsuccessful. What the prevailing spirit of nationalism favored was not cooperation but isolation in the form of "autarky," a policy designed to make individual nations economically self-sustaining.

Economic crisis, the failure of Briand's European plan, and the success of Hitler's aggressive nationalist movement, the reverberations of which were already being felt throughout Europe, prompted a group of Danubian politicians to organize, in February 1932, an unofficial Comité Permanent pour Rapprochement Economique des Pays Danubiens. Austria, Czechoslovakia, Hungary, Romania and Yugoslavia were represented in the committee under the chairmanship of Paul Auer, a Hungarian advocate of Danubian federation. The committee favored economic cooperation, with a view to closer future union of the five Danubian countries. The suggestions of the committee found favorable reception by the French Foreign Minister André Tardieu, and served as a basis for his memorandum issued in March 1932. The Tardieu memorandum displayed, relatively speaking, the most serious initiative of the inter-war period toward bringing about cooperation among the peoples of the former Habsburg Monarchy. In effect, Tardieu's plan, if successful, could have restored the economic unity of the former Habsburg Empire — and this was a goal which many deemed desirable but which nobody had known how to achieve.

Tardieu's memorandum proposed preferential reciprocal tariffs and mutually favorable quota allotments among the five Danubian countries, Austria, Czechoslovakia, Hungary, Romania and Yugoslavia. It was strictly a plan of economic cooperation in line with the school of thought that the more complicated political reconciliation in the Danube Valley must be preceded by economic rapprochement. The memorandum was modest in setting the goals of economic cooperation. Tardieu thought it would not be opportune to consider a customs union between the Danubian countries, because the formation of such union would meet with insuperable difficulties. The memorandum stated that "it will be best to leave the initiation of the discussions to the five countries concerned," and it pointed out that so far as possible "the interests of the states outside the Danubian combination" should be taken into account. The Tardieu plan failed even before the Danubian governments had had much chance to discuss it, because "states outside the Danubian combination" were opposed to it. Not only Germany and Italy, as could be expected, but even Britain, reacted unfavorably to the French proposal.[9]

The British government harbored the suspicion that the Tardieu plan was just another ruse to promote French interests in Central Europe. Germany, never enthusiastic over any Danubian plan which did not recognize her leadership, had an additional reason to oppose the Tardieu plan: a year before, in 1931, the project of a German-Austrian customs union — the so-called Schober-Curtius plan — had been killed by a vigorous protest from the French, Italian and Czechoslovak governments. As for Italy, she viewed the Tardieu plan with as much antipathy as she had the Schober-Curtius plan, because both ran counter to her own ambitions for an Italian sphere of influence in Central Europe and the Balkans. Italy's treaty of friendship with Hungary in 1927, and with Austria in 1930, were precursors of the Rome Protocol of 1934, which provided for closer economic cooperation among the three countries. With revisionist Bulgaria also, Italy forged intimate relations. Mussolini's sympathy with all these revisionists was fairly Machiavellian. His claim for "justice" for his revisionist friends was above all a smokescreen behind which he promoted the power interests of Italy. In the Balkans he was interested in isolating Italy's rival, Yugoslavia, from her neighbors, Bulgaria and Hungary. In the Danube Valley he tried to strengthen Italy's position vis-à-vis France and Germany. This motivation of Mussolini's Central European policy was even "clearly" understood — or, at least, Admiral Horthy said so in his memoirs — by the government of Hungary, Italy's protégé in the Danube Valley.[10]

The Danubian governments, whose cooperation was anticipated in the Tardieu plan, never met to discuss the implementation of the plan. Their reactions, however, were symptomatic of the mistrust and suspicion with which they eyed each other.

Hungary's point of view was summed up most distinctly by Count Stephen Bethlen, under whose premiership the Horthy regime had been consolidated, and whose influence remained considerable even after his resignation in 1931. In one of the revisionist lectures he delivered in

England in the autumn of 1933, Bethlen said: "The Tardieu plan, the scheme of a Danube confederation, as well as a long line of other variations, are all suffering from a common disease: they are economic conceptions which, however, do not solve the economic problems, having been born in a bed of a political mental reservations. . . . Practically all of them have the ultimate hidden end of drawing Hungary into the sphere of interest of the Little Entente, by offering to this country superficial economic favors, without, however, previously satisfying her rightful demands of a fair and just revision of the peace treaty."[11]

On the other hand, for almost opposite reasons, the Tardieu plan did not please the Little Entente countries either. They would have nothing to do with the plan should it change the political status quo. They suspected that the plan, if further developed — as some of its supporters hoped it would be — might introduce a new form of cooperation which would supersede the Little Entente. These fears were aired by Eduard Beneš, Foreign Minister of Czechoslovakia, on March 22, 1932, when he said: "If this cooperation should evolve political obligations of any kind, or its aims or consequences should tend towards some sort of organization, so-called confederation, or similar political combination, then, I believe, there is no doubt on our part that we would reject this cooperation, and in this respect the countries of the Little Entente stand united."

Indeed the spirit of the Tardieu plan was in many ways incompatible with the spirit of the Little Entente. If the plan could have been properly carried out, economic cooperation could have become the first step toward political reconciliation; then mutual recognition of parity among the Danubian nations would have become imperative, and revision of the Trianon Treaty's inequalities so stubbornly defended by the Little Entente would have become unavoidable. However, considering the general trend of European diplomacy, the Little Entente's worries over the Tardieu plan were unfounded. So too were Count Bethlen's worries lest Hungary be drawn into the Little Entente's "sphere of interest," with consequent impairment of her chances to regain domination of the Carpathian basin.

How slim the Tardieu plan's chances of success were, even among France's Danubian allies, could be seen from the diplomatic activities of the Little Entente. They did not conceal their view that the plan represented a rival scheme to their existing alliance system. Shortly after the launching of the Tardieu plan in March 1932, the Little Entente was revamped into an even tighter organization. The three foreign ministers, Beneš of Czechoslovakia, Titulescu of Romania, and Jevtić of Yugoslavia, met in Belgrade in December 1932 and agreed on the so-called Statute of the Little Entente, which was signed at Geneva on February 16, 1933.

By this Statute of 1933, a permanent council consisting of the foreign ministers of the Little Entente was set up, to which was added an economic council and a permanent bureau with an office in Geneva. The Little Entente, it was said, had developed from a military alliance into a "diplomatic federation." Moreover, the Statute described it as a "higher international unit open to other States under the conditions applicable to each particular case." The propaganda of the Little Entente accordingly began to speak about a Central European federation in the making, a slogan which found its way even into scholarly literature in the West. For instance, a publication of the University of California Press described the Little Entente as an excellent beginning, a definite step in the right direction, an organism which, whatever its faults, looked forward to the federal idea.[12] It is difficult to comprehend how anyone could view the Little Entente as the nucleus of a Central European federation, save by ignoring the difference between a federation and an imperialistic alliance concluded for the defense of selfish national interests.

The true purpose of the Little Entente was somewhat similar to the Austro-Hungarian Compromise of 1867. Both displayed liberal trends which earned them respect; in the Compromise, Hungary was put on equal footing with Austria, and in the Little Entente, nations once oppressed asserted their freedom. Nevertheless the Compromise was really designed to maintain the hegemony of Germans and Hungarians, while the Little Entente really favored the domination of the Danube Valley by the Czechs, Serbs and Romanians. It was characteristic of the spirit of Danubian politics that those who saw clearly the imperialistic aims of the Austro-Hungarian Compromise failed to recognize the very same objectives in the Little Entente, and vice versa.

The Little Entente's role was to enforce a new order in Central Europe which certainly was more equitable than the old one established by the Austro-Hungarian Compromise. National and social freedom was greater under the Little Entente era than under the Habsburg regime. Yet complaints like those from the past, when the Serbian nation was split into four parts, were still voiced — only this time they came from the Hungarian nation split into four parts. Also, Czech supremacy in multinational Czechoslovakia, as well as Serbian supremacy in multinational Yugoslavia, curtailed the full freeedom even of the so-called liberated nationalities. Furthermore, each of the small succession states into which the former Habsburg Empire was divided tried to carry out mutually irreconcilable nationalistic programs which, instead of paving the way for reconciliation, actually tended to keep the Danube Valley in a state of permanent conflict. The Little Entente, therefore, as the defender of this status quo, blocked rather than promoted peaceful development toward a Danubian federation of equal nations. Unless the purposes for which the Little Entente had been designed were discarded, federalism in Central Europe was as impossible as it would have been under the Habsburg Monarchy without complete revision of the Austro-Hungarian Compromise.

After its reorganization in 1933, the Little Entente took to boasting that it was well on its way to becoming the beginning of a Central European federation. Nothing could have been farther from the truth, as subsequent events have shown. The Little Entente remained, as before, mainly an anti-revisionist coalition directed against revisionist Hungary. The same held true of the Balkan Pact, signed in 1934 by Romania, Yugoslavia and Greece, which was directed against revisionist Bulgaria. This pact too was mainly an anti-revisionist platform, even though Bulgaria's neighbors who brought the pact into being preferred to regard it as the harbinger of Balkan federalism.

3 *The Nazi Challenge*

In combating the campaign for the revision of the peace treaties, a favorite contention of the victors was that the status quo needed to be maintained in the interests of democracy and peace. This rather controversial view came closer to the truth when Hitler came to power on January 30, 1933, and when, shortly after, Nazi Germany assumed leadership of the revisionist bloc. But the stronger the totalitarian revisionist threat grew, the weaker the democratic status quo front became. In the end the status quo front — or more precisely the French alliance system created for the defense of the status quo — collapsed without fulfilling its professed role as defender of democracy and peace.

The duels in diplomacy between the Nazi challengers and the democratic defenders of the European status quo got off to a rather ominous start in the summer of 1933. France, main defender of the status quo, and Great Britain, a hesitant partner, signed in Rome a treaty with the two principal revisionist powers, Mussolini's Italy and Hitler's Germany. This Four Power Pact reiterated adherence to the existing treaties. The pact never came into force; with Germany's exit from the League of Nations and from the Disarmament Conference in October 1933 the Four Power experiment ended. Nevertheless, the attempt to strengthen the status quo through cooperation with its challengers drew after itself two adverse consequences. On the one hand it emboldened the revisionists by making them believe that the status quo defenders lacked confidence in their own cause. On the other hand it tended to confuse the members of the French alliance system by making them suspicious of their leader's intentions.

Following this miscarried experiment, French and British diplomats began probing new avenues in their quest for "collective security." In an effort to counterbalance Hitler's Germany, they tried to cooperate with the two older types of European totalitarianism, Fascist Italy and Soviet Russia. And all this left Hitler undisturbed in building a new center of tyranny in the heart of Europe.

Fascist Italy stood ideologically closer to Nazi Germany than to the

Western democracies; nevertheless in the first years of Hitler's rule she preferred the partnership of the Western Powers. With her interests in the Danube Valley and the Balkans, Italy was particularly disturbed by Hitler's plot against the independence of Austria. In February 1934, Italy joined Britain and France in issuing a common declaration which pledged the defense of Austria's independence. During the Nazi coup which miscarried in Vienna, in July 1934, Italy mobilized and massed her troops along the Brenner Pass. The rapprochement between Italy and the Western Powers reached its zenith in 1935: in January of that year France signed a treaty of friendship with Italy; in April Britain, France and Italy met at Stresa, where they condemned Germany's repudiation of her obligations under the Versailles Treaty, and again pledged themselves to defend Austria's integrity and independence.

In the diplomatic battle against Germany, this cooperation between Italy and the Western Powers scored a rather dubious success — and it cost France an appreciable loss of prestige among her allies in the cordon sanitaire. The intentions behind the moves of French diplomacy and the conclusions which could be drawn from them were highly disturbing to France's allies. Czechoslovakia's Beneš, the guiding spirit of the Little Entente, was worried lest a new power grouping in the West might reduce the Little Entente's collective role as a "Great Power." Yugoslavia felt betrayed by the French-Italian pact, for she looked upon Italy as her principal foe. Poland, ambitious for the rank and title of a Great Power, felt slighted at being left out of the new moves, which seemed to indicate a regrouping in the European system of alliances.

The crisis that hit the French alliance system in the cordon sanitaire, when Hitler's rise to power ended the relative tranquility of Europe, was long drawn out. France's satellites in the Middle Zone were in agreement with the basic aim of French policy in defending the territorial status quo, but the problems of French security were different from those which France's allies were facing, wedged as they were between Russia, Germany and Italy. From the very beginning, the cordon sanitaire was for France a *faute de mieux* arrangement; French diplomacy did not hesitate to improve France's security by moves that her satellites found it hard to keep pace with. Such a move was the rapprochement between France and Germany during the Locarno period in the twenties; such was the stillborn Four Power Pact of 1933; and such were the French-Italian and especially the French-Russian rapprochements of the thirties.

It was not surprising that the rebirth of an aggressive Germany should revive the idea of an East-West alliance against Germany. But the great change in Russia, the Communist revolution of 1917 which had installed a regime so alien and so hostile to the bourgeois-democratic order of Europe, considerably complicated the resumption of old ties. Territorial conflicts between the Soviet Union and her independent western neighbors was another problem which Western diplomacy had not faced when before the First World War the foundations of the Franco-British-Russian Triple Entente were laid.

When France embarked upon a policy of rapprochement with Soviet Russia, the aim of the French alliances in the cordon sanitaire had to be revised in order to make room for the new orientation. Originally the cordon sanitaire had a double mission to fulfill, as an instrument both for Germany's encirclement and for Soviet Russia's containment. Now the containment mission had to be toned down, if not abolished altogether. But it was much easier for France than for her allies in Central and Eastern Europe to switch on and off the missions of the cordon sanitaire — not to mention that France's allies were entangled in conflicts of interests among themselves which made difficult indeed any united move for any purpose whatever.

Soviet Russia was not deterred by scruples from assuring her neighbors of her good will. In addition to separate peace treaties, she later signed one neutrality and non-aggression pact after another with her western neighbors. In 1929, the Litvinov Protocol signed in Moscow with Russia's neighbors pledged adherence to the provisions of the famous Briand-Kellogg Pact (1927) outlawing war. In 1933 the London convention for the definition of aggression was signed between Russia and her neighbors. The definition of the term "aggressor" could only be greeted with satisfaction, in view of the much-dreaded clandestine methods of communist warfare. The Russians, eager to please their neighbors, agreed that so-called indirect aggression — that is, "support to armed bands on the territory of another state, or refusal to take all the measures to deprive these bands of all assistance or protection" — should be put in the same category with direct aggression. But Soviet assurances of good will did not make France's eastern allies willing partners of the Russian orientation. Distrust of Russia and fear of communism left Poland, Romania and Yugoslavia cold, if not hostile, toward the French-Russian rapprochement. Only Czechoslovakia's foreign policy, directed by Beneš, acclaimed the new trend.

Even before the French-Russian rapprochement, Beneš had never missed an opportunity to stress the importance of Russia in the defense of the European status quo. With the crisis in Central Europe approaching, he often reiterated his credo. For instance, in 1931 he said: "The question of Russia will always play a great part in our destiny, if only because of our geographical position. . . . For that reason, the conception of our foreign policy will not be definitely completed until Russia becomes an active factor in Central Europe with her full might and interest engaged there. Russia is thus indispensable to us if we are to ensure our definitive position in Europe."[1]

Czechoslovakia followed France's Russian orientation, but not because she was a progressive democratic country; nor did Poland, Romania and Yugoslavia reject Russian orientation because of their reactionary regimes. Views which stressed ideological considerations often overlooked the primary factors shaping the foreign policies of these countries. In fact, geographical position and territorial disputes were of far greater importance than ideologies in deciding the question of whether an alliance with Stalin against Hitler was advisable or not. This explains also why none of the countries involved was in a position to view the Russian alliance so unequivocally as Beneš did. Czechoslovakia had a huge German minority, she bordered on Germany and had never had any disputes with Russia. Poland, on the other hand, bordered on both Germany and Russia, and had a long record of hostility with both, but far greater territorial disputes with Russia. As for Romania, she was far from Germany, bordered on Russia, and had grave territorial disputes with the latter over Bessarabia. And Yugoslavia, far from both Russia and Germany, reacted more sensitively to Italian than to German pressure on Central Europe.

Nor was the policy of France, to begin with, directed by democratic ideological considerations. With the rising tide of totalitarian revisionism the French alliance system was no doubt the potential defender of democracy in Europe; but collective defense of democracy was nobody's primary concern — each member of the alliance system was concerned primarily with the security of its own status quo, France as much as those whom she was supposed to lead.

The country least inclined to follow French leadership was Poland. She was suspicious of French aims; she was also irritated by the French fondness for the Czechs, of whom the Poles were not particularly fond; she was critical of the whole policy of the League of Nations. Polish policy was directed by Marshal Joseph Piłsudski — constitutionally only Minister of War and Inspector General of the army, but actually the head of state with dictatorial powers. His principal aide was Colonel Joseph Beck, Foreign Minister since 1932. Both distrusted the French alliance system. Poland began to go her own way even before the great French diplomatic efforts of the Hitler era. In July 1932, Poland signed a non-aggression pact with Soviet Russia; it was extended for ten years more in 1935. But Poland's treaty with Russia never became a part of the new, Russia-oriented, French policy in defense of the status quo. At the very time when France was making great efforts to include the Soviet Union in her collective security system, Poland signed (January 1934) a separate non-aggression treaty with Nazi Germany, without even consulting France. Although Poland voted for Soviet Russia's admission to the League of Nations in September 1934, this did not narrow the gap between her own and France's policy; and apprehensive lest the Soviet Union as a League member interfere with Polish minority policies, the Warsaw government declared that it did not recognize any longer the right of the League to concern itself with the Polish minority question.

Polish leaders felt their independent course of action was justified by the weaknesses of the alliance system led by France. They were greatly deluded, however, in thinking that they would strengthen their own position by separate treaties. They weakened all the defenders of the status quo, including themselves. They helped Hitler achieve the first resounding victory of his "peace policy," which aimed at concluding bilateral treaties in order to undermine the Franco-British collective diplomatic efforts.

France and Britain, although fearful of communism, agreed on the usefulness of Soviet Russia in counterbalancing the threat of German imperialism and militarism revived by Hitler. These views were shared by President Roosevelt. An important event of East-West rapprochement took place in 1933 when Maxim Litvinov, the Soviet Commissar for Foreign Affairs, journeyed to Washington and diplomatic relations were established between the United States and Soviet Russia. American foreign policy, however, was drifting toward isolationism, and the United States remained absent from the European scene as the crisis stirred up by Hitler moved rapidly to a climax.

The Russians endorsed Western diplomacy's aim of collective security; in fact they supported it even more energetically than the British, who, although not yet appeasers of Nazi Germany, continued in their traditional aversion to entanglements in Eastern Europe. Meanwhile French diplomacy, directed by Foreign Minister Louis Barthou, worked toward a renewal of France's alliance with Russia. The Soviet response was favorable. The alliance, in its first form, was to be embedded in a broader security pact, an "Eastern Locarno," which would include Germany too. In July 1934 a draft treaty sponsored by both the French and the Soviet governments was proposed, under which the Soviet Union, Germany and France, as well as France's allies in the cordon sanitaire, Poland and Czechoslovakia, were invited to sign a mutual guarantee pact. To all intents and purposes this meant that Germany and the Soviet Union would guarantee the cordon sanitaire which had been built against them, or in other words that they would encircle and contain themselves. Strange as it may seem, the Soviet Union was willing in this instance to contain herself. Germany, on the other hand, showed no willingness to participate in her own encirclement.

This "Eastern Locarno" came to nothing. It was supplanted by a simpler formula, in which France and the Soviet Union entered into a bilateral mutual assistance treaty on May 2, 1935. Among France's satellites only Czechoslovakia was pleased, and she too signed a mutual assistance treaty with the Soviet Union, two weeks after the Franco-Soviet pact, on May 16. In the Czechoslovak-Soviet treaty, however, mutual assistance was made dependent upon the fulfillment of France's obligations to assist Czechoslovakia or the Soviet Union, in case they were victims of aggression. Yet, Beneš's efforts to see Russia among the guarantors of the existing order were crowned with success at long last. He had the privilege of being chairman of the League Council when in September 1934 the Soviet Union entered the League of Nations — the "robbers' den," as Lenin had once defined it — a step Beneš favored strongly and helped to effect.

Thus the Soviet Union, recently a castigator of the Versailles system, entered the ranks of the status quo supporters. Litvinov became the most ardent and eloquent advocate of collective security — so ardent and so eloquent that collective security, originally a platform of Western diplomacy, became as much a Communist watchword as were some of the teachings of Lenin. Stalin evidently took seriously the aggressive plans against Russia which Hitler outlined in *Mein Kampf*. Even before Hitler proved, in the years to come, that more serious than his violent outbursts against communism was his hatred of the Slavs, Stalin seemed to understand that the old contest between Germans and Slavs had been reopened under the disguise of nazism versus communism.

The change in Soviet thinking was reflected in the platform of the Seventh Congress of the Comintern in 1935, when the so-called Popular

Front policy was adopted. Communists throughout the world were encouraged to cooperate, not only with the Social Democrats — who had been branded as "Social Fascists" at the Sixth Congress in 1928 — but even with the nationalist-capitalist bourgeoisie and practically everybody who opposed Hitler. In response, Hitler proclaimed himself the defender of Western civilization against the menace of communism. Absurd as was Hitler's claim, it was far from unsuccessful in making his brand of tyranny appear a lesser evil than communism and even an effective counterpoise to it.

The Franco-Soviet-Czechoslovak treaties in the spring of 1935, supplemented by the Franco-British-Italian agreements, marked the culmination of France's effort to strengthen the status quo front against the growing menace of Nazi-German revisionism and totalitarianism. The treaties and agreements were nothing more nor less than products of power politics, but this was the best Europe was able to produce in defense of democracy.

The stabilization of the status quo front against Hitler had begun under Barthou's foreign ministry, when France was more alert to the Nazi danger than at any other time during those critical years. It was completed under Barthou's successor Pierre Laval — who later distinguished himself as a collaborator of Hitler. Barthou was assassinated at Marseilles in October 1934. Another victim of the Marseilles assassination was the dictator of Yugoslavia, King Alexander. The assassins were Croat and Macedonian nationalist extremists — Yugoslav subjects, that is. The Yugoslav government, anxious to explain the assassination as the work of outside enemies rather than the result of fratricidal domestic strife, charged the Hungarian and Italian governments with complicity. But whatever the complicity of Yugoslavia's outside enemies, France lost in King Alexander one of her friends and allies; after the king's death, Yugoslav policy came increasingly under the influence of the Germanophile Premier Milan Stojadinović and veered away from France. French diplomacy in Central Europe suffered another setback in 1936, when Romania's king, Carol II, began to lose faith in the French security system and dismissed his Francophile foreign minister, Titulescu.

No less serious than the crisis in the old ties of the French alliance system was the crisis in the new ones. French-Italian cooperation ceased in the autumn of 1935, when Italy invaded Abyssinia. The French-Soviet alliance, while still in effect, was more a source of confusion than one of strength. Its Western opponents became especially vociferous when in May 1936 Léon Blum formed his Popular Front government in France. The Communists, although not formally members of the government, attained great strength and influence, mainly through the new united labor organization, the Confédération Générale du Travail. In reaction, the fear of communism, latent when the Franco-Soviet pact was concluded, burst into the open. The anti-Communist reaction was strengthened, both in France and throughout Europe, by the outbreak of the Spanish civil war in July 1936, Russia's informal intervention in Spain on the Republican side arousing far greater fears than Italy's and Germany's similar intervention on Franco's side. The chasm between the European "Right" and "Left" was growing, the former showing concern over the threat of communism, the latter over that of nazism and fascism. And as one observer, standing on the Left, characterized the temper of Europe, these events "struck fear into the hearts of the middle classes, stirring latent sympathy for fascism and fanning distrust of Russia."[2]

Meanwhile in Britain a new ideology of peace crystallized which suited well the temper of the West. This new ideology, if not born from sympathy for fascism, was nevertheless distrustful of Russia, and it gave Hitler the benefit of the doubt which he assuredly did not deserve.

Up to 1935 the British government was in sympathy with the idea of enlisting Russia as a counterweight to Hitler's Germany, though it abstained from making such formal commitments as France had made in her mutual assistance treaty with the Russians. But no sooner had the French-Soviet-Czechoslovak alliance become a reality than Britain turned against the Soviet orientation. German propaganda, denouncing the French and Czech alliances with the Russians as "a threat to European civilization," was too scurrilous to affect British public opinion. The change in Britain's mood was rather the result of another, more subtle, type of propaganda, the one which had been directed for years against the inequalities of the Versailles peace settlement. The historian Edward Hallett Carr described very well this change in Britain: "A growing body of opinion came round to the view that the only effect of the French understanding with Italy and the Soviet Union was to isolate and encircle Germany and perpetuate the inequalities of the Versailles Treaty — in short, to maintain those very conditions which had been largely responsible for the Nazi revolution."[3]

The policy of appeasement which resulted from this view treated Hitler as a nationalist leader whose only ambition was to undo the injustices inflicted upon Germany by the Versailles Treaty. In a somewhat similar fashion the Western Powers, during the Second World War, allowed themselves to believe that Stalin was becoming a nationalist, interested mainly in Russian security. Democratic vigilance could have discovered promptly that the inequities of the Versailles Treaty were a poor excuse for the violent agitation, let alone for the brutalities, committed by Hitler and his Nazis. But, as a result of the long years of revisionist propaganda, the Western democracies were "materially and psychologically disarmed", in the words of Hans Kohn, a keen commentator of the tragic first half of the twentieth century — they were "unprepared to understand the totalitarian challenge and much too peace-loving to take it up."[4]

Mounting fear of war began to paralyze the will of the nations whose destiny it was to defend Western civilization against Hitler. Far stronger than democratic vigilance or democratic solidarity was the longing for peace and tranquility. Unfortunately the West was as ill-prepared for Hitler's diplomatic offensive in the middle thirties as it was ill-equipped for Hitler's shooting war which followed in 1939.

Meanwhile the small nations of the Danube Valley, who lay in the path of Hitler's eastward expansion, were engrossed in their mutual fears and jealousies. Democratic Czechoslovakia, chief target of Hitler's wrath, was relying on friendly Great Powers for support against her enemies. Meanwhile her chief Danubian antagonist, revisionist Hungary, was watching with manifest delight the erosion of the status quo, hopeful of satisfying her national aspirations and like the others forgetful of the small nations' common destiny. Czech-Hungarian collaboration could have laid the cornerstone for defense of national independence in the Danube Valley. Czech-Hungarian antagonism paved the way for Hitler's aggression against the small nations of Central Europe.

This Czech-Hungarian antagonism has been generally viewed as a conflict between two diametrically opposed social systems — Hungary being portrayed as the standard-bearer of conservatism and reaction, Czechoslovakia as the champion of progress and democracy. Some such conflict undoubtedly existed; but a closer look at Czech and Hungarian policies reveals that, above all, conflicting nationalist aspirations pitted the two nations against each other and frustrated all chances of compromise and cooperation between them.

4 Czechs and Hungarians

Since the First World War no Central European country had enjoyed more sympathy from the West than Czechoslovakia. During the Second World War Czechoslovakia's reputation rose even higher. Her shameful betrayal at Munich weighed heavily upon the conscience of the West. Praise of her as *the* democratic country of Central Europe became more widespread than ever.

If Czechoslovakia was the darling of the West, admired and recognized as the builder of peace and democracy in Central Europe, Hungary on the other hand was the whipping boy, rebuked for her reactionary regime and blamed for the failure of peaceful evolution in post-Habsburg Central Europe. A.J.P. Taylor, during the Second World War, expressed quite a common belief when, writing with admiration about Czechoslovakia, and the "Beneš system," he said of Hungary: "The failure to establish wider, deeper, political and economic cooperation in Central Europe between the wars was the fault of the Hungarian governing class alone."[1] Although by no means "alone" responsible for the failure of cooperation, the Hungarian governing class was certainly the chief obstacle to the consolidation of the peace settlement in the Danube Valley. Post-war Hungary, surrounded by Austria, Czechoslovakia, Romania and Yugoslavia, occupied the center of the Danube Valley, and the viability of the new system, which Taylor called the Beneš system, depended largely upon Hungary's cooperation. The Hungarian governing class, however, was the least interested of all in making this system work. And, considering the anti-Hungarian bias of the peace settlement, there was no reason why any Hungarian regime should wish the new system to prosper.

It was often said by the leaders of Czechoslovakia that had Hungary been a democracy, relations between the two countries would have developed amicably. The antipathy of Hungary's reactionary rulers toward the Czechs on account of their democracy was undeniable. On the other hand, Czechoslovakia's hostility toward the Hungarians was not motivated merely by the Czech democrats' contempt for Hungary's reactionary ruling classes. The conflict between the two countries was rooted in nationalistic rivalry. The true nature of this conflict was clearly revealed following the two world wars. The most flagrantly hostile actions against Hungarians by Czech democrats were committed at these times: the forcible incorporation of Hungarians into Czechoslovakia after the First World War, and the forcible expulsion of Hungarians from Czechoslovakia after the Second; yet at both times Hungary happened to have incipiently democratic governments: under the Károlyi regime in 1918–19, and under the coalition regime in 1945–47.

Professor Taylor was right, of course, in pointing out that "the failure of the Károlyi regime, which held out the promise of a democratic Hungary, was a disaster both for Hungary and for Europe. . . ." It was a "disaster" indeed that the failure of Károlyi's revolution swept away from the Danubian scene those Hungarians who, deeply conscious of the causes of the Habsburg tragedy, held the most enlightened views about peaceful cooperation among the Danubian peoples. They were keen guardians of Hungarian national interests (they even hoped for a while to maintain the unity of historical Hungary by federalizing it), but they were free of the excessive national ambitions which motivated the imperialistic territorial demands of Czechoslovakia, Romania and Yugoslavia. Under democratic leadership, post-war Hungary would have had a soothing effect on the turbulent nationalism of the whole Danube Valley. Moreover, the Hungarian democrats held so much in common with the Czech democrats that Czechoslovakia, instead of launching the Little Entente against Hungary, could perhaps have entered into partnership with Hungary to build democracy in Central Europe; and then the injustices inflicted on Hungary by her neighbors in the post-war atmosphere of hatred might have been adjusted peacefully.

Such a development, although far from certain, would not have been entirely impossible had the Károlyi regime survived the revolutionary crisis of 1918–19. But it did not survive, and it should be remembered that one of the major causes of its failure was the hostile pressure of Hungary's neighbors.[2] After Károlyi's failure came Béla Kun's Communist rule of terror, then Horthy's counterrevolution. Thus, under Admiral Horthy's regime, Hungary slid back into the hands of the old ruling class, which combined in its policies some of the worst features of social reaction and chauvinistic nationalism. There was of course plenty of social reaction and chauvinistic nationalism elsewhere in post-Habsburg Central Europe, but it was a disaster that Hungary, the geographical center of the Danube Valley, did not come under a progressive and enlightened leadership.

The double tragedy of the lost war and the unsuccessful revolution destroyed Hungary's chances to help in building a new Central Europe. Humiliated and isolated, gutted and dismembered, helpless against her neighbors' greed and vengeance, Hungary started her post-war career in a pitiful condition indeed. Opinions differ as to which was Hungary's greater tragedy: the Trianon Peace Treaty or Horthy's counterrevolution. The counterrevolution certainly frustrated Hungary's chances, whatever they were, of extricating herself from the disastrous consequences of the Trianon peace settlement.

The counterrevolution, under Admiral Horthy's regency, restored the power of the pre-war oligarchy: the coalition of big landowners and lesser gentry, supported by high finance. Even worse, it entrenched in power the clique of army officers and bureaucrats, who had been accomplices in the "white" terror of the counterrevolution. However, the difference between the old and new strata of the post-war ruling class was one of degree rather than kind; they were all one in their dislike of democratic ways of life. The conservative wing of this oligarchy lingered in the aristocratic past, eager to keep society in a paternalistic system, with themselves of course as the privileged rulers, at the top of the hierarchy. The radical wing of the counterrevolution had no understanding of noble refinements; they indulged in the hollow mannerisms of the "Hungarian gentleman," but fundamentally they were neither gentle nor humane: they found their ideals ultimately fulfilled in Hitler's brutalities. The crucial shift of power toward the latter elements began under Gyula Gömbös's premiership in the thirties.

Premier Gömbös, not unlike his colleague in Austria, Chancellor Dollfuss, was an admirer of Mussolini. But Gömbös, unlike Dollfuss, was also an admirer of Hitler, and when the latter assumed power (1933) Gömbös hurried to Berlin to assure the Nazi Führer of Hungary's loyalty and traditional friendship toward Germany. Under Gömbös's premiership (1932–36), the leadership of the aristocracy decreased in favor of the lesser gentry and middle classes. This "democratization" of the regime was, however, detrimental rather than beneficial for both the country and Central Europe as a whole; it enhanced the influence of those counterrevolutionary forces which identified "reforms" with anti-Semitism, and "struggle for independence" with blind pursuit of revisionist policy in alliance with Nazi Germany and Fascist Italy.

The conditions of democratic progress were actually far less favorable under the post-war counterrevolutionary regime than they were in pre-war Hungary. The liberal-democratic spirit, always the expression of a minority, did not succeed in recapturing even its pre-war position. True, Budapest, the capital, was still one of Europe's great cities, an island where cosmopolitan culture flourished; in the Parliament and in the press a democratic opposition, though weak, nevertheless voiced its views; and the outer façade of liberalism was restored under Count Stephen Bethlen's premiership in the twenties, though the government carefully limited the freedom of democratic dissent. Advocacy of radical reforms proved futile in pre-war Hungary, but, in a comparatively liberal atmosphere, progressive ideas had a better chance for development than in the post-war times. Pre-war radicals could agitate more freely for democratic reforms than their spiritual heirs in post-war Hungary. For instance, in the thirties a group of writers called the "village explorers," who exposed the unhappy lot of the peasantry, were persecuted for subversion. No such "writers' trials" had ever occurred in pre-war Hungary. The post-war regime resisted especially stubbornly the two long-overdue basic reforms without which the country could not even start living the life of a truly democratic society: universal suffrage with the secret ballot, and the redistribution of land.

In 1920 some land reform was instigated; it redistributed less than two million acres, and not exactly among those who most needed the land. In 1939 the government announced another "reform," which promised approximately two million acres to the peasants. This second "reform" was never carried out, because of the Second World War. However, even if it had been, it would scarcely have solved the agrarian problem. Very different intentions from those of which the old regime was capable, and much more radical reforms, were needed. After the first "land reform" the distribution of land ownership in Hungary (a predominantly agrarian country with a population of nine million) was scarcely less outrageous than before. About a thousand families owned one-third of the land, while about three million people, who comprised two-thirds of the rural population, did not own any land at all, or not enough to sustain themselves as independent farmers. The Little Entente propaganda was alert in pointing out that the Hungarian government, while protesting the unjust treatment of the three million Hungarians outside the country, was in no hurry to cure the injustices of the "three million beggars" inside. Indeed the Horthy regime, which called itself "Christian and national," was moved neither by Christian ethics nor by national interests to end the plight of the Hungarian peasantry.

Government propaganda rejected charges against Hungary as a "feudal" country, arguing that the medieval system known in the West as "feudalism" had never taken root in Hungary. In a strict historical sense they were right, but such arguments did not improve the social conditions of twentieth-century Hungary. According to another theory popular with the ruling class, the failure of the democratic revolution, ending in Bolshevik terror after the First World War, and the unjust Trianon Treaty, dictated by the democratic powers, should be sufficient to discredit democracy in the eyes of the Hungarian people. Certainly the democratic program was discredited, but mainly as a result of vicious propaganda. The Horthy regime was most eager to convince the Hungarians that Károlyi's mistakes were responsible for the nation's tragedy. The democratic revolution was slandered and despised; it was described as a criminal act of traitors, unpatriotic Jews and Communist sympathizers, whose aims and deeds hardly differed from those of the Bolshevik terrorists. A public opinion was thus created which, as one observer remarked, attributed "an evil connotation" to the very term "democracy."[3] The extension of this line of thought was that Western betrayal of democratic principles of justice in the Trianon Treaty drove Hungary into the arms of Nazi Germany; this was the Hungarian variation of the Czech thesis, according to which Western betrayal of Czechoslovakia in Munich drove Beneš into the arms of Soviet Russia.[4] The Trianon Treaty was unjust; or, as Rustem Vámbéry (incidentally, a passionate castigator of the Horthy regime) expressed it, "worse than unjust or wrong, it was, indeed, stupid."[5] The separation from Hungary of about three million Hungarians — that is, over one-quarter of the entire nation — was a great injustice. This flagrant offense was the more unbearable inasmuch as the majority of the detached Hungarians lived along the new frontiers — forcibly separated, and only by the frontiers, from the rest of the nation. Their bitter opposition to the Trianon Treaty was justifiable; their protest was genuine and spontaneous. It was flimsy propaganda on the part of the Little Entente to represent the whole revisionist movement as the work of the Hungarian ruling class, eager to recover their estates in the neighboring countries, or anxious to divert the people's attention from the social ills inside Hungary. No doubt the Hungarian ruling class found it convenient to talk about the injustices the Trianon Treaty had inflicted on the nation, rather than to abolish the injustices they themselves were perpetrating against their own people; nevertheless the treaty was bad, and the Little Entente was wrong to defend its injustices.

Hungary, ever since her foundation a thousand years before, had always been an ethnically heterogeneous state, although politically she was united under Hungarian dominance. Following the First World War, she was reduced to a purely Hungarian state, ethnically almost homogeneous. Under no circumstances could such a great historical metamorphosis have taken place without stirring up bitter controversies. Unfortunately everybody concerned did his best to make the change as difficult as possible.

No hope whatsoever appeared that Hungary and her neighbors could come to an agreement on the revision of the Trianon peace settlement. There was no sign that the Little Entente would be willing to give serious consideration to Hungary's just claims. Moreover, there was no indication that Hungary would be satisfied with what could be considered her just claims, namely the reunification of the Hungarians living along the frontiers and the granting of autonomy to the rest, living farther away from the Hungarian ethnic bloc. The lofty "idea of Saint Stephen" envisaged the restoration of historical Hungary on a federal basis, with all the various nations enjoying autonomy and the Hungarians occupying the position of "*primus inter pares,*" first among equals.[6] Such exaggerated claims of the revisionist propaganda, the great stress it laid on the "perfect union" of "thousand-years-old Hungary," gave the Little Entente at least an excuse to oppose any revision; it was, however, far from certain that they would have been more responsive to revision if Hungary's revisionist propaganda had been more reasonable.

If there was a chance to gain the confidence of Hungary's neighbors (who were naturally resentful of the past) and to convince them of the necessity of replacing the vindictive peace treaty with a new deal, the Hungarian ruling class was certainly not qualified to reach such a pinnacle of statesmanship. Although they believed themselves to possess superior political abilities, they were neither capable of creating a modern democratic society for their own people, nor able to work toward an up-to-date compromise with their neighbors.

In contrast with Hungary, Czechoslovakia was most successful among the Danubian countries in building a modern democratic society. Nevertheless the much sought-after compromise between the ruling Czech nationality and the multinational population of the young republic proved unattainable, much as in the other states of post-Habsburg Central Europe where old struggles for national prerogatives continued.

The Czechs, dazzled by their undreamed-of triumph over Austria-Hungary, embraced enthusiastically the program of the national state. From the very beginning it was obvious that Czechoslovakia was not going to be "a sort of Switzerland." The Czech nation, with its will and talent, was the primary prop of the Czechoslovak national program and Czech supremacy was unavoidable if there was to be a Czechoslovak national state. For only the Czechs were in a position to make the new state a going concern, by defending it against the hostile pressure of the massive minorities, and by educating for leadership the two backward members of the fragile majority, the Slovaks and Ruthenes.

The linguistic affinity between Czechs and Slovaks was close enough. Their differences, however, resulting from long historical separation, proved in the long run to be stronger than their similarities. With the freedom they enjoyed in Czechoslovakia, the Slovaks developed into a distinct nation; and while their pro-Czech elements succeeded in merging Slovak nationalism with loyalty to the Czechoslovak state, their autonomist elements, imbued with local patriotism, clamored for independent rights. Thus, though the natural process of national growth, which the Slovaks had been unable to attain under Hungarian rule, was completed in Czechoslovakia, it ended also in a split within the Slovak nation. A somewhat similar process took place in Ruthenia, with even more confused results. The Ruthene nationalists were wavering not merely, like the Slovaks, between Czechoslovak loyalty and local patriotism, but also between Ukrainian and Russian sympathies.

The Czechs had troubles with the nationalities they intended to invest with majority rights (Slovaks, Ruthenes) as well as with those who were granted so-called minority rights (Germans, Hungarians, Poles). These troubles persisted in spite of the enlightened principles of President Masaryk which guided Czechoslovakia's policy. Czechoslovakia carried out progressive social, political, economic and cultural reforms. Her policy toward national minorities was more liberal than that of any other country of Central Europe, and in particular the Sudeten Germans of Bohemia enjoyed broad rights. However, in comparison with the status of the Czechs in old Austria, the Sudeten Germans had a somewhat less favorable position. This was because old Austria, though her supranational ties of loyalty to the dynasty were fading away, never was a German national state; whereas Czechoslovakia was the national state of the Czechs from its very beginning, and therefore parity between majority Czechs and minority Germans was, so to speak, by definition an impossibility. As far as Slovakia was concerned, there the Hungarians enjoyed incomparably more rights than the Slovaks had had in pre-war Hungary. But this was no consolation to the Hungarians; the change of their status from majority to minority was as painful for them as for the Germans in Bohemia.

The leaders of Czechoslovakia thought the democratic progress of the country — and the progress was remarkable — would appeal to both majority and minority, and would strengthen the ties of loyalty to the state; but in spite of the blessings of democracy and liberal minority rights, loyalty to the state which had conferred them was conspicuously lacking in vast portions of the population. In fact, only the Czechs were unconditionally loyal, for they not only enjoyed their national rights in full, but also occupied a privileged position as leaders of the country.

The ambition of the Czechs to create a unitary Czechoslovak nation on the one hand, and their mistrust of the non-Czech half of the population on the other, prolonged the rule of centralized government despite repeated promises of decentralization. A substantial part of the Slovaks, the centralists, accepted unity of their nation with the Czechs as final. Nevertheless, the Slovak "autonomists," whose leader in the inter-war period was the impulsive priest-politician Andrej Hlinka, were not merely clerical reactionaries (as Czech propaganda often called them) who turned into Fascists during the Hitler era; among Slovaks of various political beliefs there was a genuine and growing demand for autonomy, which had been pledged in the controversial Pittsburgh Convention of May 31, 1918, signed by T. G. Masaryk and some American citizens of Slovak descent. Similar to the feelings of the Slovaks were those of the Ruthenes. Moreover, the Ruthenes' right to autonomy was secured unequivocally both in the Minority Treaty of 1919 signed in St. Germain and the Czechoslovak constitution of 1920. Autonomy was also the popular battle cry of the Germans, Hungarians and Poles against the centralism of the Prague government. They had, however, no legal basis for claiming collective national minority rights, since the Minority Treaty and corresponding Czechoslovak laws provided them with minority rights for individuals only, not with rights for the national minority as a whole.

If all of the claims for autonomy had been fulfilled, Czechoslovakia would have been transformed into a federal state; but considering the lack of loyalty of the various nationalities toward their common state, federalization might have led to dissolution. During the great crisis in 1938, when the government's resistance to federalization was finally broken, the claims of the nationalities for autonomy turned out to be mere pretexts for ultimate complete secession. Perhaps an earlier federalization would have had the same effect, but this no one can know for certain. Obviously, however, the denial of autonomous rights was a source of permanent tension and irritation. The Slovaks felt insulted not to be allowed even to call themselves a nation, being obliged to say

"Czechoslovak nation." And the resentment of the Germans and Hungarians against the state was only intensified by such contentions as that the Germans of Bohemia, or the Hungarians of Slovakia, were colonists and foreign intruders in "millennial Czechoslovakia." The Germans and Hungarians, in turn, called Czechoslovakia a "Saisonstaat," a country which owed its birth in 1918 merely to favorable "seasonal" circumstances and would collapse if the international political climate should cease to favor her existence. The Czechs countered these angry charges with skillful propaganda.

Western scholars, through sympathy for the democratic Czechs, often endorsed the theory of a millennial Czechoslovakia in European history. The American historian S. Harrison Thomson, for instance, looking at the minority problems of Czechoslovakia, concluded that these problems were due to "the gradual infiltration of foreign influences into the territory occupied by the Czechoslovak people. . . . Germans came from several directions, Magyars from the south, into the living space of the Slovaks."[7] This was the same argument with which the Prague government defended its thesis that Czechoslovakia was the national state of the Czechs and Slovaks and that the Germans and Hungarians (that is, Magyars) were entitled to minority status only. The Germans, however, thought the question of "who came first" was meaningless from the point of view of how much privilege one should enjoy; moreover, they rejected the minority classifications on the ground that there were at least one million more Germans than Slovaks in Czechoslovakia. The Hungarians on the other hand labelled the theory of Slovak historical prerogatives as mere propaganda, and argued that their minority status was simply the result of artificial boundaries which separated them from the bulk of the Hungarian nation.

In order to gain the loyalty of the non-Czech half of the population, the Prague government, which was essentially controlled by the Czechs, used a variety of tactics. It appealed to the Slovaks and Ruthenes mainly in nationalistic terms. The gist of the argument laid before the Slovaks and Ruthenes was that Czechoslovakia saved them from Magyarization, assured their national development, and also endowed them with the blessings of democracy. Meanwhile in an effort to capture the loyalty of the Germans and Hungarians the government toned down the nationalist program, emphasizing the supranational and democratic mission of Czechoslovakia. The Germans were reminded of the old ties of Bohemian patriotism and, especially after the Nazi seizure of power in Germany, of the advantages of living in a democratic country. The

Hungarians were told how much better was their position in democratic Czechoslovakia than in semi-feudal Hungary.[8]

The German and Hungarian "activist" movements in Czechoslovakia, which advocated loyalty to the state and cooperation with the Prague government, were not altogether unsuccessful. Also, assimilation, a natural process of adjustment, which was strongly fostered by the government's loyalty drive, tended to lessen the hostility of the minorities to the state. Nevertheless the loyalty thus evolved proved ephemeral. Under the impact of Nazi propaganda the Sudeten German masses were alienated almost completely from the Czechoslovak state, which they had never liked anyway. And all the other dissatisfied nationality groups — with the exception of Jews and leftist elements among their numbers — also deserted the state without scruple during the 1938–39 crisis. The Jews were terrified by Hitler's anti-Semitism, and the leftist element regarded the defense of liberal Czechoslovakia against the Nazi German foe as a matter of democratic duty.

The inner cohesion of Czechoslovakia was diminishing apace, as the threat of hostile forces began to engulf the Republic from without. Whether the Czechoslovak state was a "Saisonstaat" or not, her existence depended on preservation of the European balance of power as it existed in 1919. The Czechs owed their national state, with a non-Czech population twice as great as that of the Czechs, to the conviction of the peacemakers that such a state would serve as a bulwark against Germany; and its unusually prominent role in post-war international affairs rested upon its position in the system of alliances created by France as a counterpoise against the threat of German imperialism. Once the Western Powers allowed Germany to rearm and overthrow the European balance of power, Czechoslovakia's security was doomed. Isolated from without, and undermined from within by disloyal citizens, she stood alone before the revived threat of German imperialism under Hitler's aggressive Third Reich.

5 *Appeasement of Hitler*

In the spring of 1935, France was working most actively for Nazi Germany's encirclement. The Franco-Italian agreements had been signed and the Franco-Soviet-Czechoslovak treaties had been concluded. At the same time, however, Hitler himself was not idle. In March, he brashly announced the creation of a German Air Force and the introduction of compulsory military service. The French government called for a special session of the League of Nations. Response was slow. In April, finally, at the Stresa Conference, Britain, France and Italy condemned Hitler's treaty violation. But in June the political effects of the new British appeasement attitude were felt in earnest for the first time. Britain signed the notorious Naval Agreement with Hitler, by which she acquiesced in a restoration of German naval strength to thirty-five percent of her own. In vain did Stanley Baldwin's Conservative government argue that the Naval Agreement would limit the armament race, which had got out of control when the Disarmament Conference collapsed in 1933. The fact remained that one of the leading democratic powers of the West had complied with Hitler's violation of the Versailles Treaty and, in a way, had cooperated in Germany's rearmament. Between British and French policies a serious rift occurred; but if the rift was serious, the eventual healing of it was disastrous, for it entailed France's adjusting her policy to Britain's fully-fledged appeasement policy.

The display of British-French disunity encouraged Hitler. His remilitarization of the Rhineland and denunciation of the Locarno Pact precipitated a new crisis in March 1936. Poland's Foreign Minister Beck, although at odds with French diplomacy, appealed to France and suggested armed action against Germany, and a similar suggestion had been made by Piłsudski in 1933, when Hitler seized power in Germany — though opinions differ about the seriousness and motivations of the Polish moves.[1] At any rate, Hitler was able to get away with his new violation of the Versailles Treaty. He further strengthened his position by making common cause with Mussolini, the invader of Abyssinia. In

October 1936, Count Galeazzo Ciano visited the German capital and signed a pact which laid down the foundations of the Rome-Berlin Axis. Called a league of "have-nots" against the league of the "haves," the Axis proved an effective instrument of aggressive policy. Another move of Hitler's diplomacy was the theatrical Anti-Comintern Pact signed with Japan in November 1936. Japan, the invader of Manchuria, was another suitable partner for Hitler. Thus, in uniting himself with the aggressors in Asia and Africa, Hitler was preparing for his eastward expansion in Europe. The year 1936 was truly a turning point. While the West was drifting ever more distinctly toward appeasement, Hitler was stepping up ever more boldly his aggressiveness.

The prospects for resistance to Hitler's *Drang nach Osten* were gloomy. The smaller countries east of Germany were disunited and perplexed by the appeasement currents of Western diplomacy, and their social ills and national strifes were skillfully exploited by Nazi diplomacy and propaganda.

Economic conditions in the predominantly agricultural eastern half of Europe played into the hands of the Nazis. Countries suffering from economic crisis generally benefited by Hitler's economic policies, because Germany bought their agricultural products. Material interests called for cooperation with, rather than resistance to, Hitler. Moral resistance to Nazi ideology was greatly undermined by Hitler's appeal to the base instincts of anti-Semitism. The ratio of Jews in the more lucrative free professions, which was out of proportion to their percentage of the total population, aided the spread of anti-Semitism throughout Central and Eastern Europe. The spearheads of Nazi infiltration were the many large German minorities of the Middle Zone, who readily embraced the aggressive and perverse ideas of national-socialism. In fact, Hitler's program appealed to many malcontents, irrespective of nationality, who were dissatisfied with the existing social or political order. The revisionist governments, of course, agreed with Hitler's loudly proclaimed aim of undoing "the injustices of the peace treaties." But the defenders of the status quo, too, in their confused and disorganized state, more and more deemed it opportune to curry the favor of the new and powerful German Reich.

While stamping out liberalism at home, the Führer advertised his foreign policy in terms of lofty liberal principles. His aim was, so he boasted, to apply for the benefit of the German nation too, the right of self-determination proclaimed by Woodrow Wilson's peace program of 1918. He wanted, so he said, nothing but the liberation of the German nation from the shackles of Versailles. The first goal of his expansion was the annexation of Austria.

The countries of the Middle Zone succumbed to Hitler's aggression one by one. Although the circumstances of the various conquests were different, there were some common causes of the tragedy of the small nations. First, their inner weaknesses undermined their individual power of resistance. Second, their strifes with each other destroyed whatever abilities they might have had for resistance through cooperation. Third, the blunderings of the Western Powers left them without guidance and aid.

The inner weakness of Austria was greater than that of any other country threatened by Hitler's aggression. She had led an aimless sort of life since the dissolution of the Habsburg Empire. The program in favor of union with Germany, the so-called "Anschluss," had always been popular in Austria. It remained popular after Hitler's seizure of power in Germany. Austria was no longer a democratic state which could reject union with Nazi Germany for reasons of political ideology. The most powerful source of anti-Nazi resistance could have been the socialist movement. But this had been crushed by the Dollfuss government in the winter of 1933–34 when Vienna had become the scene of a full-scale civil war. The battle against the highly civilized and once powerful Austrian social democracy had actually begun in the early twenties. The attack was led by the Heimwehr, a private army organized mainly by monarchists who aped the Italian Fascists and looked upon Mussolini as the champion of Habsburg restoration. The Heimwehr and the Fascist course of Austrian policy managed to grow under Ignaz Seipel, the Catholic priest-Chancellor, as the reactionary elements succeeded in taking control of the Christian Social party. The Fascist trend culminated in 1934 with Chancellor Engelbert Dollfuss's establishment of a dictatorship on the Italian model.[2]

Dollfuss relied upon his own brand of dictatorship to foil the Nazi dictator's project for annexing Austria. However, the conservative-clerical regime which Dollfuss had helped to create was unable to unite the country against Hitler. Dollfuss was murdered in the miscarried attempt of Austrian Nazis to seize power in the summer of 1934. Dollfuss's successor and the heir to his policy, Chancellor Kurt von Schuschnigg, was fighting a losing battle against the rising tide of Nazi-German nationalism as the showdown with Hitler approached.

Austria's Danubian neighbors were unable to bring themselves and

Austria with them into any kind of unity to oppose Hitler's aggression. An eleventh-hour attempt to integrate the Danubian countries was made by Milan Hodža, Premier of Czechoslovakia, in 1936. His original aim was to establish cooperation between the three countries of the Rome Protocol (Italy, Austria, Hungary) and the three countries of the Little Entente (Czechoslovakia, Romania, Yugoslavia). But Mussolini, after his pact with Hitler in 1936, ceased to be a protector of Austrian independence, and the Rome bloc lost its anti-Hitler potentialities. Hodža therefore had to drop Italy from his scheme. The resulting so-called Danubian Plan — which, like Tardieu's plan, proposed to link together the Danubian states by means of a preferential system — never materialized; it shared the fate of many pious desires aimed at the recreation in modern form of the economic unity of the old Habsburg Empire.

Hodža discussed with Schuschnigg the possibility, also, of the restoration of a Habsburg ruler in Austria as a means of bolstering the country's threatened independence. Meanwhile, in sharp contrast to the plans for saving Austria by Danubian cooperation directed against Germany, or by a Habsburg restoration, Schuschnigg flirted with a pro-German course, too. In his conversations with Franz von Papen, the German envoy to Vienna, Schuschnigg suggested that Austria's political and moral forces might be placed at the disposal of the German nation in its struggle to regain world position. Schuschnigg was alleged to have argued that Austria had a German mission in southeastern Europe; therefore she should be permitted to retain the character she had formed in the course of a millennium and not be yoked to any sort of centralized system directed from Berlin.[3]

Schuschnigg, in his attempt to save Austria, played with a surprising variety of possibilities, none of which led to Austria's salvation. Otto Habsburg, the man whom the legitimists — Schuschnigg included — thought of as being most competent to perform the miracle of Austria's salvation, could hardly have succeeded either. In the first place, opinion in Austria was widely divided over the Habsburg restoration. Furthermore, rumors of the Habsburg restoration did nothing to enhance Danubian unity, without which any attempt to stop Hitler was doomed to failure.

The only Danubian country with latent sympathies for the Habsburgs was Hungary. This was not because the Hungarians were "loyal to the dynasty," as the legitimists alleged, but because the revisionist propaganda, conservative and nationalistic, glorified the past, thus spreading the conviction that a Habsburg restoration in the Danube Valley might also help restore pre-war Hungary. In the countries of the Little Entente, nationalistic passions were inclined to swing in exactly the opposite direction, for the very name of Habsburg was a symbol of the past they hated. Therefore when rumors from Austria about Habsburg restoration reached the Little Entente countries, Belgrade's reaction was: "Rather Anschluss than restoration." Bucharest's reaction was similar in tone. Prague, the third capital of the Little Entente, did not join the anti-Habsburg chorus at this particular time. The Czechs had always before been solidly opposed to Habsburg restoration, and the fact that they did not react vigorously to such plans at this time did not imply a change of heart on the Habsburg issue. It denoted, rather, a realistic evaluation of the situation created by Hitler's determination to annex Austria. This Anschluss would have almost surrounded the Czech lands by Nazi Germany. No wonder that the person with whom the Czechs were concerned was Adolf Hitler, and not Otto Habsburg. Prague's concern was epitomized by the slogan, "Anschluss means war," coined by Eduard Beneš, President of the Czechoslovak Republic since December 1935.

The Western Powers, whose guidance and aid were badly needed in Central Europe, remained passive onlookers of the growing crisis. In May 1937, Stanley Baldwin, who "knew little of Europe and disliked what he knew," retired. He was succeeded by Neville Chamberlain, who on the other hand "was imbued with a sense of a special and personal mission to come to friendly terms with the dictators of Italy and Germany."[4] In January 1938 President Roosevelt, alarmed by the European situation, proposed to take the initiative by calling an international conference. No event, as Churchill saw it, would have been more likely to stave off, or even prevent, war than "the arrival of the United States in the circle of European hates and fears." Opinions differ as to who is to be blamed for the failure of the American initiative. At any rate the United States did not arrive, and "the last frail chance to save the world from tyranny otherwise than by war" was lost.[5] Foreign Secretary Anthony Eden resigned, in February 1938, in protest against Chamberlain's appeasement policy. He thus steered clear of responsibility for that which was soon to follow and which he was unable to stop.

On March 12–13, Hitler occupied Austria. The Western Powers merely protested, which did not discourage Hitler from sighting his next goal — the "liberation" of the Germans in Czechoslovakia.

The inner weakness of Czechoslovakia was of a nature different from Austria's. Czechoslovakia, unlike Austria, was a multinational state. The 3.5 million Sudeten Germans were the most powerful of Czechoslovakia's so-called national minorities — and the best united, under the leadership of Konrad Henlein. In giving expression to their national grievances, they were greatly emboldened by Hitler's successes. Other discontented groups were the Slovak and Ruthenian autonomists, the Hungarian and Polish separatists. They remained calmer than the Sudeten Germans — not out of greater loyalty to the Czechoslovak Republic, but because of lesser numerical strength.

Henlein, in the spring of 1938, demanded autonomy in his Karlsbad program. The Sudeten Germans pretended to be fighting for equal rights, as if their aim were the strengthening of Czechoslovakia by transforming it into a federal union of equal nations. President Beneš pretended, too, that he was ready to forget about the original Czech mission of the Republic as a bastion against German power. In four successive "plans" the Prague government showed itself willing to grant autonomy to the Sudeten Germans and, under pressure of the growing crisis, to the other discontented nationalities. But no one really believed that federalization would be feasible. The government was bidding for time. The discontented nationalities, above all the Sudeten Germans, were ready to desert the Republic.

Besides her masses of disloyal citizens, Czechoslovakia's other fundamental weakness was her isolation from her neighbors. After the Anschluss, the "head" of the Czech state was caught in the German pincer, while the "tail" was squeezed between two countries, Poland and Hungary, which had never had any sympathy for even the existence of Czechoslovakia. Only the easternmost tip of Czechoslovakia was connected with allied Romania, a member of the Little Entente. But Romania, as well as Yugoslavia, was more anxious to get along with Hitler, master of nearby Austria since the Anschluss, than to go to the rescue of hard-pressed Czechoslovakia. Italy too, a neighbor of Germany since the Anschluss, preferred cooperation with, rather than the role of counterpoise against, Hitler. In vain did the Western Powers expect Italy to play the latter role in exchange for the Italo-British agreement, signed in April 1938, which tacitly condoned the Fascist conquest of Abyssinia.

In August 1938, the British government sent Lord Runciman to Czechoslovakia to investigate and to mediate between the Czech government and the Sudeten Germans. The Runciman mission reported that the two nations, Czechs and Sudeten Germans, could not continue to live in one state. The finding was accurate. Czechoslovakia was not, and could scarcely become, the true home of the Sudeten Germans or of the other discontented national groups, inasmuch as they were forced against their will into the national state of the Czechs. But two separate issues existed which were never clearly distinguished: the chronic problem of conflict among the former Habsburg peoples on the one hand, and the acute struggle against the Nazi threat to civilization on the other.

Hitler had appealed to the right of national self-determination on behalf of the Sudeten Germans. But whereas President Wilson in 1918 had conceived the principle of national self-determination as a means of spreading democracy, Hitler invoked it to expand the rule of nazism, the deadly enemy of democracy. The Paris peacemakers committed an initial blunder when they failed to recognize that the principle of national self-determination cannot make Central Europe safe for democracy except in combination with a broader federal principle. The appeasers repeated the blunder and precipitated the final defeat of democracy in Central Europe when they conceded Hitler's right to the Wilsonian principle.

That Czechoslovakia should submit to the application of the principle of national self-determination, by virtue of which, and by the violation of which, she was originally created, was proposed publicly by *The Times* on September 7. In a leading article *The Times* called on the Czechoslovak government to consider "the project, which has found favor in some quarters, of making Czechoslovakia a more homogeneous national state by the cession of that fringe of alien populations who are contiguous to the nation to which they are united by race." Thus, the "homogeneous national state" was acknowledged on the eve of Munich as the possible basis of a new peace settlement in Central Europe.

The Czech government tried to federalize the country, a program originally proposed by the Sudeten Germans. But the federalization of Czechoslovakia in the summer of 1938 proved to be just as belated an attempt at saving the country as had been the federalization of the Habsburg Monarchy, proclaimed by Emperor Charles' pathetic Manifesto, in the autumn of 1918.

In the Danubian countries there was a vague notion of common danger in the summer of 1938. There were even a few conciliatory gestures exchanged between the old antagonists. Hungary was invited to attend the Little Entente Council at Bled, Yugoslavia, in August 1938 — which incidentally was the last session of that institution. At the same time, the tension also eased between Bulgaria and the countries of the Balkan Pact. Both Hungary and Bulgaria were freed of the disarmament clauses of the peace treaties. Meanwhile Yugoslavia and Romania, watching closely the deterioration of Czechoslovakia's domestic situation, both made efforts to relieve their own nationality tensions. In Romania, a so-called Nationalities Statute promised to the minorities what they were supposed to possess already according to the peace treaties, namely equal rights without distinction as to race, language or religion. In Yugoslavia, the spirit of compromise improved Serb-Croat relations, producing a year later (in August 1939) the so-called *Sporazum,* which pledged the long-sought autonomy to the Croats. But all these efforts, domestic and international, were merely improvized steps rather than the well-planned actions needed to make Central Europe cohesive and resistant to common dangers.

Even the great realist of the day, Winston Churchill, was a victim of illusions in gauging the strength of Central Europe. On March 14, 1938, in a House of Commons debate following the Anschluss, he evaluated the strength of the Little Entente, then on its way to disintegration, in these words: "Taken singly, the three countries of the Little Entente may be called powers of the second rank, but they are very powerful and vigorous states, and united they are a great power." The Little Entente was at no time really a "great power" and in its state of disintegration in 1938, it represented even less power than before. Far more realistic than Churchill's faith in the Little Entente's power was his view that the combined power of Russia and the West could deter Hitler from aggression.

During the critical summer of 1938, Churchill was urging upon Lord Halifax, then Foreign Secretary, the idea of a British-French-Russian "Joint Note," for which he expected also to gain President Roosevelt's support. In this note Hitler would be warned that world war would inevitably follow an invasion of Czechoslovakia.[6] Churchill's suggestion apparently was linked to an earlier move by Soviet Foreign Commissar Litvinov, who had proposed to the British, French and United States governments, on March 18, that they, with Russia, should confer in order to discuss means of preventing further aggression.[7]

A firm Britain, ready to take such a course of action as Churchill urged, could have thrown its weight into an anti-Hitler coalition, the nucleus of which already existed in the French-Soviet-Czechoslovak alliance. Such a coalition, had Britain adhered to it, could perhaps have been made effective and palatable to all those nations threatened by Nazi Germany but distrustful of Soviet Russia. A firm Britain, more than any other factor, could have ended the confusion and indecision of the nations in Central and Eastern Europe, exposed as they were to

German aggression, fearful of the Bolshevik menace, and disunited by their petty rivalries. But Prime Minister Neville Chamberlain opposed the idea of a Soviet alliance, and he seemed to be annoyed rather than concerned with the problems of "far-away" small nations in Central and Eastern Europe.

The French government, led by Premier Daladier and Foreign Minister Bonnet, presided over a nation badly split between the Right and the Left; they possessed neither the strength nor the conviction to base the country's foreign policy on the French-Soviet-Czechoslovak alliance. Somewhat reluctantly they yielded the command to Neville Chamberlain, while Chamberlain's appeasement policy was increasingly supported by a growing body of pacifist opinion throughout the West. The West, it seemed, was willing to compromise with Hitler, especially since the success of such a policy did not require tangible sacrifices from either France or Britain. Also, Nazi propaganda made inroads on European public opinion, with the result that the Soviet alliance was ever more sharply criticized as exposing the Continent to the dangers of communism.

The pro-Soviet Left was, no doubt, nurturing an illusion when it thought of the Soviet tyranny as a progressive form of democracy. Nevertheless the Left's advocacy of alliance between the Western democracies and the Russians against Hitler was well founded. As Churchill, certainly no "leftist," realized, such an alliance was the combination of power that could tip the balance in favor of the anti-Nazi forces in Europe. Even had the Western alliance with the Russians entailed great risk for the countries of Eastern Europe, this risk should have been considered worth taking by everybody concerned in view of the alternative of letting Nazi tyranny expand in the heart of Europe.

But very few of those concerned were of this opinion. The Polish and Romanian governments, upon whose attitude the effectiveness of an East-West alliance depended, were particularly distrustful of Soviet Russia. Their distrust was enhanced by the fact that they both ruled over territories with Ukrainian and Russian populations. They feared the Red Army would be more willing to enter than to leave their territories. They therefore could not bring themselves, in case of war against Germany, to grant the Red Army the right of passage. Moreover, they were most unwilling to take any risks for the sake of Czechoslovakia in a situation which they shortsightedly considered no concern of their own.

Poland's shortsightedness was especially striking. Like Czechoslovakia, she too had German minorities; but apparently the Polish government was caused no uneasiness by the thought that the Polish Germans, after the Germans of Czechoslovakia, might become the next target of Hitler's "liberation" policy. Actually, the Polish government seemed to approve of Hitler's demands in Czechoslovakia, and even considered demanding the simultaneous liberation of the eighty thousand Poles there. The governments of Great Britain and France, too, looked at the Czech crisis with singular shortsightedness. They viewed the Sudeten-Czech conflict merely as a local quarrel between two nations. They were ready to accept the explanation that this quarrel had been caused simply by the peace settlement's failure to draw frontiers according to the ethnic principle.

The "moral" justification for the West's appeasement attitude was found mainly in the belief that the time had come for the revision of the unjust peace treaties. But even if the treaties were unjust, Hitler was the last person in the world entitled to claim justice. Moreover, as a device of "peace making" the appeasers reinforced the nation-state principle. This was a capital error in itself — without even considering that the Nazi brand of nationalism was the worst the world had ever seen. Not only was the peace lost by this appeasement; but also revisionism (in contrast to rigidity) as a policy of change, a sane program in itself if taken away from the revisionists, was discredited.

6 *Munich: Hopes and Lessons*

In his notorious Sportpalast speech on September 25, 1938, Hitler demanded the annexation of the Sudeten territories and threatened to use force against Czechoslovakia if this "last territorial claim" of Germany in Europe was not fulfilled. Czechoslovakia had been under general mobilization since September 23, but her decision to fight, in the event of Hitler's fulfilling his threat, depended upon the decision of Czechoslovakia's allies to honor their treaty obligations. One of these allies, Soviet Russia, stood by her treaty obligations. This, however, meant merely that Russia would fight if France did the same. France on the other hand made her decision depend upon Britain's decision, which meant that Czechoslovakia's defense was caught in a vicious circle of indecision.

After dramatic tension, during which the decision to fight would have been the greater surprise, the forces of appeasement prevailed. In order to save peace, Britain and France decided to surrender the Sudeten territories of Czechoslovakia to Germany. Agreement was reached with Germany on September 29, at the Munich Conference attended by Adolf Hitler, Benito Mussolini, Neville Chamberlain and Edouard Daladier. Czechoslovakia was not consulted. The Soviet Union was not invited.

In Munich the Big Four agreed that within ten days, beginning October 1, a territory with a population of 3,600,000 should be handed to Germany. About 600,000 of this population were Czechs, who were to pass under German rule, while after this cession some 300,000 Germans were to remain in Czechoslovakia. A declaration attached to the agreement provided that the problems of the Polish (80,000) and Hungarian (800,000) minorities of Czechoslovakia, if not settled within three months by direct agreement between the governments of the countries involved, should be the subject of another meeting between the four Great Powers.

Next morning, on September 30, the Czechoslovak government capitulated and accepted the Munich dictate. The peace settlement, dictated by the victors to the vanquished after the First World War, lay in ruins. Hitler had achieved his goal without having to resort to force.

What would have happened if Hitler had met resistance? General Halder, Hitler's chief of the Army General Staff, testified after the Second World War that a plot to arrest Hitler and his principal associates was called off at the last minute on September 14, 1938, when it became known that Chamberlain was going to meet Hitler at Berchtesgaden. And General Keitel, who was head of the supreme command of the German armed forces in 1938, when asked at the Nuremberg trials after the war whether or not the Reich would have attacked Czechoslovakia if the Western Powers had stood by Prague, answered: "Certainly not. We were not strong enough militarily."[1] These and other stories certainly indicate that inside resistance to Hitler existed which could have been touched off into action if, and apparently only if, Hitler had met outside opposition. But though the British government was informed about the plot of the German generals, it did not believe Hitler would be overthrown if the West resisted. Therefore appeasement prevailed, and therefore the generals did not act. This sequence was part of the whole chain reaction of impotence which began with the indecision in regard to defending Czechoslovakia.

Winston Churchill thought the vicious circle could have been broken by Eduard Beneš, President of Czechoslovakia. He believed Beneš was wrong in yielding to the Munich dictate. Beneš's resistance would have infuriated both Hitler and his generals, and probably would not have deterred them from attacking Czechoslovakia. But, in Churchill's view: "Beneš should have defended his fortress line. Once fighting had begun . . . France would have moved to his aid in a surge of national passion, and Britain would have rallied to France almost immediately."[2] Stalin too thought Beneš had made a mistake in not resisting Hitler. The very day Beneš arrived in Moscow for his first visit during the war, in December 1943, Stalin confronted him with the question: "And why didn't you fight in September 1938?"[3]

But actually would the West (on which Russia's action in turn depended) have moved to the aid of Czechoslovakia in 1938 if Beneš had refused to yield? Beneš thought not, and he was probably right.

Churchill, in a statement to the press a week before Munich, said: "The partition of Czechoslovakia under pressure from England and France amounts to a complete surrender of the Western democracies to the

Nazi threat of force." Unfortunately Churchill's battle cry, that the Western democracies were in danger, did not arouse the spirit of resistance. Peoples in the West were hardly aware of the forces threatening to destroy the foundations of their civilization. The defeat of the West at Munich was not a sudden disaster, but a slowly ripening catastrophe.

Domestic policies in the West, dominated by economic and social problems, widened the gap between the upper and lower classes, and split their views on the aims and purposes of democracy. Foreign policies, formulated out of narrow-minded nationalism, could not produce understanding for the broader common interests of the West. "Western democracy" was for many people an empty slogan; and for many it meant even something quite different from what Churchill was trying so desperately to defend, for they thought of Hitler rather than Churchill as the defender of the West — quite a number of Europeans were misled by Hitler's boast that he was defending Western civilization against Bolshevik barbarism.

The target of Hitler's fury, Czechoslovakia, was a popular country in the West; but this popularity was mainly the result of earlier propaganda through which Czechoslovakia had acquired the reputation of being the mainstay of peace and democracy. The French, especially, thought of the Czechs as pillars of their own security. But in the summer of 1938 the growing feeling of the French was that Czechoslovakia, instead of keeping them out of trouble, was dragging them into it. Czechoslovakia's reputation rapidly dwindled as the country became a center of crisis rather than of security. Both the fear of war and the hope of peace were overwhelming in Europe during the Czech crisis. The peoples of the West saw no reason why they should take up arms and sacrifice themselves for Czechoslovakia. Their sentiments were expressed in Chamberlain's words when at the height of the Czech crisis he spoke about a "quarrel in a far-away country between people of whom we know nothing." Czechoslovakia was "far-away" for them — and for that matter far away also was the whole danger zone between Germany and Russia; they were only too ready to disengage themselves from those "far-away" countries, peoples and problems.

The independence of the Middle Zone, dominated for so long by the empires of the Hohenzollerns, Habsburgs, Romanovs and Sultans, had been proudly proclaimed after the First World War as the victory of Western democracy. But the Western governments were never really interested enough to become organizers, leaders or peacemakers of the many quarreling nations of this area. The French concluded only alliances dictated by sheer national interest, while the British always refused to take up any direct commitments there. The Czech crisis brought to the surface the latent disgust of the West with the intricate problems of this unhappy half of the Continent. Beneš, who knew the West well, must have realized all this when he perceived the futility of defying the Munich dictate, because the Western Powers would not come to his rescue anyway. Under the conditions then prevailing, Czech defiance could easily have resulted not in what Churchill expected but in the very opposite — that is to say, in condemnation of the Czechs and their total isolation.

Nor was the population of Czechoslovakia in such a fighting mood as was later declared in propaganda. Not even the Czech part of the population (7.2 million in a country of 15 million) was really united, and its unity with the Slovaks (roughly 2.8 million) had been greatly undermined by the Slovak autonomist movement. The condition of the Czech-Slovak union was sad indeed; the Slovak autonomists, despite their close cooperation with the Sudeten German enemies of the state, were rapidly gaining popularity with the masses. Among the Czechs, on the other hand, powerful elements organized by the Agrarian party opposed Beneš's pro-Soviet orientation and blamed Beneš personally for the disastrous situation of the Republic. And some of the critics of Beneš's policy believed that if the Czech-Soviet alliance had been renounced, the showdown with Hitler could have been avoided. Under such circumstances, even if some Soviet help could have been rendered to a defiant Czechoslovakia after the Western betrayal in Munich — as some patriots of the Left, preferring defiance to submission, expected — it could only have fanned the flame of inner division and confusion.

Beneš had no reason to fear that his two hostile eastern neighbors, Poland and Hungary, would unite with Germany in a joint attack on Czechoslovakia. Anxious though they were to annex those Polish and Hungarian territories which had been awarded to Czechoslovakia after the First World War, they were no less anxious to avoid a military campaign in alliance with Nazi Germany. On the other hand, Czechoslovakia could expect nothing more than strict neutrality from her two allies in the Danube Valley, Romania and Yugoslavia. It must have appeared to Beneš as almost certain that Czechoslovakia would be left alone if she rejected the Munich dictate. And Beneš must have been tormented by the thought that Czech resistance not only would not arouse the conscience of the West, but also would probably result in the disintegration and inglorious collapse of the multinational army and population of the Republic, rather than in their heroic resistance, should Hitler decide to take by force what he already had been given in Munich by agreement.

Thus Beneš was in no position, by resisting Hitler, to transform the West's appeasement policy into a Grand Alliance of the Second World War. He was in no position to wrest the leadership from Neville Chamberlain. Broken and sick, President Beneš resigned the week after Munich; he left his unfortunate country three weeks later for London.

The views of Prime Minister Chamberlain on the hopelessness of the Czechoslovak situation lie buried now in documents of British foreign policy;[4] but in 1938 more people — from the Left as well as from the Right — shared these views than can remember the fact today. Chamberlain decided to accept Hitler's demands and pressed the Czechs to accept them because he was convinced that Czechoslovakia could not be defended against a German attack. Both London and Paris had a rather poor opinion of the Czechoslovak army; indeed, under the impact of the Sudeten crisis, they developed a rather poor opinion of the very existence of the Czechoslovak state. As one of the British documents bluntly stated the matter: why fight a European war for something you cannot protect and do not expect to restore?[5]

Moreover, the British and French governments thought uneasily of the Soviet alliance in a European war. Chamberlain not only distrusted the intentions of Soviet Russia but doubted her military power as well. (Skepticism concerning Russia's military strength was widespread in the West after the great Stalinist purges of the mid-thirties.) On the other hand, Chamberlain neither doubted the military power of Germany nor, at the time of Munich, distrusted Hitler's intentions. Because Chamberlain trusted Hitler, he believed peace would reign in Europe once Hitler's "last territorial demands" were fulfilled. An Anglo-German declaration, signed at the time of the Munich Pact, expressed the desire of the two peoples "never to go to war with one another again." Furthermore, Munich provided for a new "method" of assuring peace, outlined in a passage of the Anglo-German declaration which read as follows: "We are resolved that the method of consultation shall be the method adopted to deal with any other question that may concern our two countries, and we are determined to continue our efforts to remove possible sources of difference, and thus to contribute to assure the peace of Europe." A French-German agreement was signed in the same spirit on December 6, in Paris.

Munich cancelled the anti-German edge of the cordon sanitaire, leaving the Middle Zone open to German penetration. But since Chamberlain seemed to trust Hitler's intentions, he could hardly have expected Eastern Europe to become exclusively German *Lebensraum,* subservient to German interests. It is reasonable to assume that even Beneš, a politician more astute than Chamberlain, believed, for a while at least, in a *modus vivendi* between Hitler's Germany and post-Munich Czechoslovakia.[6] The relationship between Germany and the countries of the Middle Zone was expected to develop along somewhat the same lines as the relationship of Russia to this area was supposed to develop according to the Yalta agreements seven years later. Governments friendly toward Germany were to cooperate with their mighty neighbor, while their quarrels — such as that over the unsolved problem of the Polish and Hungarian minorities in Czechoslovakia — were to be settled by the judicial court of the Big Four.

Soviet Russia was excluded from this new era of "European cooperation." She was not invited to Munich; there was evidently no room for her in the new system. The anti-Russian edge of the former cordon sanitaire remained in force, and there could be no doubt about the hostile attitude the Big Four had taken, according to their temperaments, toward Russia. But Chamberlain, a believer in peace, did not mean to incite Hitler against Russia — as the Soviet interpretation of Munich has claimed. Chamberlain believed, rather, that a new and steady balance of power was being created in Munich, in which Germany would be a natural counterweight to the Soviet Union.

The guiding principles of the Munich peacemaking, therefore, can be summed up as follows: friendship to Germany, hostility to Russia, and recognition of the rights of national self-determination. None of these principles was suitable for European peacemaking in September 1938. In fact, Nazi Germany was the indomitable enemy of the Western democracies, Soviet Russia was their indispensable ally, while the right of national self-determination was a weapon of Hitler's *Machtpolitik* only. The complete misunderstanding of the situation is immortalized in Chamberlain's famous comment on Munich: "This is . . . peace with honor. I believe it is peace in our time."

The "method of consultation" provided by the Anglo-German declaration never went into effect. Not even the problem of the Polish and Hungarian minorities of Czechoslovakia, explicitly mentioned in the Munich agreement, was settled in the way agreed upon.

Poland, instead of resorting to a Four Power decision as provided by the Munich agreement, chose unilateral action. After an ultimatum, she took possession on October 2 of the Teschen region of Czechoslovakia, which included not only 80,000 Poles, but also not less than 150,000 people of Czech, Slovak, or German nationality. The problem of the Hungarian minority of Czechoslovakia, handled first in Komárom by direct negotiations between Hungary and Czechoslovakia which ended in failure, was finally decided in Vienna on November 2 by a German-Italian verdict. The Hungarian government headed by Béla Imrédy, a man of pro-Western reputation at that time who later became one of the pro-Nazi extremists, would have preferred a Four Power decision; but to turn down the German-Italian offer for "mediation" in the Czech-Hungarian controversy would have been tantamount to open rebellion against Hitler's "new order" in Central Europe. For such an action Hungary, eager at long last to pluck the fruits of her revisionist policy, was not qualified.

At the Vienna meeting of the Axis dictators, Hungary's exorbitant territorial claims were opposed by Hitler as a sort of punishment for Hungary's unwillingness, during the pre-Munich crisis, to enter into a military alliance with German against Czechoslovakia. (Horthy had refused this German offer, at a meeting with Hitler in Kiel, in August 1938.) With Mussolini's help, however, the decision was still favorable to the Hungarians. Hungary regained about 700,000 of her nationals, taking along with them about 300,000 Slovaks, Ruthenes, Germans and Romanians, while about 100,000 Hungarians were left in Czechoslovakia. Imperfect ethnically as it was, the new frontier between Slovaks and Hungarians nevertheless followed the ethnic principle more closely than did the line drawn by the Trianon Treaty after the First World War. The Hungarians, of course, rejoiced over this first revision of the Trianon frontiers. They were blind to the tragedy of Munich: they did not know that Munich, being the collective tragedy of all Central Europe, was before long to toll the bell for Hungary too.

The injustices of the new frontiers were decried by the Czechs and Slovaks, whose turn it was to become revisionists and to reclaim the lost boundaries. The Czechoslovak revisionists did essentially the same as the Hungarian revisionists had done since the First World War: they repudiated the frontiers forced upon them. Yet the circumstances under which these two revisionist claims originated and developed were so different that their similarities passed, so to speak, unnoticed. R. W.

Seton-Watson, a great British friend of Czechoslovakia, as early as 1939 termed the injustices of the new Hungaro-Czechoslovak frontier "scandalous" and "still more contrary to all reason than that [the frontier] adopted between Bohemia and the Reich,"[7] while Winston Churchill, in a calmer atmosphere after the Second World War, in his memoirs branded Hungary and Poland as "beasts of prey."[8]

Harsh words like these were not entirely without justification. They were applicable, however, not merely to the 1938 situation, when Czechoslovakia suffered injuries, but also to the 1918 situation, when Czechoslovakia inflicted injuries upon others. In fact, seen from a broader perspective, the Czechoslovak tragedy of 1938 was conceived in the womb of the great nationalist revolution of 1918, when the small victors, like "beasts of prey," carved out their nation-states from the Habsburg Monarchy and set up frontiers "contrary to all reason" among interdependent peoples. Unfortunately, during the Second World War, "Munich" became so much the symbol of Czechoslovakia's betrayal by the West that it was never really seen for what it was: a demonstration of the failure of the peace settlement in the Danube Valley. The wartime temper of the West was not favorable to such interpretations. Since appeasement led to the revision of the peace settlement in Munich, it followed in logic that when the blunder of appeasement was exploded, the peace settlement should appear to be vindicated. Criticism of the peace settlement seemed so completely enmeshed in the disastrous policy of appeasement that, under the pressure of wartime political expediency, it was thrown out of the Western thinking, together with the shameful memory of appeasement. During the Second World War, approval of the pre-Munich status quo in the Danube Valley was considered, so to speak, a full proof of repudiation of Munich in the same way that pro-Soviet orientation (after 1941) was considered a full proof of democratic anti-Fascist sincerity.

While, as a rule, the mistakes of the peace settlement in the Danube Valley were lightly glossed over, the mistakes of the Western Powers' policy toward Nazi Germany were heavily concentrated on by the critics of Munich. A.J.P. Taylor, for instance, defended the pre-Munich Danubian status quo by arguing that it "would have been permanent and stable had it not been for the breakdown of the Versailles settlement of Germany." In his picturesque parable: "To attribute the fall and dismemberment of the national states in central and south-eastern Europe to their own defects is comparable to condemning Sir Christopher Wren as an architect because of the collapse of the City churches in the blitz of

1940–1."[9] Another English historian, C. A. Macartney, was of the opinion, though, that "it is obvious and tautologous to say that an overwhelming outside force in favour of the status-quo would have preserved it. But the ideal which the treaty-makers hoped to achieve was not a structure, unstable in itself, which had to be propped up by titanic efforts from outside, but rather something possessed of inherent vitality and solidarity. And in fact, when the test came, the solidarity was conspicuously lacking and the vitality insufficient."[10] Such views, however, drew few followers.

Lack of solidarity among the nations of the Middle Zone was not, of course, the sole cause of their undoing. One of the leading historians of the Middle Zone, the Polish Oscar Halecki, was right in pointing out: "The liberation of that whole region after World War I could have changed the destiny of its peoples if they had shown more solidarity, if German and Russian power had not been so quickly reborn under particularly aggressive totalitarian regimes, and if the system of international organization, inseparable from lasting self-determination in one of the most exposed regions of the world, had worked more satisfactorily."[11]

Indeed, it was a grave misfortune to live in Europe's danger zone; and the blunders of Western policy in the inter-war period were most unfortunate; nonetheless, the essential harm done the Middle Zone nations was of their own doing. Their energies had been consumed in wrangles over national prerogatives and boundaries; free development of their great human resources was impeded to a large extent by reactionary class rule and ethnic rivalries; their economic progress was hampered by artificial political frontiers. They had attained national independence after the First World War, but they had overlooked, and so had their Western protectors, the iron laws of interdependence. Preoccupied with quarrels among themselves, they failed to protect themselves against the common dangers of their precarious geographical location between Russia and Germany. Munich and its consequences reminded them again of the old truth that only in federation could they develop and maintain their freedom and independence.

7 *From Munich to Moscow*

The Munich surrender invited Nazi Germany to further aggression. Within half a year Hitler was in full control of what was left of Czechoslovakia. Within another half-year the Nazi-Soviet pact was signed in Moscow, and the Second World War was on. Thus did Hitler, the winner of Munich, lead his country and the world, via Moscow, to the ruin of war. Meanwhile President Beneš, the loser of Munich, took a different road to Moscow, which proved ruinous too. Disgusted with the Western betrayal of his country in Munich, he drew the conclusion that once Czechoslovakia was reestablished, her security should rest on a close cooperation with the Soviet Union. Both developments belonged to the consummation of the Munich tragedy.

The post-Munich Czech government, which was formed hurriedly from the Agrarian critics of Beneš's policy and included some Czech Fascists, tried to collaborate with Nazi Germany in fitting mutilated Czechoslovakia into the "new order" of Central Europe. The "Second Republic" (distinguished from the first by a hyphen, Czecho-Slovakia) also granted autonomy to the Slovaks and Ruthenes. But neither the change in the orientation of foreign policy, nor the reform in the relations among the three Slavic groups of the state, could give a new lease of life to post-Munich Czechoslovakia. Hitler carried out his determination to smash her completely by resorting to the terroristic methods which had previously paid him such nice dividends.

The same threat of force which had softened the two Western powers on the eve of Munich compelled Emil Hácha, President of post-Munich Czechoslovakia, to sign a treaty during the night of March 14–15, 1939, which turned the Czech lands into a "protectorate," a Nazi term which meant occupation. Meanwhile the Germanophile Slovak autonomists, under Msgr. Jozef Tiso's leadership, proclaimed independence. "Independent" Slovakia was of course a Fascist state and a German satellite. In spite of this, and not because of it, the Slovak Republic enjoyed a remarkable popularity. It was the first national state the Slovaks had ever had and it appealed to their pride, a quite normal sin in the age of nationalism.

The Ruthene remains of Czechoslovakia, after two days of "independence" proclaimed by the local autonomists, were occupied by Hungary, with Hitler giving only reluctant approval inasmuch as he would have preferred to keep them under direct German control. Thus, in the Carpathians, where Ukrainians live on one side of the mountains and Ruthenes on the other, a restoration of the "Polish-Hungarian" frontier — a favorite aim of both the Warsaw and the Budapest governments — was celebrated. The myth about the desirability of a Polish-Hungarian frontier as a mighty source of strength — believed in with equal naivety by both governments — was soon to be exploded when Germany attacked and defeated Poland; the only practical gain drawn from the common frontier was that after Poland's collapse masses of refugees were received into Hungary with the warmth of a romantic friendship which had long existed between the two nations. Meanwhile the Hungarian government pledged autonomy to the Ruthenes, boasting of giving them the rights they had never secured from the Czechs; but the "autonomy" granted by Budapest was a disappointment even to those Ruthenes who were Hungarophiles.

After Munich, with help from Germany and Italy, Hungary began to recover her lost territories. Together with the Hungarians came people of other nationalities, and Hungary became again a multinational state. Here was the opportunity to prove the superiority of the "Saint Stephen idea" over the much criticized minority policies of Hungary's neighbors. But the "Saint Stephen idea" — as the author of the idea, the historian Gyula Szekfű, himself had to concede — failed the test of history.[1] The national minorities, returned to Hungarian rule between 1938 and 1941, although better treated than they had been in pre-war Hungary, did not receive the rights anticipated by those who believed in the modern mission of historical Hungary. In addition, Hungary's reactionary social fabric was bitterly resented by everyone, the returning Hungarians included.

After the final liquidation of Czechoslovakia, Nazi pressure turned against Poland. On March 21, Hitler notified Poland that the Free City of Danzig, lying in the corridor between East Prussia and Germany, must return to the Reich; also the Warsaw government was violently attacked for mistreating the million-strong German minority in Poland. On April 27, Hitler denounced the German-Polish non-aggression pact of 1934. The threat of war was greater than ever. On May 19, Churchill asked: "If we are ready to be an ally of Russia in time of war, why should we shrink from becoming an ally of Russia now, when we might by that very fact prevent the breaking out of war?"

Hitler's march into Prague, in violation of the Munich agreement, had cured Neville Chamberlain and the non-Fascist world at large of the illusion that, since Hitler was fighting against the injustices of the Versailles Treaty, a compromise with him by satisfying Germany's aspirations for "national self-determination" was possible. But the collapse of the appeasement policy did not yet make the long-pending alternative, alliance between Russia and the West, a reality. On the contrary, the chances of East-West cooperation against Hitler grew worse. East-West estrangement and the Russo-German rapprochement were the results of Munich. And the sly assumption of some people in the West that antagonism between nazism and communism would precipitate a war of mutual extermination between the two dictatorships proved as wrong as all the other Western assumptions which sought the easy way out of the European quandry.

In April, Britain and France extended guarantees to Poland, Romania and Greece. But the protracted negotiations in the spring and summer of 1939 between the Western Powers and Russia, which could have made these guarantees effective, ran into the same obstacles as had already barred the East-West alliance against Hitler before Munich. Thus no satisfactory formula could be found to ensure cooperation between Russia and her western neighbors, Poland, Romania and the Baltic states, within the broader framework of an alliance among the Soviet Union, Britain and France. The position maintained by the Russians was that the proposed Anglo-French-Soviet treaty should go into effect in the case of either "direct" or "indirect" aggression. In the annex to the proposed treaty, Molotov defined "indirect aggression" as "an internal *coup d'état* or a political change favorable to the aggressor." Moreover, the Russians were anxious to reserve the right of any one of the interested countries to determine whether an act of "indirect aggression" had been committed. This meant in effect that the Soviet government would have been entitled to determine what kind of internal changes in the neighboring countries, exposed to German aggression, would be favorable to the aggressor. This, in the opinion of Russia's neighbors, would have constituted a serious encroachment of their sovereignty and a pretext for Soviet westward expansion.[2]

The fears of Soviet expansion among Russia's neighbors have been amply justified by subsequent events; but at that late hour in 1939, the Anglo-French-Soviet alliance was even more than at any time before, the only possible means of knocking Hitler out, either with or without war; and the sooner this alliance could have been concluded, the less, in all probability, would have been the danger of Soviet westward expansion. And although Munich was no excuse for what Soviet Russia did in partnership with Nazi Germany, one thing seems almost certain; it was the Munich blunder that cleared the way for the conclusion of the Nazi-Soviet pact and for its awful consequences.

When the Nazi-Soviet pact was signed in Moscow on August 23, Stalin knew that Hitler was determined to attack Poland. Also, Stalin had assured for himself a share in the event of Poland's "territorial and political rearrangement." However, the intent imputed to him of unleashing war between Germany and the West was based on no more evidence than the Soviet assertion that "Britain and France, supported by the United States ruling circles . . . were maliciously inciting Hitler Germany against the Soviet Union."[3] Stalin could not know, nor could he take it for granted, judging the West on the basis of Munich, that Britain and France would go to war to save Poland — he might have expected a second Munich. But no Munich materialized. On August 25, two days after the Nazi-Soviet pact, Britain had signed an agreement of mutual assistance with Poland. On September 1, Hitler invaded Poland. And three days later, on September 3, Britain together with France declared war on Germany. This was a decision of a Britain whose fighting spirit was aroused — but it was not a decision capable of saving Poland. No aid from the West could save the Poles from disaster. The Poles fought heroically, but succumbed to the superior force of the Nazi war machine, while the Russians entered the last phase of Poland's hopeless struggle to cash in on their share of the Nazi-Soviet deal.

With the Nazi-Soviet pact and the outbreak of the Second World War the tragedy of Munich had been consummated. But seldom have victims of historical tragedies learned the lessons of their misfortunes — more often, tragedies have given birth to myths; and Munich was no exception.

The exiles from Nazi-occupied Czechoslovakia who found refuge in the West were in the best position to initiate a new policy of future cooperation among the Danubian nations. After a short eclipse, their country was regaining and even improving its reputation in the West due to the fast-spreading conviction that Munich was both a shame and a blunder.

The opinions of the Czech exiles were most carefully listened to. It was a great misfortune that the leader of the Czech exiles, ex-President Beneš, bent his enormous energies and brilliant diplomatic talents to the restoration of Czechoslovakia rather than to the creation of a Danubian federation.

Humiliated and filled with vengeance, Beneš was unable to progress from the idea of a Czechoslovak nation-state to the broader program of Danubian cooperation. Furthermore, as a reaction to the West's betrayal at Munich, he concluded that only Russia could safeguard the independence of restored Czechoslovakia. Thus, he was evolving a political ideology which during the Second World War drove him ever closer to Moscow. And while seeking Russia's protection against the recurrence of German aggression, he was also evolving unprecedented nationalist plans for Czech domination. Regressing from Masaryk's liberal concepts of minority policy which had earned so much in world reputation for his country, Beneš conceived a program of expelling the disloyal national groups whom he blamed for the Czech tragedy. For reasons of expediency he glossed over the disloyalty of the Slovaks, but was the more uncompromising in his resolution to expel the Germans and Hungarians from Czechoslovakia. Czechoslovak martyrdom, Western guilt, Soviet innocence: these were the ingredients which shaped Beneš's thinking after Munich.

While Western betrayal bitterly disappointed Beneš, Soviet loyalty, in September 1938, impressed him deeply. Translating Munich into ideological terms, he saw behind Western betrayal the work of European reaction and in Soviet loyalty the proof of democratic solidarity. In his thinking, as his memoirs clearly reveal, Munich became the symbol of a bond of union between Soviet Russia and Czechoslovakia. Soviet Russia was the only European power that "kept its word"; Czechoslovakia and Soviet Russia were the only countries that consistently pursued "anti-Fascist" policy; only they were ready to fight Hitler in September 1938, and they were "left alone." Munich was "a crime as much against the Soviet Union as against Czechoslovakia."[4]

Beneš knew of course that Soviet assistance to Czechoslovakia was made conditional upon the fulfillment of France's treaty obligations to Czechoslovakia. Considering the small likelihood of French help, as well as the fact that Czechoslovakia was not contiguous to Soviet Russia (whereas Poland and Romania, who were, refused to let the Red Army cross their territories), the Soviet pledge of aid to Czechoslovakia was a platonic expression of loyalty indeed. Furthermore, Beneš suspected that if war broke out the Kremlin would prefer to intervene with "social revolutionary" aims, when both sides had been exhausted. Nevertheless, after Hitler's seizure of Czechoslovakia in March 1939, Beneš did not cease to hope for an East-West alliance against Germany, and he tried his best to dispel Western distrust of Russia.

While in the United States as visiting professor at the University of Chicago in the spring of 1939, Beneš had a meeting with President Roosevelt. The meeting was arranged by Beneš's long-time American friend, Hamilton Fish Armstrong, editor of *Foreign Affairs,* and took place on May 28, at Hyde Park. During the interview Beneš predicted the outbreak of war and also that Russia would be "on our side." He was pleased to find that Roosevelt understood well the importance of Soviet Russia in world politics; and he was no less pleased to hear the President say that, for him, "Munich does not exist." In London, where Churchill openly advocated an alliance with Russia, Beneš's views were acclaimed warmly by the group of Conservatives who opposed Chamberlain's appeasement policy; and in the Liberal and Labour ranks too, Czechoslovakia had many friends. At a dinner given in Beneš's honor, on July 27, by the pro-Czechoslovak group in Parliament, Churchill presided and the speakers included Sir Archibald Sinclair and Arthur Henderson, Jr., representatives respectively of the Liberal and Labour parties. All expressed their faith in the restoration of Czechoslovakia, without which, as Churchill said, "the peace will not be made."[5]

In contrast to the sympathies of Czechoslovakia's friends in the United States and Britain was the animosity of the French. Even after the outbreak of the war, when Beneš was visiting Paris in October 1939 Daladier refused to receive him. In Paris, where Beneš once had earned his greatest success, he gathered the impression that, for the French government, Czechoslovakia was "definitely dead."[6]

In Paris, J. Šverma, a Czech Communist leader, called on Beneš and tried to persuade him to leave the West and go to Russia.[7] Šverma thought that the liberation of Czechoslovakia would occur in the wake of a great Communist revolutionary victory in Europe. Beneš, however, rejected Šverma's ideas; he disliked the extremist views concerning Soviet Russia, of the Right as well as of the Left. Thus he disagreed also with Władysław Sikorski, the Polish leader in exile, who anticipated "some repetition of the First World War," namely that Germany would first annihilate Soviet Russia and then the West would crush Nazi Germany.[8] What Beneš believed in was an East-West cooperation, both in war and in peace; he longed for it; he was determined to work for it.

When in March 1938 Hitler occupied the remains of mutilated Czechoslovakia, events began to move according to Beneš's expectations. In September the war which he had predicted broke out. But another of his predictions, that Russia would be "on our side," was not fulfilled until June 1941, when Hitler attacked the Soviet Union.

During the early stage of the war, plans for the inner reconstruction of restored Czechoslovakia were taking shape in Beneš's mind. He was resolved to fight for the pre-Munich frontiers, which he called "the primary objective" of Czech diplomacy in exile; and simultaneously he decided to revise radically the minority policy of pre-war Czechoslovakia. To those who argued in favor of the old minority status quo, he retorted: "Do you want to prepare a new Munich?" His plan was "to reduce radically the number of minorities." This was to be achieved by expelling the minority population.

Beneš had a series of dramatic interviews with Wenzel Jaksch, the exiled leader of the Sudeten German Social Democrats, who first called on him on September 3, 1939, in London. Jaksch argued in favor of federalization and presented a plan for a broader Central European federation. Not even the Social Democrats who were loyal to the pre-Munich democracy, Jaksch pointed out, could accept the pre-Munich structure of Czechoslovakia. Beneš, however, rejected these plans and, in the course of subsequent meetings with Jaksch, revealed his plan to expel the minorities. Jaksch protested vigorously, but Beneš remained adamant. "We have to part for good," Beneš argued; "only thus shall we be able at some time, when the present pains are forgotten, to meet as neighbors and live side by side, everybody in his own new home, without bitterness and in peace." And Beneš concluded: "Yes, I recognize your tragic situation and I feel sorry for you from the bottom of my heart. But this is how it happens sometimes in the life of nations, due to historic circumstances and because of the guilt of their leaders."

To this Beneš added in his memoirs, written after the Second World War at a time when the expulsion of the minorities already was in full swing: "These were natural conclusions which had to be valid for the Hungarians and Poles, too. . . . In this sense I was defending this solution in all the discussions with Britons, Americans, Russians and French. Experiments with minority treaties, carried out after the First World War with the aid of the League of Nations, should not be repeated, because they have ended in failure and disappointment. They have led us . . . to Munich."[9]

Chamberlain had believed in saving peace by detaching the minorities from Czechoslovakia. Beneš believed in making peace by expelling them. So the modern myth of a homogeneous national state stood at both the beginning and the end of the Munich tragedy.

No dramatic farewell meeting like the one between Jaksch and Beneš took place between Beneš and a representative of the second largest minority of Czechoslovakia, the three-quarters of a million Hungarians, who were also marked by him for expulsion. The few Hungarians from Czechoslovakia who followed the Czech leader into exile were, unlike the Sudeten Social Democrat Jaksch, completely subservient to Beneš. They also were slow to realize what Beneš's post-war plans were; and some of them grew so bitter, during the war, against Admiral Horthy's reactionary regime, that they not only did not protest against, but on the contrary actively supported the Czech effort to brand Hungary's collaboration with Hitler as the collective guilt of the entire Hungarian nation.

The small group of democratic exiles from Horthy's Hungary, headed by Count Michael Károlyi, who had been President of the short-lived Hungarian Republic in 1918–19, were also not in a mood to criticize Beneš; they were as much impressed by the democracy of the Czechs, whose hospitality many of them had enjoyed during the inter-war period, as they were depressed by lack of democracy in their Hungarian homeland. Sincerely, but naively, they were hopeful of a "compromise" between Hungary and Czechoslovakia leading to a Danubian federation. In Károlyi's words: "Such a nucleus of permanent cooperation between Prague and Budapest would provide the Danubian region with a center of attraction well-fitted to become a stable foundation for that democratic grouping of peoples which the federation is to be."[10]

Beneš, however, was thinking in terms very different from Károlyi about the future of Czechoslovak-Hungarian relations. Infuriated with Horthy-Hungary's part in the tragedy of Czechoslovakia, Beneš's feelings toward the Hungarians, as toward the Germans, were directed almost exclusively by desires of revenge and punishment. To equate the hated Germans with the Hungarians was nothing new. Lumping together the crimes of Germany and Hungary was a Czech practice which had already been carried out effectively during the First World War. Now again the Czechs took the view that the main trouble in Central Europe was the German-Hungarian alliance. Czech propaganda went so far as to describe the "Axis" as not so much a German-Italian, as a

German-Hungarian, alliance. In Beneš's popular interpretation, Hungary was, in effect, the villain of Central Europe: "Hungary was following doggedly the so-called revisionist policy which marred for many years all the attempts and possibilities of establishing friendly relations between the countries of Central Europe in general, and was above all helpful in preparing Germany's aggression against its smaller neighbors."[11]

This one-sided interpretation was, if not excusable, at least explicable by the Hungarians' even greater single-mindedness in blaming Beneš, usually, for all the troubles of Central Europe.[12] As a matter of fact, the antagonism between Czechoslovakia, main pillar of the post-Habsburg system, and Hungary, its implacable foe — the rivalry, that is, between Czechs and Hungarians, their mutual hatred and recrimination — was more responsible for the ruin of Central Europe than any of the other small-nation jealousies in the Danube Valley. The Czech-Hungarian rivalry was an antagonism between the principal democratic and the principal reactionary forces of the Danube area, but it was also a struggle between two rival nationalist "solutions" of the problem of Central Europe; and while the Trianon tragedy failed to teach the Hungarians that their "solution" was wrong, the Munich tragedy failed to teach the Czechs that their "solution" was wrong too.

Convinced that democratic Czechoslovakia created conditions superior to any that had existed before in Central Europe, the Czechs considered dissatisfaction with Czechoslovak policies *a priori* as an act of hostility against democracy. They viewed their struggle *against* disloyalty among their multinational citizens as a struggle *for* democracy. This conviction grew especially strong as Czechoslovakia became a target of Nazi aggression. No doubt the disloyal groups were always honeycombed with elements hostile to democracy, and obviously at the time of Munich the enemies of Czechoslovakia were identical with the enemies of democracy; but it was a gross distortion to explain the lack of loyalty to the Czechoslovak state as a conspiracy against democracy. The essential trouble with multinational Czechoslovakia was the same as plagued multinational Austria-Hungary. As Walter Kolarz, a Sudeten German scholar of unimpeachable democratic loyalty, pointed out: "In essentials there was a repetition in Czechoslovakia of what had occurred in the case of the Austro-Hungarian Monarchy: those nationalities which had no full share in the state power deserted when circumstances allowed."[13]

The Czech leaders were unwilling to concede the fact of "essential repetition" in the tragedy of their nation. They had identified their national aspirations with the cause of democracy and they therefore branded disloyalty to Czechoslovakia as a crime against democracy. This was the moral basis upon which President Beneš, when driven into exile after Munich, constructed his thesis which claimed that Czechoslovakia had the right to expel its disloyal German and Hungarian subjects. This was a *Verwirkungstheorie,* a theory of forfeiture, similar to the one invoked by the Viennese absolutists after the defeat of the revolutions of 1848–49, according to which the nations, by their revolt against Austria, forfeited their rights to constitutionalism. It was also an ugly program for forcibly expelling those forcibly incorporated. After the First World War, Germans and Hungarians, with their land, had been incorporated into the Czechoslovak state against their will; after Munich, according to Beneš's *Verwirkungstheorie,* they were to forfeit not only their right to self-determination but also their right to their land. They were to be treated, indeed, as intruders into an imaginary "thousand-years-old" Czechoslovakia. Beneš, in terms reminiscent of the Hungarian revisionist vows, expressed the hope that "Czechoslovakia will return to its original thousand-years frontiers";[14] but, while he bent his efforts to the restoration of Czechoslovakia's territorial integrity, his *Verwirkungstheorie* foreshadowed the worst of all defeats: the betrayal of the Czech nation's hard-won democratic legacy.

The Czech program of the ethnically pure national state was a bad augury for the prospects of Danubian reconciliation. Perhaps the worst of it was that it precluded future cooperation even with the democratic elements of those nations who were branded collectively guilty of crimes against democracy. The Czechs, who could have contributed more than anybody else to the building of a truly democratic Central Europe, committed themselves to a program incompatible with democracy. So when the long night of the Hitler era was over, Beneš's program of statemaking was not a fit instrument for the revival of Western principles of freedom; instead, it fitted into Stalin's plans, and abetted the victory of Soviet tyranny.

Part Two: The Triumph of Tyranny

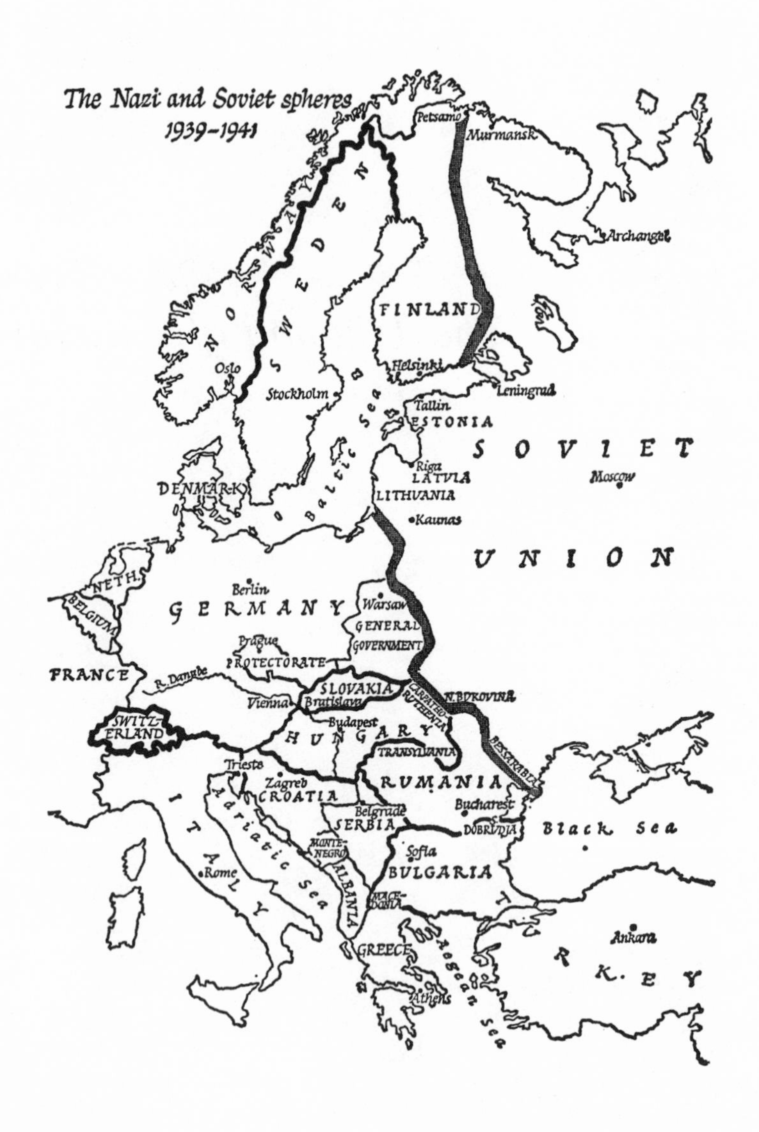
The Nazi and Soviet spheres
1939–1941
Petsamo
Murmansk
Archangel
NORWAY
SWEDEN
FINLAND
Oslo
Helsinki
Stockholm
Leningrad
Baltic Sea
Tallin
ESTONIA
SOVIET UNION
Riga
LATVIA
Moscow
DENMARK
LITHUANIA
Kaunas
NETH.
BELGIUM
Berlin
GERMANY
Warsaw
GENERAL GOVERNMENT
Prague
PROTECTORATE
FRANCE
R. Danube
SLOVAKIA
Vienna
Bratislava
CARPATHO RUTHENIA
N. BUKOVINA
SWITZERLAND
Budapest
HUNGARY
TRANSYLVANIA
BESSARABIA
Trieste
Zagreb
CROATIA
RUMANIA
Bucharest
Belgrade
SERBIA
DOBRUDJA
Black Sea
Adriatic Sea
MONTENEGRO
Sofia
BULGARIA
ITALY
Rome
ALBANIA
MACEDONIA
GREECE
Athens
Aegean Sea
Ankara
TURKEY

8 *German Hegemony*

The capitulation of the Western Powers at the Munich Conference in 1938 started the avalanche of events which almost a decade later, following the Second World War, ended in Soviet Russia's tyranny over half of Europe. Munich enabled Hitler to seize Czechoslovakia and to deliver the decisive blow against the Middle Zone of small nations which separated Germany from Soviet Russia. During the period of Nazi-Soviet cooperation which followed (1939–1941), two concurrent movements took place: the expansion and consolidation of German hegemony in the Middle Zone continued, and the Russian advance began. The Russian expansion westward was disrupted when Nazi Germany attacked Soviet Russia in 1941, forcing a great eastward retreat; but the tide of the war turned, and the Russian advance extended in final victory well beyond the confines fixed for Soviet rule by the Nazi-Soviet pact of 1939.

The secret protocol to the Nazi-Soviet non-aggression pact, which was signed on August 23, 1939, by the German Foreign Minister, Joachim von Ribbentrop, and the Soviet Commissar for Foreign Affairs, Vyacheslav M. Molotov, divided the territories between Russia and Germany into spheres of interest. Finland, Latvia, Estonia, eastern Poland and, eventually, Bessarabia were to pass into the Soviet sphere, while western Poland and Lithuania were to go into the German sphere. After the defeat of Poland, the secret protocol to a new treaty, signed on September 28, 1939, transferred Lithuania to the Soviet sphere and enlarged somewhat the German sphere in Poland.

While ruthless power politics was the essence of these arrangements, Russia's territorial claims against Poland and Romania were based also on ethnic principles. The frontiers of the Soviet sphere in East Poland, called the Molotov-Ribbentrop Line, ran slightly to the west of the so-called Curzon Line, which had been proposed as the Polish-Russian ethnic frontier after the First World War, but was rejected by Poland. There were about four million Poles living in this area, but the majority of the population was Ukrainian and Russian. Bessarabia, too, had a slight Ukrainian majority. In these instances the Soviet Union acted as Mother Russia, anxious to recover her lost territories. Her claims were not unlike those of the other revisionist countries, Hungary, Bulgaria, or, for that matter, Poland. The Poles, only a year before, in October 1938, had utilized the ethnic principle, stretching it to doubtful capacity, in their seizure of Teschen from Czechoslovakia. What was novel in Russia's claims was that the Russians should employ revisionist slogans in the same vein as the Hitlerite propaganda, demanding the liberation of "blood brethren from Polish yoke." On the other hand, there was nothing novel in the fact that Soviet Russia's aspirations based on ethnic principles went far beyond ethnic limits. The ethnic principle in the age of nationalism was always a convenient pretext for imperialistic expansion, no matter whether the government which invoked "the right of national self-determination" was democratic, reactionary, Fascist, or Communist.

In the war against Poland, in September 1939, Germany gained control of her sphere of interest immediately. In the closing phase of the war Russia invaded East Poland and annexed it, but moved into the rest of her sphere only gradually. In fact, Finland never passed under her control. Although Russia attacked Finland on November 30, 1939, the "winter war" ended in a compromise, with Stalin satisfied by frontier rectifications. The Soviet annexation of the Baltic states was completed in June 1940. At the same time Romania, under German pressure, ceded to Russia not only Bessarabia but, as an addition to the Soviet sphere, North Bukovina, too.[1]

During the winter of 1939–40 there was some hope that Mussolini might stay out of the war, despite the "pact of steel" he had signed with Hitler in the spring of 1939. There was vague talk about a neutral bloc in the Danube Valley and the Balkans under Italy's leadership. Italy's "powerful, non-belligerent influence" as a counterpart of the United States' "great neutral influence" was discussed by Sumner Welles, Under-Secretary of State, during his mission to Europe in early 1940. Mussolini told Sumner Welles in March 1940: "You may wish to remember that, while the German-Italian Pact exists, I nevertheless retain complete liberty of action."[2] Hitler's stupendous successes in his war against the West, however, soon dispelled Mussolini's desire for independent action. Instead, eager to share in the spoils of what not a few considered Hitler's final victory, Mussolini hurried, in June 1940, to declare war on France and Britain.

France's defeat and Italy's entrance into the war dashed the hope for neutrality in the Danube Valley. German continental hegemony seemed overwhelming. German pressure in southeastern Europe increased rapidly. Governments, including those of Yugoslavia and Romania, which not long before had been friends of France, vied with each other for the friendship of the Hitlerite Third Reich. Hungary and Bulgaria, the two old revisionist partners of Germany, meanwhile waited impatiently for the fulfillment of their territorial claims.

The old feud between Romania and Hungary over Transylvania had developed to the verge of war when the Nazi and Fascist Foreign Ministers, Ribbentrop and Ciano, met in Vienna on August 30, 1940, to continue the revision of the Trianon Treaty which had been started, in principle at least, by the Western Powers at Munich. The two Axis ministers attempted to draw an ethnic frontier between Hungary and Romania. They bisected Transylvania and gave the northern part of it, with a population of two and a half million, to Hungary. This so-called Second Vienna Award left about half a million Hungarians still in Romania, while it transferred to Hungary roughly as many Romanians as Hungarians — altogether, two and a half million people. The massive Hungarian island of the Székelys in eastern Transylvania was returned to Hungary but only with a Romanian-settled corridor lying between Transylvania and Hungary. This solution was not satisfactory. But as long as it was between Romanian and Hungarian *national* states that Transylvania remained a bone of contention, no true solution was possible. A federated Transylvania within a Danubian union could have solved the problem. Such a solution, however, was as remote from fulfillment at the time of the Second Vienna Award as at any time before or since.

As a matter of fact, the Vienna frontier favored the Hungarians less than the Trianon frontier had favored the Romanians. The deputies of the Nazi and Fascist dictators committed no worse crimes against the principle of national self-determination than did the democratic peacemakers of Paris twenty years earlier; nor did Hungary and Romania become worse neighbors after the Second Vienna Award than they had been after the peace settlement of 1919–20. The gain for Hitler, however, was significant.

In Hungary, gratitude for the revision of the Trianon Treaty strengthened pro-German sentiment and made nationalist public opinion insensible to the Nazi danger. The Hungarian government also signed an agreement in Vienna with the Reich, granting to the German minority in

Hungary special privileges which were actually incompatible with Hungarian sovereignty. But the people of Hungary, overjoyed at recovering more of the territory of their thousand-years-old country, hardly took notice of Nazi encroachments on their national sovereignty. Meanwhile in Romania, after proud possession for twenty years, the loss of the greater part of Transylvania was viewed as a catastrophe. In the wave of national indignation that followed, King Carol II was swept from his throne. But the Romanian upheaval, though precipitated by indignation against the Nazi-sponsored Vienna Award, in fact helped the pro-Nazi elements to power. Romania came within the German sphere of influence, and it was now the Romanian Fascists' turn to claim that, on the strength of their friendship and loyalty to Nazi Germany, they were the saviors of their fatherland. Thus, while young Prince Michael became king, the pro-Nazi General Ion Antonescu established himself as virtual dictator of Romania.

In this ominous autumn of 1940, the amputation of Romania's minority population was completed. On September 7, under German pressure, she ceded Southern Dobrudja to Bulgaria. This process was similar to what had happened to Czechoslovakia in 1938–39, with the difference however that the remainder of Romania was still a good-sized country, and militarily she became a substantial ally of Hitler. In October 1940 a German "instructor corps," in fact an entire panzer division, arrived by way of Hungary. Before long, Romania became the principal operational base of the Nazi war machine in southeastern Europe.

The transformation of southeastern Europe into a German sphere of interest, a prospect which had not been envisaged in the Nazi-Soviet secret protocols, proceeded rapidly. Meanwhile Mussolini, anxious to expand the Italian sphere of interest in the Balkans, invaded Greece on October 28 from Albania, which the Fascists had occupied over a year before. This cumulative Axis activity in the Balkans greatly disturbed Russia, herself a power with long-standing interests there. The changes in the status of Romania prompted the Soviet government to lodge protests in Berlin. At the end of October, Russo-German rivalry over the Danube delta came into the open at a conference held in Bucharest, when the Axis Powers rejected the Soviet demand for a Soviet-Romanian control authority.

While Nazi-Soviet tension was mounting, Soviet Foreign Commissar Molotov arrived in Berlin on November 12, 1940, to discuss broader Nazi proposals for a worldwide cooperation on the basis of spheres of interest. Plans to partition the world between Germany, Italy, Japan and the Soviet Union were laid before Molotov. The Soviet sphere, in addition to what had been previously agreed upon, was to lie south of the U.S.S.R. in the direction of the Indian Ocean. Furthermore, the status of the Straits was to be revised, by bringing joint pressure on Turkey; in the future only Black Sea powers were to have the right to send warships through the Straits to or from the Mediterranean. Molotov, however, demanded also a Soviet base in the Straits and the inclusion of Bulgaria in the Soviet "security zone,"[3] and over these demands the Berlin negotiations broke down.

The Axis thereafter, in defiance of Russia, tightened its control over southeastern Europe. In November, between the 20th and 25th, Hungary, Romania and Slovakia adhered to the German-Italian-Japanese Tripartite Pact. German pressure on Bulgaria and Yugoslavia, too, was increased during this period, as Italian military setbacks in Greece gave Hitler special concern lest Greece, allied with Britain, become a British bridgehead in the Balkans. The German position vis-à-vis both Britain and Russia was strengthened when on March 1, 1941, Bulgaria joined the Tripartite Pact. Thereafter German "instructor corps" entered Bulgaria to make it a German bridgehead against Greece, and to defy Russia's claim that it fell within the Soviet "security zone."

The only Danubian country not a member of the Tripartite Pact was now Yugoslavia. Its regent, Prince Paul, was maintaining an uneasy balance between the Axis and the Western Powers. A treaty of friendship, signed in December 1940 with Hungary, a member of the Tripartite Pact, was one of the friendly moves Yugoslavia made toward the Axis, although the Budapest and Belgrade governments, rather naively, conceived the treaty as a means of strengthening their neutrality. When Berlin continued to press Belgrade for adherence to the Tripartite Pact, Prince Paul submitted, and Yugoslavia signed the pact on March 25, 1941. The next day, however, an officers' coup overthrew Paul's regime, elevating the minor, Prince Peter, to the throne.

The motivations for this coup were rather obscure. British and American diplomatic encouragement to resist German pressure probably had little effect. The coup, almost exclusively a Serbian affair, was mainly a spontaneous protest against the threat of German encroachment on Yugoslav national sovereignty. But it represented a violent outburst of Serbian nationalism in more than one direction. Hugh Seton-Watson seems to be right in observing that "there is some ground for the suspicion that they were more interested in undoing the concessions made to the Croats by Prince Paul in 1939 than in resisting the Axis."[4]

The new government of General Dušan Simović assured the Axis of Yugoslavia's loyalty to the Tripartite Pact, but Hitler was filled with distrust. It will never be known whether Yugoslavia, under the new regime, would have cooperated with the Axis as the German satellites, willingly or unwillingly, did. Nor is it clear what Russia's true intentions were. On April 4, 1941, a Soviet-Yugoslav treaty of non-aggression and friendship was signed in Moscow, but at the same time Molotov assured Count Schulenburg, the German Ambassador, that Yugoslavia intended to adhere to the Tripartite Pact.[5] Molotov's friendly assurance to Germany with regard to the Soviet-Yugoslav treaty probably was not a single piece of deception. It was, rather, a reminder that on the terms of the Berlin negotiations, if Soviet interests in the Balkans were recognized, Russo-German cooperation might still have a future.

According to subsequent Soviet official interpretation, every move during the period of cooperation with Nazi Germany served the purpose of "probing the German position" and building up an "eastern front" against the Germans. As an official Soviet document expressed it, "the point was to build up a barrier against the advance of the German troops in all areas where that was possible, to organize a strong defense and then to launch a counteroffensive, smash Hitler's armies and thereby create the conditions for the free development of . . . [the Eastern European] countries."[6]

If the Soviet-Yugoslav treaty was intended to build up a "barrier" against Hitler, then the treaty failed to attain its purpose. It succeeded, however, in "probing the German position." On April 6, Germany invaded Yugoslavia. And when Hitler ruthlessly attacked the country with which, two days before, the Soviet Union had signed a treaty of friendship, he also intimated what he thought of the friendship treaties which Germany had signed two years before with the Soviet Union.

Hitler had several springboards (Austria, Romania, Bulgaria) for launching his attack against Yugoslavia, but to speed up victory he needed Hungary too. The pro-Nazi Hungarian General Staff, without the knowledge of the government, agreed to the passage of German troops. Premier Count Paul Teleki, realizing the *fait accompli,* committed suicide while the German troops were beginning their march across Hungary toward Yugoslavia. Teleki's tragedy was symbolic of the impasse in which Hungary found herself and of the hopeless situation of the Danubian nations in general, which one by one had submitted to the Nazi will.

With the ring around Yugoslavia closed, Hitler launched his attack from the four small countries of the Danube Valley: Austria, Hungary, Romania and Bulgaria. If united, these four countries, together with Yugoslavia, Czechoslovakia and Poland, could have stopped Hitler from destroying any one of them. Within a few years Hitler conquered them all, without once meeting even two of them deliberately united. There were individual acts of solidarity, like Hungary's refusal in 1939 to let German troops cross Hungary against Poland. And refugees from one invaded country were received as friends in another country not invaded. But it never happened that any two of the countries intentionally formed a united front of resistance. Only by coincidence, and for a very short time, did such a bond of union materialize: when Hitler launched his attack against Yugoslavia, Greece was at war with Italy; Hitler's attack was aimed therefore against Greece as well as Yugoslavia, and also against the British, who were rushing aid to the hard-pressed Greeks. But this united resistance of Yugoslavia, Greece and Britain in the Balkans was too little and came too late. Hitler's war, on the other hand, was greatly aided by dissensions inside multinational Yugoslavia, which collapsed after a brief struggle. With the victory in the Balkans, Hitler completed his destruction of the Paris peacemakers' work in the belt of small nations between Germany and Russia.

Hungary, the principal revisionist country of the area, concluded her revisionist career by annexing from defeated Yugoslavia approximately one million people, less than half of whom were Hungarians. However, the suicide of Count Teleki, one of the leaders of the revisionist policy, had been a dramatic confession of what he, like many other Hungarians, thought of the actual value of the territorial gains which Hungary achieved with Hitler's aid. Statistically, the ethnic composition of the enlarged Hungarian national state after this last revision of the Trianon Treaty compared not unfavorably with that of the states favored by the Paris peacemakers after the First World War. In 1941 the Hungarians held an 80 percent majority in their enlarged country, whereas the majorities in the victor states after the First World War, according to official figures, were as follows: the Czechs, Slovaks and Ruthenes made only 69 percent in Czechoslovakia; the Poles 69 percent in Poland; the Romanians 72 percent in Romania; the Serbs, Croats and Slovenes 83 percent in Yugoslavia. In other words, the ratio of ethnic majority and minority in enlarged Hungary was not worse, but rather better, than in most of the Central and Eastern European countries which after the First World War were beneficiaries of the Paris peace settlement.

This comparison is significant only because it shows that Hungary's territorial gains, decried as outrageous violations of justice by the former beneficiaries of the Paris peace settlement, were not, comparatively, outrageous at all. The real significance of the new situation lay elsewhere.

After Yugoslavia's dismemberment, when the last phase of the "revision" of the Paris peace settlement was concluded, the peoples of the once-independent Middle Zone were all in the grasp of Nazi Germany; and Nazi Germany herself now felt it safe, from her bases in Eastern Europe, to launch the invasion of Soviet Russia which followed in June 1941. The citadel of democracy, as Czechoslovakia was called, had fallen first. Poland and Yugoslavia had been crushed by military force, suffering more than any other countries during the Hitler era. Satellite governments of different shades continued to function in the conquered lands — except in Poland, where the Germans did not care even to maintain the semblance of self-government — but the forces of freedom had been brutally suppressed or paralyzed everywhere. Horrors of Nazi inhumanity, especially against the Jews, marked the reign of terror.

A strange island of relative freedom survived in Hungary, at least until the German occupation of the country in March 1944. The revisionist bond of union with Germany enabled Hungary to adjust to the Hitler era without revolutionary changes in her regime. Thus Horthy's Hungary — the most reactionary country in post-war Central Europe — was, with its limited freedom, after Nazi rule had engulfed Europe, the freest Danubian country of the Hitler era, an asylum for many refugees from all over Europe. The same reactionary forces which for so long had resisted the democratization of Hungary became the forces of national resistance against Hitler. This was the last achievement of the old Hungarian ruling class which called itself Conservative-Liberal. Their reliable representative at the head of the government was Nicholas Kállay, a member of the gentry class; he took over the premiership in March 1942, when Regent Horthy dismissed Ladislas Bárdossy, an advocate of unequivocal alliance with Nazi Germany in the war against Soviet Russia. It was Kállay's job to keep both Hungary's war effort and her further adaptation to Nazi norms in domestic affairs at a minimum. Kállay was well fitted for this task. For two years, with great dexterity, he kept the Hungary which had been enlarged with Nazi Germany's help safe from Nazi domination. Hungary was allowed temporarily to enjoy the fruits of her revisionist policy.

Revisionist Bulgaria, too, benefited from the dismemberment of Yugoslavia. She annexed Macedonia on the basis of a controversial claim that Macedonians were more Bulgarian than Serbian. In addition, Bulgaria regained access to the Aegean Sea by taking western Thrace from Greece. Although less an "island of freedom" than Hungary, Bulgaria nevertheless succeeded in preserving her full freedom of action (or rather inaction) in at least one respect: she was the only country among Germany's satellites that did not declare war on Soviet Russia.

Nazi Germany's victory in the Balkans enabled Fascist Italy victoriously to conclude her two years of war against Greece, and Italy shared also in the spoils of German victory over Yugoslavia. She annexed the greater part of Slovenia and all of Dalmatia. Montenegro was proclaimed "independent" under Italian protection. Germany annexed the rest of Slovenia and occupied Serbia. Neither Germany nor Italy, however, controlled the inaccessible mountains from which, four years later, Josip Broz Tito was to emerge as the victor, not only over Hitler and Mussolini, but also over Draža Mihailović, leader of the Serbian partisans even before Tito had gone to the mountains to organize resistance to the Axis invaders. (Incidentally, other Communists, who were to become stars in the post-war Soviet era, did not take to the mountains but found refuge in Moscow through the good offices of the Nazis. The future Communist boss of Hungary, Mátyás Rákosi, and the Romanian Ana Pauker, belonged to this latter category; they were released from jail and extradited to Russia by the two Axis satellites, Hungary and Romania, under the aegis of Nazi-Soviet cooperation.)

Out of the Balkan chaos the medieval kingdom of the Croats was resuscitated as an Axis satellite. She even got a king in the person of the Italian Duke of Spoleto; but the duke never cared to assume his throne. The Croats had longed for national autonomy while they were a member-nation of Serbian-dominated Yugoslavia, but "independent Croatia," headed by the Fascist fanatic Ante Pavelić, was anything but the fulfillment of their national aspirations. Satellite Croatia was an even less solid creation of the Hitler era than its northern counterpart, the National Socialist Slovak state. Pavelić's Croatia lacked the quite considerable popular support which Tiso's Slovakia enjoyed, and Croatia was torn by partisan war, which Slovakia was spared until the uprising in the summer of 1944.

Hitler's "new order" in the Danube Valley did nothing at all to advance reconciliation among the rival nations there. Although all the

Danubian states were Hitler's allies, among themselves they continued their old hostilities by nurturing revisionist aspirations of one kind or another. Romania was anxious to recapture the lost half of Transylvania; Slovakia too was desirous of recovering territories from Hungary; while Hungary was eager to restore her rule over the whole of Transylvania, or for that matter over the whole of the Carpathian basin. Sympathies and antipathies among the Danubian states remained pretty much the same as they were before. Hungary and Bulgaria, traditional allies of the revisionist era, remained friends, while Romania, Slovakia and Croatia were mutually attracted by their hostility toward Hungary, thus tending to continue the tradition of the defunct Little Entente. And those who believed in the permanence of Hitler's mastery over Central Europe were hopeful also that they might eventually, if loyal to Nazi Germany, be rewarded at the expense of their rival neighbors. All this of course suited Hitler well, to keep his satellites in line, and to extort from them whatever he needed to further Germany's war effort.

Russia's westward advance as a result of the Nazi-Soviet pact was relatively minor in comparison with Germany's eastward expansion between September 1939 and April 1941. From Poland to Greece the Germans were in the saddle. This was a development Stalin certainly had not foreseen and could not have approved, yet he seemed ready to cooperate in maintaining the status quo. But Hitler felt that all advantages he could derive from "peaceful coexistence" with Soviet Russia had been exhausted. He left unnoticed such Soviet gestures of amity as the expulsion of Belgian, Norwegian and Yugoslav diplomatic representatives from Moscow in the spring of 1941, or proposals for further German-Russian economic cooperation. Much as Hitler tried to avoid the dangers of a two-front war, he nevertheless came to the same conclusion as Napoleon fighting the same enemies had reached before him, that the road to London led through Moscow. On June 22, 1941, Germany invaded the Soviet Union.

Shortly after — on July 12 — the British-Soviet mutual aid pact was signed. Thus Churchill, Prime Minister since May 1940, was able to conclude the Grand Alliance for which he had been pleading relentlessly as leader of the opposition to Chamberlain's appeasement policy. Tsar or Commissar, Kaiser or Hitler: the laws of geography and power politics asserted themselves to restore the East-West alliance of the First World War. But many other circumstances were different. Now, France had already been knocked out of the war and Churchill was Lloyd George and Clemenceau in one person. Hitler, on the other hand, ruled over more territory and people than the former realms of the Hohenzollerns and Habsburgs combined.

Had the East-West alliance functioned sooner, there could not have been a Munich and Hitler could have been knocked out, probably without a second world war. And had a democratic federation of the Danubian nations been formed when the realm of the Habsburgs collapsed after the First World War, Hitler could hardly have conquered Central Europe, if indeed he could have arisen at all from obscurity in a Europe capable of creating a Danubian federation. And above all: had France, Britain and the United States remained united, the entire course of European history would have been different. Had the United States not left Europe to a separate destiny after the First World War, she would not have been called back less than a quarter of a century later to fight in the Second World War, and there would have been no need for calling in Soviet Russia to rescue the crumbling defenses of the West.

The Grand Alliance of East and West, urged originally by Churchill for the purpose of stopping Hitler's aggression, was entrusted now with an even greater task: the liberation of Europe from Hitler's tyranny.

9 *Federalist Interlude*

Hitlerism was the most hideous product of the age of European nationalism. The German Nazis and their accomplices among the European nations, who were supposedly Christians of the Western civilization, rendered terrible evidence of Europe's debasement in the age of nationalism. Moreover, Hitler's conquest of Europe proved the total incapacity of nationalist Europe to defend itself against the destructive forces that had undermined Western civilization from within.

Meanwhile the Soviet conquest of the Baltic states, East Poland and Bessarabia, during the period of Nazi-Soviet cooperation, provided a fresh reminder of the brutalities which the harbingers of a purported new age of social justice could inflict upon European civilization. It was a grave mistake for the West not to enter into a military alliance with the Soviet Union against Hitler at a time when such an alliance could have prevented the Nazi conquest of the Continent. But Soviet Russia, according to the laws of geography a natural ally of the West against Nazi Germany, could not help the West solve its inner crisis. The very fact that an enemy of Western democracy like Soviet Russia was needed as an ally of the West against Hitler was an alarming sign of Europe's troubles.

The causes of Europe's decay were manifold, but the principal cause was the disintegration of the European community through nationalism. Without drastic changes in the outward political structure, the inner crisis of the Continent could not be ended. There was, indeed, but one way out of the anarchy of the past: the reorganization of Europe into a federal union. The cataclysm of war should in all logic have led to a revival of federalist movements. Indeed, as it turned out, the tragic collapse of national independence in the Middle Zone did seem to work as a stimulus toward federalist planning on an unprecedented scale. The century-old warning that the nations lying between Russia and Germany could not defend their freedom unless they were welded into federations came to be reechoed in many quarters.

Federalism became a popular watchword among the exiles from Central Europe. Eduard Beneš, ex-President of Czechoslovakia, reached an agreement in November 1940 with Władysław Sikorski, Premier of the Polish government in exile, an agreement whose details were worked out in a declaration signed in January 1942, to the effect that after the war Poland and Czechoslovakia would form a "Confederation of States." This agreement did not envisage a Danubian union, which had been a traditional aim of Central European federalists. Also, as it turned out, in Beneš's plans cooperation with the Soviet Union took priority over cooperation with any of the Middle Zone nations. In retrospect, the suspicion arose that Beneš availed himself of a Czechoslovak-Polish rapprochement for opportunistic purposes only in order to strengthen temporarily the international position of the Czech exiles; for, until Soviet Russia's entry into the war, Czechoslovak foreign policy operated almost in a vacuum.[1] Nevertheless at the time of the signing of the Polish-Czech confederation agreement, hopes rose high that this might signify the beginning of a new era of cooperation among the Middle Zone nations. This belief had been strengthened by the proclaimed aim of the Polish-Czech declaration that "other states" should eventually be included in the planned confederation.

When Yugoslavia and Greece fell victim to Nazi aggression, the scope of the exiles' federalist planning was broadened. At a New York meeting in November 1941 the International Labor Conference issued a declaration, signed by "the government and employers' delegations" of Czechoslovakia, Greece, Poland and Yugoslavia, which emphasized the unity of Central Europe and the Balkans. In January 1942 federal agreement on the Czechoslovak-Polish model was reached between the Greek and Yugoslav émigré governments, concerning the constitution of a "Balkan Union." A Central and Eastern European Planning Board was established in New York in January 1942 and entrusted with the study of federalism. The charter members of the board were the government representatives of Czechoslovakia, Greece, Poland and Yugoslavia, countries which already had signed the federalist agreements. In London, the so-called "Peasant Program" was published in July 1942 by a group composed of exiled representatives of peasant parties who favored a federal union of all the peoples from the Baltic to the Balkans.

Another group, the London Danubian Club, in October 1943 proposed a "Central and South-east European Union," in the form of a detailed draft constitution for a federation of the entire Middle Zone. Both plans were drawn up in cooperation not only with representatives of the four countries (Poland, Czechoslovakia, Yugoslavia, Greece) engaged officially in federalist planning, but also with exiles from Austria, Hungary, Romania, Bulgaria and Albania.

Vague federalist programs appeared frequently too in the clandestine press of the Nazi-occupied Central and Eastern Europe. In Hungary, where the press was relatively free until the German occupation (March 1944), both the progressive and conservative anti-Nazi Budapest newspapers — such as the Conservative-Liberal *Magyar Nemzet,* the Socialist *Népszava,* and the organ of the Smallholders party, *Kis Újság* — occasionally advocated Lajos Kossuth's ideas of a Danubian confederation.

The federalist planning of the Central and Eastern European nations seemed to meet with approval from the Western Powers. In fact, federalism became something of a popular watchword in the West too. Some of the conclusions the Western nations began to draw from their tragedy seemed to parallel those the Central and Eastern European nations were drawing from their catastrophe. Winston Churchill seemed to understand better than anybody the necessity for Europe's federalist reconstruction. He knew that democratic states were weak "unless they are welded into larger organisms," and he knew that the complete break-up of the Austro-Hungarian Empire was a "cardinal tragedy" for Europe.[2] Churchill was the sponsor of a revolutionary proposal which could have changed the course of European history had it been accepted — the proposal of a French-British Union in the summer of 1940, just before France collapsed.

"At this fateful moment in the history of the modern world," Churchill proposed, "the Governments of the United Kingdom and the French Republic make this declaration of indissoluble union. . . . The two Governments declare that France and Britain shall no longer be two nations but one Franco-British union. The constitution of the union will provide for joint organs of defence, foreign, financial, and economic policies. Every citizen of France will enjoy immediate citizenship of Great Britain, every British subject will become a citizen of France."

In comparison, the signing of the Atlantic Charter a year later, on August 14, 1941, was an anticlimax. The Charter, which came to be recognized as the fundamental declaration of principle of the United

Nations, spoke out against "territorial changes that do not accord with the freely expressed wishes of the peoples concerned" (Point 2). It defended "the right of all peoples to choose the form of government under which they will live" (Point 3). But it did not embrace, not even by implication, the federalist program as a principle of future peace. In effect, the Charter reasserted the old principle of national sovereignty. President Roosevelt and Prime Minister Churchill, instead of declaring the necessity for "larger organisms" for the defense of peace and democracy, expressed in Point Six of the Charter their hope that a peace would be established "which will afford to all nations the means of dwelling in safety within their own boundaries. . . ."

Considering the fact that Europe, and especially Central Europe, had been torn for so long with struggles over boundaries, Point Six of the Charter, emphasizing boundaries, gave a most inadequate program for future peaceful cooperation between nations. In omitting the federal principle from their program, the authors of the Atlantic Charter failed to devise the best means by which nations could achieve peace and safety. The absence of the federalist program from the Charter was the more deplorable because the time of the Charter's publication in the summer of 1941 coincided with Soviet Russia's entering the war as an ally of the West against Nazi Germany. With a resolute endorsement of the federal program, in which — as so many seemed to agree, lay Europe's only salvation — the Western Powers could have provided themselves in defense of the West's interests with the best possible basis for any future discussions of peace aims with their Soviet ally.

As for Soviet Russia, she always opposed the idea of European federation even though she herself was, at least nominally, a federal union of several nations. (Incidentally, that the Russians, who master this "federation," represent only a little over 50 percent of the total population, is among the little-known facts of the Soviet state of affairs.) In the late twenties when Briand proposed his plan for a European union, Stalin had declared emphatically: "For the slogan 'the United States of Europe' we will substitute the slogan 'the federation of Soviet republics of advanced countries, which have fallen, or are falling, away from the imperialist system of economy.'"[3] The German attack in the summer of 1941, however, turned Russia into an ally of the "imperialist" West and it remained to be seen whether Russia would be willing to change her anti-federalist stand for the sake of East-West cooperation.

Soviet Russia's well-known antipathy toward federal union of the countries along Russia's borders did not discourage the exiles from Central Europe from continuing their federalist planning. In fact, most of the already mentioned émigré announcements concerning the federalization of the Middle Zone were dated after the German attack on Russia. Nor, at the beginning of East-West cooperation, did the Soviet attitude appear stiff. Great military setbacks and the realization of the vital importance of Western aid to Russia (during the Teheran Conference in 1943 Stalin acknowledged that without American production the war would have been lost) seemed to soften Soviet hostility toward European federalism. Thus, in a report from Moscow on January 5, 1942, Eden quoted Stalin as saying that "the Soviet Union had no objection to certain countries of Europe entering into a federal relationship, if they so desired."[4]

In London, on June 4, 1942, Beneš discussed the Czechoslovak-Polish federal plan in detail with Molotov, who told him that Russia had no objections to the project. Five weeks later, however, on July 16, Jan Masaryk, the foreign minister of the Czech government in exile, was informed by Alexander Bogomolov, the Soviet minister in London, that Russia could not approve the plan. This was interpreted as a "drastic reversal of policy in the Kremlin between June 4th and July 16th,"[5] although more probably it was only a move to probe and test the Western policies, at a time when discussion of post-war plans was beginning between the Western Powers and the Soviet government. Ivan Maisky, the Soviet ambassador in London, told Eden almost a year later, in March 1943, that in his opinion the Soviet government, although "not enthusiastic about the proposal for a future federation of Europe . . . would not oppose a Balkan federation provided it excluded Romania, and a Scandinavian federation which excluded Finland." Maisky also spoke "of the possibility of a Polish-Czech federation, saying that all such considerations depended on whether or not Poland was to have a government friendly to the Soviet Union."[6] Other Soviet pronouncements in the meantime emphasized Russia's wish to see "free, democratic, sovereign nations with governments friendly to the Soviet Union" rise in the Middle Zone, especially a "strong" Poland, Czechoslovakia and Yugoslavia, while the federal plans were denounced as "reactionary attempts" to revive the old anti-Soviet cordon sanitaire of the inter-war period.

Czechoslovakia's government in exile was the only one that responded promptly and favorably to the Soviet point of view. Moscow's program, envisaging the restoration of sovereign nation-states in the Middle Zone, appealed to Beneš — partly because he never felt enthusiastic about the federal plans anyway, and partly because he found ready support in Moscow for his pet project, the restoration of Czechoslovakia as a "homogeneous" Slav nation-state. The memory of Munich, and the fact that the Soviet government took the lead in supporting Beneš's diplomatic struggle for the repudiation of Munich, further nurtured his pro-Soviet leanings. Foreign Minister Molotov, while visiting London in the spring of 1942, assured Beneš that Russia recognized the pre-Munich frontiers of Czechoslovakia. One year later, in June 1943, the expulsion of Czechoslovakia's non-Slav population was approved by Moscow. The note informing the Czechs of the Soviet decision was conveniently timed. Coinciding, as it did, with Beneš's visit to Washington, it helped the Czechs in winning President Roosevelt's assent to their plans.[7]

The Western Powers were reluctant to take action during the war prejudicing post-war territorial questions in any way. Nevertheless in August 1942, upon Beneš's insistence, the British government declared itself free of any engagements undertaken at Munich, repeating thus Molotov's similar assurances given two months earlier. Meanwhile Foreign Secretary Eden agreed also — actually one year ahead of the Russians but in less general terms than they — to "the transfer of minority populations, *guilty* against the [Czechoslovak] Republic."[8] Beneš repeated his London success a year later in Washington, during his official visit to the United States in May and June 1943. Secretary of State Cordell Hull gave assurances that the U.S. government considered Munich null and void. With Roosevelt, Beneš discussed the population plans "twice in detail," and the President approved the transfer of "the greatest *possible* number" of Germans.[9] Western approval of Beneš's expulsion plans, so alien to Western thinking, was granted in somewhat guarded terms. Nevertheless it was granted — evidently in the belief that this too would promote the then avidly sought cooperation between East and West.

Thus Beneš pioneered East-West cooperation in the Middle Zone, based, however, not on a federal plan, but on restoring the sovereign nation-states as homogeneous ethnic units. Other exile governments also subscribed in principle to cooperation with Soviet Russia, but without the enthusiasm of the Czechs. The Poles had especially grave problems to face. No agreement had been reached on the future of Russo-Polish frontiers. The fate of Polish prisoners of war and civilian internees in Soviet territory was another explosive issue. General Sikorski, the Polish premier in exile, was for Soviet cooperation but (until his untimely death in 1943) he remained an advocate of a federated Middle Zone.

Beneš, on the other hand, combined Moscow's program of "sovereign nations" with the plans for Czech-Polish union into a new scheme of close association between Czechoslovakia, Poland and Soviet Russia. This he called the future "cornerstone of peace in Europe." Elaborating upon this concept, Beneš said, addressing the Czechoslovak State Council in exile on November 12, 1942: "The present war is a decisive historical opportunity for stopping definitely the Pan-German *Drang nach Osten.* The present war has proved that this cannot be attained except by a true, friendly and loyal cooperation between Poland, Czechoslovakia and the Soviet Union. If we succeed, the whole future of Poland and Czechoslovakia is guaranteed, and the whole of Europe is helped by it. If not, a new catastrophe will come, in some form provoked by Germany."[10]

Actually this plan of a tripartite Czech-Polish-Soviet cooperation was superseded by bilateral Czech-Soviet cooperation, which led in December 1943 to the signing of a treaty of friendship, mutual assistance and post-war cooperation between Czechoslovakia and Soviet Russia. Poland's adherence was envisaged in the pact, but in the meantime Polish-Soviet relations became worse than ever. The Soviet government broke off diplomatic relations in April 1943, when the Polish government asked the International Red Cross to investigate the mass grave of Polish officers massacred, according to the German pronouncement, by the Russians in the forest of Katyn. Diplomatic relations were never resumed. During the liberation of Poland, in 1944, the Russians created for themselves a subservient Polish partner in the form of the Communist Lublin Committee of National Liberation.

The Czechoslovak-Polish federal project died unceremoniously and the Czech and Polish governments in exile went their separate ways in their struggle for the future of their nations. The other federal pilot-project, the Balkan Union planned by the Yugoslav and Greek governments in exile, fared no better. Struggles for power among the partisans at home, as well as among the exiles, dominated Balkan politics. How to return home, rather than how to form a union between Yugoslavia and

Greece, was the problem of the two governments in exile. The Greeks succeeded in getting home, with British help, while all that the Yugoslavs achieved was an agreement, signed in liberated Belgrade in December 1944, between Ivan Šubašić, the premier of the exiles, and Tito, who possessed the real power at home, a compromise which turned out to be a complete victory for the latter.

It was the aim of Soviet policy to deal with each nation in the Middle Zone separately, not with groups united by federal ties. The liberation of Eastern Europe by the Red Army was of course the decisive factor in enabling Russia to carry out her intentions. But then, too, the Western allies made no attempt to carry out the federal plans; nor is there much ground for assuming that these plans would have been carried out even if the Middle Zone had been liberated by armies of the West. For despite the wartime vogue for federal plans, the intentions of the planners remained ambiguous.

As Oscar Jászi, dean of the Danubian federalists, saw it, there was not even a real will aiming at "true federalism." For a truly democratic federation — that is, a system in which autonomous nations would be united with equal rights for all under a supranational federal government — had little or no backing among the planners of various federal projects. Conservative legitimists, trying to regain power under a Habsburg restoration, paid lip service to federalism, as did also those who intended to establish the dictatorship of the proletariat in Central Europe under Russia's leadership. But most frequently the federalists were simply nationalists, primarily interested in restoring the pre-war system of national states and planning to make the state even more nationalistic by expelling the minorities. This was what Beneš, for instance, planned to do in Czechoslovakia.

Professor Jászi called Beneš's decision to expel the minorities an "amazing conclusion." Jászi denied "the right of any state to experiment in uprooting national minorities, which for centuries have lived and worked on a territory which they regard as their beloved home." He branded the efforts to restore the small independent nation-states in Central Europe as a "reactionary policy, impotent and hopeless," and pointed out that "the governmental organs of sovereign states cannot generate a common will for common action, but will be directed inevitably towards selfish national interests."

Jászi deplored especially the way federalist slogans were being used as a screen for nationalist ambitions. In 1944 this life-long champion of Danubian federation, then a retired professor of Oberlin College, commented: "Most amazing to the friends of a lasting peace is the frequent emergence of so-called peace plans, which, in a more or less hidden language, emphasize the necessity for the re-establishment of the prewar system of distinct national sovereignties. Of course the authors of such plans express their admiration for certain vague forms of federalism, or pay compliment to a new 'better' League of Nations; but, discounting their rationalization, the realistic observer will not fail to understand that what they have in mind is really not true federalism, but the reconstruction of a new balance of power system, planned primarily to operate against a defeated and humiliated Germany, but occasionally also against Russia."[11]

In Western statesmen's attitudes, too, the realistic observer could detect no more than superficial expressions of admiration for certain forms of federalism. The records show various statements complimentary to federal plans; the plans themselves, however, were extremely vague and the actions taken on their behalf, if they can be called actions at all, were such haphazard improvizations that it is no wonder they did not affect in the slightest the actual course of wartime diplomacy.

In a message reproduced in his memoirs, Prime Minister Churchill said to Foreign Secretary Eden on October 21, 1942: "I must admit that my thoughts rest primarily in Europe — the revival of the glory of Europe, the parent continent of the modern nations and of civilization. It would be a measureless disaster if Russian barbarism overlaid the culture and independence of the ancient states of Europe. Hard as it is to say now, I trust that the European family may act unitedly as one under a Council of Europe. I look forward to a United States of Europe in which the barriers between the nations will be greatly minimized and unrestricted travel will be possible. I hope to see the economy of Europe studied as a whole. I hope to see a Council consisting of perhaps ten units, including the former Great Powers, with several confederations — Scandinavian, Danubian, Balkan, etc. — which would possess an international police and be charged with keeping Prussia disarmed. . . . unhappily," Churchill concluded, "the war has prior claims on your attention and on mine."[12]

A few weeks later, in December 1942, Foreign Secretary Eden was asked in the House of Commons whether the British government desired to encourage the formation of federations, and specifically whether a

Danubian federation would include such states as Austria, Hungary, Czechoslovakia and Poland. Eden replied: "In my spech at Leamington, on September 26th, I referred to the existing Polish-Czechoslovak and Greek-Yugoslav agreements and said that, as far as we were concerned, we should continue to foster agreements of this kind and to encourage the smaller states to weld themselves into larger, though not exclusive, goupings. Whether it will be possible, or desirable, to include Austria and Hungary within a federation based upon Poland and Czechoslovakia must clearly depend, among other things, upon the views of the Polish and Czechoslovak Governments and peoples and upon the future attitude of the Austrians and Hungarians, who are now fighting in the ranks of our enemies."

Churchill discussed publicly the subject of regional federations in his famous Council of Europe broadcast on March 21, 1943, when he said: "It would . . . seem, to me at any rate, worthy of patient study that side by side with the Great Powers there should be a number of groupings of states or confederations, which would express themselves through their own chosen representatives, the whole making a Council of great states and groups of states. It is my earnest hope, though I can hardly expect to see it fulfilled in my lifetime, that we shall achieve the largest common measure of the integrated life of Europe that is possible without destroying the individual characteristics and traditions of its many ancient and historic races. All this will, I believe, be found to harmonize with the high permanent interests of Britain, the United States, and Russia. It certainly cannot be accomplished without their cordial and concerted agreement and participation. Thus and thus only will the glory of Europe rise again."

While Churchill was talking about regional federations, the American State Department, in its post-war planning, was also discussing certain types of regional organizations. According to Under-Secretary of State Sumner Welles, at the beginning of 1943 the members of the Departmental Committee on International Organization were almost unanimously of the opinion that any new world structure would be built upon regional organizations.[13]

American and British views on regionalism and federation were exchanged during Churchill's third wartime visit to Washington, in May 1943, especially at "an important conversation on the structure of a post-war settlement," held at a British Embassy luncheon on May 22. The Prime Minister, as he recounted in his memoirs, expressed the view that the real responsibility for peace after the war should rest on a Supreme World Council formed by the United States, Great Britain, Russia, and — if the United States wished — China. Subordinate to the World Council there should be three Regional Councils: one for Europe, one for the American hemisphere, and one for the Pacific.

The European Council, Churchill suggested, might consist of about twelve "States or Confederations." He expressed the hope that in Southeastern Europe there might be several confederations, among others "a Danubian Federation based on Vienna and doing something to fill the gap caused by the disappearance of the Austro-Hungarian Empire." Incidentally, Churchill's "Danubian Federation" bore little resemblance to former Austria-Hungary. It tied Austria and Hungary to Bavaria rather than to the surrounding Danubian nations of the former Habsburg Monarchy. Churchill spoke also of a "Balkan Federation," and referred to Poland and Czechoslovakia as yet another grouping, having in mind, evidently, the federal pact agreed upon a year before by the Czech and Polish governments in exile. "Poland and Czechoslovakia," he said, "should stand together in friendly relations with Russia."

The American guests present at the British Embassy luncheon were: Vice-President Wallace, Secretary of War Stimson, Secretary of the Interior Ickes, Senator Connally, chairman of the Foreign Relations Committee, and Under-Secretary of State Sumner Welles. They all agreed with Churchill and said they themselves had been thinking along more or less similar lines. Stimson voiced the farsighted view that agreement on post-war plans should be reached while the war was still proceeding, inasmuch as after the war there would be a tendency to relax and a reluctance to embark upon new international experiments.[14]

However, no Anglo-American agreement was reached on the regional councils. Moreover, the views of the Western leaders on the creation of "larger organisms" showed more discrepancy than harmony during the Russo-American-British discussions of post-war plans at Moscow and Teheran, which followed shortly after the British-American conference in Washington.

In contrast with Under-Secretary of State Sumner Welles's views, Secretary of State Cordell Hull showed, during the Russo-American-British negotiations, no understanding at all of the regional plans. Nor, it seems, did federal union as a means of curbing the dangers of nationalism figure in Hull's thinking, even though, according to his public statements, he was fully aware of the evils of nationalism. For instance, he condemned nationalism in the strongest terms in a speech of July 23, 1942. "Nationalism, run riot between the last war and this war," he said, "defeated all attempts to carry out indispensable measures of international economic and political action, encouraged and facilitated the rise of dictators, and drove the world straight towards the present war." But he put all his faith, as did Roosevelt, in a new worldwide international organization which would curb international rivalry. He even considered regionalism a dangerous trend which "might imperil the future post-war organization."[15]

This view that regional or federal plans might impair the success of Allied negotiations concerning the creation of a post-war world organization was upheld by Cordell Hull at the conference of the foreign ministers of the Big Three (Hull, Eden, Molotov) which took place in Moscow between October 13 and October 30, 1943. At the October 26 meeting the question of confederation of the smaller European nations, with particular reference to the Danubian area, came up for discussion on the basis of a proposal sanctioning such confederations, submitted by Anthony Eden. This British plan had been rejected previously by the State Department, and in Moscow Hull reiterated his stand by saying that agreement should first be reached on a broad set of principles, capable of worldwide application, which would then guide the three powers in consideration of separate and specific questions. Thereupon Soviet Foreign Minister Molotov read a statement which emphatically criticized the idea of planning federations of small nations at that time. The Soviet government, Molotov said, felt the active consideration or encouragement of such schemes to be premature and even harmful, not only to the interests of the small countries, but also to general matters of European stability. Some of the plans for federation, he continued, reminded him of the old cordon sanitaire against the Soviet Union. Eden replied that his government was not interested in creating a cordon sanitaire against the Soviet Union, but was very much interested in creating one against Germany. Acknowledging, however, that there was a "great force" in Molotov's statement, Eden dropped the issue.[16]

The forces behind Eden's Danubian plan must have been negligible, because it never came up again for discussion during the subsequent international conferences. Not even Churchill seemed to go along with Eden's plan. Churchill was in favor of detaching Bavaria from Germany to set it up as a separate state with Austria and Hungary. Eden's view, on the other hand, held it advisable to restore the separate states created from the old Austro-Hungarian Empire and to form them into a Danubian group.[17] Actually, Eden distinguished himself more as a restorer of the national states than as an advocate of a Danubian federation. Already, in the summer of 1942, he had assured Beneš that the British government not only recognized the pre-Munich frontiers of Czechoslovakia but also would support the Czech plan for expelling the minority populations from Czechoslovakia, an ultranationalist Czech demand absolutely alien to the idea of federalism.[18]

The sole decision of the Moscow conference of the foreign ministers relating to the Danubian area was the "Declaration on Austria." In line with the Allied principle that Hitler's conquests should be repudiated, the three foreign ministers agreed that the annexation imposed upon Austria by Germany on March 15, 1938, was null and void; and in line with the general principle of restoring the pre-war national states they declared that Austria should be re-established as a free and independent country.

The "dangerous trend" toward regionalism was carefully avoided in another decision which set up a European Advisory Commission. In Cordell Hull's own words: "We could agree to the creation of a European Commission for dealing with the terms to be imposed on the enemy, but we opposed entrusting to such a body long-range peace-time functions. We took this up at the Moscow Conference and agreed to create the European Advisory Commission with functions limited to the formulation of terms of surrender and plans for their execution."[19]

Regionalism and federalism fared no better when, a month later, between November 28 and December 1, 1943, in Teheran, the Big Three, President Roosevelt, Prime Minister Churchill and Marshal Stalin, met for the first time; there the European federal plans were discussed by all three top leaders of the Grand Alliance, also for the first time, and, so far as the available evidence goes, for the last time.

On the first day of the Teheran conference, on November 28, Churchill improvised a few after-dinner remarks on what he called the "Danubian Confederation," outlining again the plan he had broached at the Washington meeting in May. Churchill expressed his feeling that Prussia should be isolated and reduced, and that Bavaria, Austria and Hungary might form a "broad, peaceful, unaggressive, confederation." The issue popped up again at the last formal meeting of the conference on December 1. In connection with the future of Germany, after Roosevelt explained his plan for splitting it up into five parts, Churchill suggested that a distinction should be made between Prussia (which he would treat "sternly") and the "second group" of less ferocious, non-Prussian states of Germany: Bavaria, Württemberg, The Palatinate, Saxony and Baden, which, he said, "I should like to see work with what I would call a Danubian Confederation."

Churchill believed it necessary to "create in modern form what had been in general outline the Austro-Hungarian Empire." His Bavarian-Austrian-Hungarian "Danubian Confederation," however, represented something unique in its purpose as well as in its geographic extension. Although it had the merit of being conceived as part of a broader European union, it was otherwise a rather extravagant plan. Its primary purpose was to dismember Germany and isolate Prussia. It had nothing to do with the traditional aim of the Danubian federalists to unite primarily the peoples of the former Habsburg Empire living along the middle and lower Danube, for whom it would have been very doubtful whether such a combination of Bavarians, Austrians and Hungarians would be desirable at all.

Stalin, referring to Churchill's "Danubian Confederation," said that he favored instead Roosevelt's plan for simply partitioning Germany. Furthermore, Stalin added: "We should be careful not to include the Austrians in any kind of combination. Austria had existed independently, and could do so again. So also must Hungary exist independently. After breaking up Germany it would be most unwise to create new combinations, Danubian or otherwise." President Roosevelt agreed warmly, Churchill recounts, supporting thus the Soviet opposition to the only federal scheme that ever came up for discussion among the Big Three.

Stalin, apparently suspecting that Churchill's Danubian plan was intended to include Romania, protested against uniting either Hungary or Romania with Germany. The matter was not discussed further, save for Stalin's emphatic assertion that "Hungary and Germany should not be coupled." Why, aside from any parts of Germany, small Danubian countries should not be coupled was a question which Stalin was spared the embarrassment of having to answer simply because nobody seemed to suggest such a union.

In favoring an independent Austria at Teheran, Stalin was adhering to the very recent decision of the foreign ministers at Moscow; but a year later he changed his mind. In October 1944, when Churchill was discussing Germany's partition with Stalin in Moscow and again mentioned his Danubian plan, Stalin said he would be "glad to see" Vienna become the capital of a South German federation consisting of Austria, Bavaria, Württemberg and Baden. But he did not change his mind about Hungary. As Churchill reported to Roosevelt: "U. J. [Uncle Joe] wants Poland, Czecho [Czechoslovakia] and Hungary to form a realm of independent, anti-Nazi, pro-Russian States, the first two of which might join together."[20]

Although Stalin rejected Churchill's Danubian plan at Teheran, with Roosevelt seconding the rejection, he went on record as not being opposed to a larger European organism. When asked by Churchill if the Soviet government contemplated a Europe of little states, all disjointed, with no larger units at all, Stalin replied that he was speaking only of Germany, not of Europe. Curiously enough, the idea of a "European Committee" was brought up at Teheran by Stalin rather than by Churchill, who was the original advocate of the "European Council." And it was discussed by Stalin and Roosevelt — in Churchill's absence. This is how it happened:

Before the December 1st meeting, at which Churchill's Danubian plan was rejected, Roosevelt had a private interview with Stalin and Molotov, during which the President's plan concerning "the government of the post-war world" was the main topic of discussion. According to Churchill's account, Stalin disapproved of Roosevelt's plan that the world should be governed by "the four policemen" (the United States, Great Britain, Soviet Russia and China), because he did not believe that China would be very powerful, nor did he think that "the four policemen" would be welcomed by the small nations of Europe. As an alternative, Stalin proposed that there should be one committee for Europe and another for the Far East. The European Committee would consist of Great Britain, Russia, the United States, and possibly one other European nation, which he left unnamed. Roosevelt replied that this was somewhat similar to Churchill's idea of regional councils, one for Europe, one for the Far East and one for the Americas. "He does not seem to have made it clear," Churchill noted in his memoirs, "that I also contemplated a Supreme United Nations Council of which the three regional committees would be the components. As I was not informed till much later of what had taken place, I was not able to correct this erroneous presentation."[21]

Certainly, there was no vestige of team-work between Roosevelt and Churchill concerning the post-war regional plans, and Churchill himself made only improvised forays into the field of federalist politics. If the decisive battle fought by the Western federalist forces took place at the Teheran meeting — and no further showdown has been recorded — then the Soviet Union won without a struggle.

The Soviet anti-federalist stand prevailed. In fact the West too preferred to return Europe to the nation-state system of the past. While the British broached their federal plans rather casually, the Americans gave them no support whatsoever. The Russians then, evidently taking advantage of this situation and almost without opposition, advocated the restoration of the pre-war national states — "free and independent states," as they called them — and easily defeated the vague Western schemes of supranational reform.

10 *Partition of Europe*

The Teheran conference, although dealing only superficially with post-war political issues, nevertheless revealed clearly that the United States and Britain did not intend to press for a reorganization of Europe which would emphasize the political unity of the Continent. As a matter of fact, these two leading Western powers gave no indication of any common effort at all to change the old political system of nation-states into a new form of supranational cooperation. Instead of concentrating on badly needed reforms in the structure of Europe, they seemed to labor under the notion that pre-war national sovereignty should remain the basis of Europe's post-war political organization. Meanwhile, with inaction on behalf of a united and federated Europe, the forces which had brought about the partition of Europe were forging ahead.

Military realities, of course, took precedence. The German attack on Russia had failed to achieve its object, which was, it should be remembered, to win a blitzkrieg victory in the east that would enable Hitler to deliver the death blow to Britain in the west. The battle for Moscow in the winter of 1941–42 was won by the Russians, and the Stalingrad battle, during the winter of 1942–43, marked definitely the turn of the tide in the war in the east. The Allied landing in North Africa in November 1942 was the prelude to the invasion of Europe from the south. Sicily was invaded in July 1943, and the Italian mainland in September. Mussolini was overthrown, but was rescued by German paratroopers and reestablished as head of a Nazi-sustained Fascist regime in northern Italy, while the new Italian regime under Marshal Badoglio signed an armistice.

Although the offensive power of the Germans was broken in the east, and Hitler's "European fortress" dented from the south, the Nazi war machine remained formidable. The Western democracies, facing another strong enemy, Japan, in the Far East, were happy to have the Red Army as their ally. They were also greatly impressed by the might of Soviet Russia.

In 1941 the prevailing opinion in the West had been that Russia would collapse. After the gigantic victory at Stalingrad, however, it was assumed that the U.S.S.R. would emerge from the war as a great power. Russia's post-war position was discussed at Quebec, where Roosevelt and Churchill met in August 1943. A memorandum which one of Roosevelt's principal advisers, Harry Hopkins, had with him at the Quebec conference recognized that: "Since Russia is the decisive factor in the war, she must be given every assistance, and every effort must be made to obtain her friendship. Likewise, since without question she will dominate Europe on the defeat of the Axis, it is even more essential to develop and maintain the most friendly relations with Russia." The memorandum also embraced the view that: "With Russia as an ally in the war against Japan, the war can be terminated in less time and with less expense in life and resources," and that otherwise "the difficulties will be immeasurably increased and operations might become abortive."[1]

At the Teheran conference, in November 1943, after some controversy, agreement was reached concerning joint strategy in both Europe and the Far East. It was decided that the cross-Channel invasion by the Allied forces should take place in May 1944, together with a landing in southern France; and Stalin gave his assurance that the Soviet Union would enter the war against Japan as soon as possible after the common victory over Hitler in Europe. Churchill had originally demurred from the landing in southern France, favoring instead continuation of the campaign in Italy with all available forces in the Mediterranean. He hoped the Allies, in cooperation with the Balkan partisan forces and with Turkey's eventual intervention in the war, could break through the Ljubljana Gap into Austria and Hungary, contributing thus, rather than by the Riviera landing, to the final defeat of Nazi Germany. Both the Americans (for strategic reasons) and the Russians (for political reasons) opposed Churchill's plans, although Stalin later changed his mind. When in the autumn of 1944 the Soviet offensive in Poland came to a halt, Stalin then strongly advocated that the Allied armies in Italy should cross the Adriatic and drive north through Yugoslavia in the direction of Vienna.[2] Also, the second Quebec conference of the Allies, in September 1944, recommended the advance toward the Ljubljana Gap and across the Alps through the Brenner Pass.[3] But the diversion of Allied forces from Italy to southern France and the stubborn German resistance in northern Italy made the breakthrough into Central Europe from the south impossible.

Not only in the light of later political developments, but also from a strictly military point of view, Churchill was probably right when he urged that Germany be given "a stab in the Adriatic armpit." However, failure to adopt this strategy certainly had far less effect on subsequent events than was later assumed by some critics. If Churchill's strategic plans in the Mediterranean theater of war could have been applied, and moreover applied successfully, armies of the West would have been the liberators in some areas of Central and Eastern Europe where at the war's end the Red Army was the master. But unless it is forgotten that the Second World War was fought against Nazi Germany, and also unless it is overlooked that without the Russian alliance the West could not have won the war, it is not possible to conceive of any strategy that could have kept the Russians within their pre-war boundaries. Not even Churchill's strategy could essentially have changed the post-war partition of Europe between the armies of the Russians and of the West.

The critics of Western blunders who assumed that Churchill's strategy could have saved half of Europe from Soviet liberation also blamed the Allied policy of unconditional surrender toward Nazi Germany. This policy, it was argued, strengthened Hitler's power by weakening the chances of his internal enemies to overthrow him, and thus the war was prolonged with the resultant Soviet thrust deep into the heart of Europe. "Unconditional surrender" was certainly not sound either as policy or as propaganda toward the enemy; but it is most improbable that any reasonable conditions of surrender could have stopped Hitler's madness or could have been a decisive aid to the anti-Nazi conspirators in overthrowing Hitler. It is true that the German underground's heroism (as well as the resistance in Germany's satellites, especially Hungary) was never fully appreciated in the West; but even in retrospect it is hard to see how the Hitler regime could have been overthrown by more clever Allied policy, or how, through cooperation with anti-Nazi Germans, the West's reliance on Soviet Russia's military might could have been modified. Only superior force could crush Nazi Germany; and in order to muster this superior force, close cooperation between Russia and the Western Powers was absolutely necessary.

Russia was as eager as the West to cooperate. Not until victory seemed certain did Stalin show anxiety to keep the eastern front as his exclusive theater of military operations. In 1941, for instance, Stalin insisted, though in vain, that a British army be sent to Murmansk or Rostov to relieve pressure on the Red Army.[4] Not until the end of 1942 was the

West able to participate in the war with forces which brought relief to the hard-pressed Russians. And the massive invasion of Europe from the west had to be delayed until the summer of 1944, a delay which caused dangerous tensions between Russia and the West. It is doubtful whether the armies of the Western democracies could have reentered the European continent had Russia not withstood the fury of the German onslaught in the east. As Cordell Hull pointed out: "We must ever remember that by the Russians' heroic struggle against the Germans they probably saved the Allies from a negotiated peace with Germany."[5]

The military might of the West was not sufficient to forestall the Russian occupation of Eastern Europe. Nor, unfortunately, were the political weapons of the West adequate to protect the nations of the Middle Zone from the consequences of Soviet liberation.

Russia's future relationship to "Eastern Europe" — as the Middle Zone of small nations between Germany and Russia came to be known after the Second World War — was a principal issue between the East and West from the moment the German attack turned the Soviet Union into an ally of the Western democracies. In fact, the future of East-West cooperation depended largely upon a mutually satisfactory solution of the problems in the belt of smaller nations between Germany and Russia.

That this area, once the cordon sanitaire of French policy, and later the German *Lebensraum* of the post-Munich era, must cooperate and live in friendship with the Soviet Union and never again become a springboard of German aggression, was the most obvious conclusion to be drawn from past experience, especially during wartime, when Germany was the enemy and Soviet Russia an ally. This conclusion however was followed by another, which envisaged no solution for Eastern Europe save to acquiesce in the fate of becoming a Soviet sphere of influence. A line of thought which anticipated such a status for Eastern Europe appeared in some famous leading articles in *The Times* shortly after the German attack on Russia.

On July 15, 1941, *The Times* said: "An . . . error of 1919 which is fortunately present in our minds today was the elimination of Russia from the settlement. Little foresight should have been needed to realize that a settlement of Eastern European affairs made without regard to Russian interests and at a moment when Russia could not make her voice heard was unlikely to endure. That error at any rate will not be repeated." On August 1, 1941, *The Times* elaborated upon the subject: "Russia may continue to be separated from Western Europe by different material conditions and by different traditions and ways of life . . . but this involves no irreconcilable divergency of policy. . . . The direct community of interest created by Hitler's invasion can be projected into the future and becomes applicable to the future settlement of Europe. Leadership in Eastern Europe is essential if the disorganization of the past twenty years is to be avoided, and if the weaker countries are not to be exposed once more to economic disaster or to violent assault. This leadership can fall only to Germany or to Russia. Neither Great Britain nor the United States can exercise, or will aspire to exercise, any predominant role in these regions; and it would be fatal to revive the Allied policy of 1919, which created a bond between Germany and Russia against Western Europe." On March 7, 1942, *The Times* further declared that "security in Europe will prove unattainable if Russia herself does not feel secure. . . ." The known author of these unsigned leading articles was the historian Edward Hallett Carr, who expressed his ideas even more bluntly in his popular wartime book, *Conditions of Peace.* There he stated: "Just as preponderant weight will properly be given in Western Europe to the views and interests of Great Britain, the same preponderant weight must be given to the views and interests of Russia in Eastern Europe."[6]

Curiously, Carr's program (which in effect outlined pretty closely the actual trend of British policy) was almost identical with the text of the secret agreement Tsarist Russia had proposed to France during the First World War. This text read: "We are prepared to allow France and England complete freedom in drawing up the western frontiers of Germany, in the expectation that the Allies on their part would allow us equal freedom in drawing up our frontiers with Germany and Austria. . . ."[7] Certainly no such secret agreement partitioning Europe into Western and Eastern spheres of influence was concluded during the Second World War; nevertheless it was taken for granted that after the war Russia would have a preponderant weight in Eastern Europe, and British diplomacy was even inclined to acknowledge this fact by preliminary agreements which came very close to dividing Europe into spheres of influence. American diplomacy, on the other hand, repeatedly rejected such devices as "power politics" and "balance of power" as unsuitable for ensuring a new type of peace in the post-war world. Churchill's simultaneous flirtations with European federation and with its direct opposite, spheres of interest, were both rejected by the United States. American diplomacy centered its efforts instead on the creation of a worldwide organization, the United Nations. This ultimately was approved as the common post-war objective of the Grand Alliance. The East European nations were expected to promote this objective by establishing governments friendly to Russia; they were to cooperate most closely with Russia against the revival of German imperialism, as were the Western nations too, under the aegis of the United Nations.

President Roosevelt became the principal spokesman for the widely shared belief that what the world needed was a global organization, supported by the leading Great Powers. Noble internationalism and broad-minded progressivism in this "One World" concept mingled with blindness for the practical details. A most regrettable concomitant of the "One World" concept was that believers in world unity tended to overlook the urgent need for European unity. Under Roosevelt's leadership the United States progressed to the stage of breaking away from its antiquated traditions of isolationism, for Roosevelt was fully aware of the great mistake his country had made a generation before, when isolationist sentiment prevented the United States from joining Wilson's creation, the League of Nations. But at the same time, American policymakers were victims of "over-simplified One Worldism," as one critic described it.[8] And this over-simplification in international affairs led to consequences after the Second World War no less calamitous than those which followed the failure of the United States to join the League of Nations after the First World War.

East-West agreement on an East European settlement proved difficult long before the Red Army wrested control of these regions from the German Wehrmacht. The first clash, which was really just the latest encounter in an old controversy, occurred during the negotiations for a formal Anglo-Soviet treaty of alliance in 1941–42. Some of the issues connected with Russia's relations to her western neighbors were the same as those which had caused the failure of Anglo-Soviet negotiations in the summer of 1939. However, Russia now took for granted that she was entitled, as an ally of the West, to retain the territorial gains she had obtained during her partnership with Hitler.

The Soviet territorial aims came to light during Eden's visit to Moscow in December 1941. The Russians demanded restoration of the borders to their position prior to Hitler's attack; that is, Russia wanted to incorporate Estonia, Latvia and Lithuania, also portions of Finland, Poland and Romania, into the U.S.S.R. The only Soviet concession was to allow the Curzon Line, which was slightly more favorable to Poland than the Ribbentrop-Molotov Line, to become the Polish-Soviet frontier. An additional Soviet demand was that Romania should give Russia special facilities for bases. In return, Romania was to receive from Hungary certain Transylvanian territories which had been awarded to Hungary by a German-Italian decision in 1940. Poland in its turn was to be recompensed by the transfer of East Prussia. The restoration of Albania, Austria, Czechoslovakia and Yugoslavia (with slight territorial gains at the expense of Italy), and a tentative plan for the dismemberment of Germany, were included in the Soviet proposals.[9]

The British, faced with these Soviet proposals, were unwilling to enter into secret agreements on the post-war territorial settlement. But Stalin continued to press the issue, letting it be known that he regarded recognition of Soviet territorial aims in the Baltic area as a test of Britain's trustworthiness as an ally. Churchill thereupon, according to Cordell Hull, "seemed reluctantly determined" to go ahead with such an accord. For the British, as Hull explained, "could not help but remember that their own protracted discussions with the Russians in 1939 over these same Baltic states might have been one of the causes of Stalin's signing an agreement with Hitler instead of Chamberlain. . . . They feared lest . . . Stalin might negotiate a separate peace with Germany." Only after a warning that the United States government would issue a separate statement "clearly stating that it did not subscribe to the principles and clauses of the Anglo-Soviet treaty" did Eden suggest a formula omitting all reference to frontiers. Molotov made a last attempt to assert the Soviet claim in May 1942, when he came to London. He proposed that a clause be inserted in the treaty whereby Britain would recognize Russia's "special interests" in the countries which were her western neighbors. But it was of no avail, and the twenty-year Anglo-Soviet treaty of cooperation and mutual post-war assistance was signed on May 25 without territorial provisions.[10]

The United States government continued to adhere to the principle that the idea of balance of power, or spheres of influence, should be banned, and that the means of keeping peace in the post-war world should be sought in the overall authority of an international security organization. British diplomacy, however, while largely sharing the American views, showed a tendency to acknowledge the fact — not really contested, in effect, by the Americans either — that the Soviet Union did have special interests in Eastern Europe. Thus Churchill, during his first meeting with Stalin in Moscow, in August 1942, conceded that the Soviet Union had "predominant interest" in Poland, Czechoslovakia, Hungary, Romania, Yugoslavia and Bulgaria, while Stalin recognized Great Britain's "predominant interest" in Greece. This agreement was, no doubt, in line with the old balance-of-power concept; but Sumner Welles's criticism that it was this agreement which started Western diplomacy on the policy of spheres of influence in Europe seems to blame Churchill for something for which he actually was not alone responsible.[11] What started Western diplomacy on the policy of spheres of influence in Europe was, rather, a mistaken belief of the Western Allies in general — the belief that if the nation-states between Germany and Russia were restored individually and protected by the authority of a worldwide international organization (though not united among themselves by supranational ties, nor with the rest of Europe as a unit), they would be capable of safeguarding their independence in the shadow of the monolithic power of a victorious Soviet Russia.

In the Kremlin there were some skeptics, who as the American Ambassador to Moscow, Averell Harriman, observed, were "unwilling to see Russia depend for her security solely on an untried world organization with associates whom they did not fully trust."[12] But similar skepticism with regard to the security of the Middle Zone did not prevail among the Western leaders. They rightly acknowledged that Soviet Russia, invaded and devastated by Germany, was legitimately entitled to obtain full security. But they viewed the security of the Middle Zone, vis-à-vis Russia, with a lack of foresight much like their attitude during the period of appeasement vis-à-vis Nazi Germany.

In actuality, Western views about the future of the Middle Zone reflected political conceptions implying the partition of Europe — despite vigorous protests, especially from the American State Department, against spheres of influence. The nations of the Middle Zone were expected to cooperate with Soviet Russia against the revival of German imperialism, a most natural and desirable program which the Western Powers themselves were trying to implement on a worldwide scale. But the sole assistance the Middle Zone nations were to receive from the West was "Big Three unity," that is, the unity of Great Britain and the United States with Russia. When translated into reality, this amounted to an amicable partition of Europe between the West and Russia, with no security for the small nations of the Middle Zone apart from an untried world organization and untried Soviet cooperation.

A few sharp-eyed critics of Western policy foresaw this coming partition of Europe. Thus, David J. Dallin, an American scholar of Russian origin, whose knowledge of Soviet affairs was no less profound than his understanding of the Middle Zone problems, made this observation in one of his books published during the war: "Most of the popular schemes proposed recently for post-war settlement of European relations envisage a durable partition of Europe into two . . . spheres; the Eastern sphere, embracing all the large and small countries from a line east of Germany-Italy to the Urals; and the Western sphere, containing all the nations lying west and south of Germany." "This trend of thinking," added Dallin, "is not confined to a few authors and diplomats. On the contrary, the idea of dividing Europe into two spheres has a multitude of adherents because it seems to indicate a peaceful solution of thorny problems." And he warned: "The idea, an agreeable one, is being uncritically digested. However, it does not ensure a stable structure, nor does it contain a guarantee of peace."[13]

Cooperation betwen Soviet Russia and the Middle Zone nations raised a series of grave problems. One set of problems was related to Russia's post-war frontiers. Some of the territorial questions, such as the status of the Baltic states, were never solved by agreement. After the unsuccessful Soviet attempt to insert a territorial clause into the Anglo-Soviet treaty of May 1942, Stalin did not even raise the question of Soviet post-war frontiers during Churchill's Moscow visit later in 1942. However, at the Teheran conference of the Big Three in November 1943 the Curzon Line was tentatively agreed upon as the future Soviet-Polish frontier; and a final decision was reached in this matter at the Yalta conference in February 1945 (the London Polish government in exile not concurring in this decision). Other Soviet territorial demands were met one by one, in the armistice treaties (concerning parts of Finland and Romania), at the Potsdam conference (concerning parts of East Prussia), and in the Czechoslovak-Soviet treaty, signed in June 1945, by which Ruthenia was ceded to Soviet Russia.

The core of the problem concerning the future of the Middle Zone, however, was not so much the territorial question, as the kind of government Russia's neighbors would have after the war. The Western Powers agreed in principle with Russia that the pro-German, Nazi and Fascist reactionary elements should be expelled from public life; also that the new governments should be based on democratic forces which would carry out necessary social reforms in the liberated countries, follow a friendly policy toward Soviet Russia, and build an effective barrier against German aggression. But it was easier to agree on the broad characteristics of the future governments than on the procedure by which these new governments should be constituted.

Later, at Yalta, the Western principle of free elections won recognition, though without any effective safeguards to ensure its observance. There was only the hope that the war against the common enemy had wiped out the controversies of the past, and that Western democracy and Soviet communism would cooperate in mutual trust to create a new world order under the shield of the United Nations.

Faith in Soviet Russia was nourished by a belief then current, that communism could progress from tyranny to democracy, a belief which reached its highest peak in the West during the war. Hatred of Nazi Germany too was transformed into sympathy toward Russia, whose soldiers had borne the brunt of the struggle against the dreadful common enemy. Also certain "changes" in the Soviet Union were interpreted hopefully as heralding a new era in the history of communism. These changes were the dissolution of the Communist International in 1943, interpreted as the end of the Bolshevik ambition to stir up world revolution; the official recognition of the Russian Orthodox Church, interpreted as the end of the Bolshevik persecution of religion; and the sudden flare-up of the Pan-Slav movement.

Soviet sponsored Pan-Slavism was especially instrumental in allaying the fears of revolutionary communism and Russian imperialism. The theory fitted well into the Western image of a post-war Europe, in which the Slavic East was envisaged as a counterbalance to Germany. Also, Pan-Slavism was interpreted as an expression of wholesome nationalism, a departure from Communist internationalism. Western experts on Russia believed the rebirth of Russian nationalism, under the impact of war, to be a salutary deviation from Communist orthodoxy. They saw the Soviet Union dropping the internationalist revolutionary elements of Marxism.

A Pan-Slav Committee, under the chairmanship of General A. S. Gundorov, was founded in Moscow shortly after Hitler's attack on Russia. The first Slav Congress, called by the committee, was held in August 1941. A manifesto, issued by the congress, exhorted the Slavs to fight against the common Fascist enemy; it disavowed the Pan-Slav imperialism of Tsarist Russia, and proclaimed the equality of the liberated Slav nations. "No interference in the inner affairs of other nations!" proclaimed Stalin on November 6, 1941, when he reiterated the guiding principles of the new Slav movement, emphasizing that the sole aim of the Soviet Union was to liberate the enslaved nations from Hitler's tyranny, and then leave them absolutely free to decide under what kind of regime they wished to live.[14]

The Pan-Slav movement during the war gained enormous popularity among the Slavs, both in enslaved Europe and throughout the free world. Hitler's insane hatred of the Slavs had accomplished what no Slav enthusiast had ever achieved during the long history of Pan-Slavism: he had made the Slav movement a reality. Two more Slav congresses were held in Moscow during the war. The publication of a monthly, *Slavjane* (The Slavs), began in January 1943. Slav congresses were organized in the United States, Canada, Chile, Peru, Bolivia, Uruguay, Argentina, Palestine, Australia and New Zealand.[15] Under the chairmanship of an old English friend of the Slavs, R. W. Seton-Watson, a congress of Slav nations met in London in 1944. Even King Peter of Yugoslavia, whose government in exile, like that of the Poles, was branded reactionary by the Moscow Slav Committee, tried to get on the bandwagon of Pan-Slavism. In January 1945, he declared that "fraternal union with Russia is one of the most deeply rooted sentiments of the Slav peoples."[16]

Of course there were Slavic dissenters who disapproved of the Slav movement. Unfortunately, however, most of these Slavic dissenters, like most of the non-Slavic critics of the West's pro-Russian policy, also were people with a "reactionary record" — such for instance were the Catholic Slovaks in the United States who supported Tiso's Fascist Slovakia — and their opinions therefore were dismissed by a line of reasoning, incidentally correct, that it was bias rather than political wisdom that prompted them to oppose the pro-Soviet Pan-Slav currents.

Least attracted by the new Pan-Slavism were the Poles, who were the closest Slavic neighbors of the Russians. Not even this heyday of Slavic fraternization improved Polish-Russian relations. On the other hand the most enthusiastic propagators of Pan-Slavism were the Czechs; they, the westernmost among the Slavs, with their homeland farthest away from Russia, had never in their history as a nation come into direct contact with the Russians. The Czech exiles, with their great democratic reputation in the West, were the most effective salesmen of the idea that the new Pan-Slavism was a happy combination of progressive democracy and Slav brotherhood, which would erect an impregnable wall against German imperialism in post-war Europe.

The few Czechoslovak democrats who entertained contrary views had no influence on exile politics. Most prominent among them was Milan Hodža, who died in June 1944. Hodža, shortly before his death, protested vigorously in a memorandum to the American State Department against the Pan-Slav policy of the Czech government in exile, which in his view was helping to build spheres of influence. Hodža recognized the attraction which Pan-Slavism held for the Czechs. "A Slav nationalist," he wrote, "may be enthusiastic about an unheard-of expansion of Slavic thought or sphere as far as Prague, a traditional center of Slavic culture and political efforts." But he warned against the pitfalls of Slavic nationalism, and called it a "dangerous error" to believe that Russian communism had become something different just because it had embraced nationalism. He believed that the nations of Central Europe between Russia and Germany could attain freedom and independence only in a federation.[17]

The Czechoslovak nationalists, however, who supported Beneš's pro-Russian policy, whether they were liberals (Jan Masaryk), socialists (Hubert Ripka), or communists (Vlado Clementis), took turns in assuring the West that the new Slav policy would be the best safeguard of peace in Central and Eastern Europe. Even the so-called federalists among them were confident of Russia's best intentions. Said one of them, Hubert Ripka: "If Soviet policy adopted an attitude of extreme reserve — if not a negative one — to confederative plans in Central Europe, the reason was that it feared lest, in this new form, the old, anti-Soviet conception of a cordon sanitaire might be revived. I do not doubt that the Soviets will regard these plans favorably once there are guarantees that they are not directed against the Soviet Union, that they cannot become an instrument in the hand of any other Great Power, and especially of Germany, and that the nations of Central Europe wish to live in friendly accord with the Soviet Union. . . . I have no doubt that events will prove that we were not mistaken in showing our faith in the friendly intentions of the Soviet government, and its determination to respect the liberty and independence of the smaller nations of Central and South-Eastern Europe."[18]

Pan-Slavism did not seem to worry the West at all. Western sympathy with Slavic nationalism was of course nothing new. After the defeat of Germany in the First World War, the liberation of the Slavs in the eastern half of Europe was viewed as a blessing conferred through the extension of Western ideas of nationalism and democracy. During the Second World War, however, sympathetic Westerners saw the Slavic nations striving for and achieving an even greater measure of freedom and security than they had previously enjoyed under Western guidance, by means of a new integration into an Eastern community under Russian leadership.

One such sympathetic Westerner, the English historian A.J.P. Taylor, wrote, "The Slav peoples have now come of age; none of them will again pass under German tutelage — nor under Anglo-Saxon tutelage either. The peoples of Western Europe, and finally of the United States as well, have learned that they can employ the Germans to enslave the Slavs only at the price of being enslaved themselves. Sooner than pay this price, Western civilization — and particularly its two Great Powers, England and America — have recognized the Slavs as equals; this is the meaning of the Anglo-Soviet alliance of 1942, and of the present collaboration between the three Great Powers. The West has at last ceased to insist that its civilization, liberal, individualistic, humanitarian, is the sole form of civilization; it has acknowledged the equal claims of Eastern European civilization, Byzantine and collectivist. . . . The collaboration of the three Great Powers means the permanent *disappearance* of Germany as a Great Power and thus an end of the German problem which has spread its shadow over the first half of the twentieth century."[19]

However, the birth of this new age of the Slavs was not as joyful an event as many Western friends of the Slavs had anticipated. And the course of history in Eastern Europe, hailed by A.J.P. Taylor, was viewed with less enthusiasm by one of its makers, Winston Churchill.

11 *Churchill's Bargain*

Churchill left the Teheran conference in December 1943 less satisfied than the Americans. Some of his ideas had differed from Roosevelt's. Roosevelt attributed paramount importance to the creation of a world organization based on "Big Three unity," and Stalin's willingness to go along with this program filled American policy-makers with great hopes. In Cordell Hull's words, "Moscow and Teheran brought Russia into a program of real cooperation for war and peace."[1] Churchill on the other hand, while not less devoted to the program of worldwide cooperation, was increasingly worried about the practical details of this cooperation in Eastern Europe. And while the Americans continued to believe in universalism as a cure for all problems, Churchill was anxious to meet the special problems with special arrangements.

The special problems in Eastern Europe accumulated with great speed as the year 1944 brought the Red Army one success after another. Only one problem, Czechoslovakia's future, seemed to be neatly settled in that disordered area. Beneš's treaty, signed with Moscow in December 1943, served as a model for future bilateral cooperation between Soviet Russia and her western neighbors; but to reproduce this model was not easy for the rest of the nations in Eastern Europe.

In January 1944, the Russians crossed the pre-war Polish-Soviet frontier, and although in Teheran the Big Three had tentatively agreed on the Curzon Line as the future frontier between Russia and Poland, agreement between the Kremlin and the Polish government in exile on both territorial and political problems made no progress at all. In Teheran it had been agreed also that the British would give full support to Tito's Communist partisans, but relations between Tito and the Yugoslav government in exile were not yet clarified. The problems of the Axis satellites, Hungary, Romania and Bulgaria, were coming to the fore too, as the Russians approached Central Europe and the Balkans. While the retreating Germans were alerted to forestall defection among their satellites, the latter were increasingly anxious to avert defeat alongside the Germans.

The situation was unique in satellite Hungary. There Premier Kállay successfully sabotaged cooperation with Germany, while his emissaries got in touch with the British intelligence and agreed on some preliminary conditions under which Hungary would turn against Germany; the most important of these conditions provided that the Hungarian army should be in a position to establish contact with the Western forces. Kállay's hopes, like those of others who were planning to desert their German allies, were based on the assumption that the Western armies would be the liberators of Central Europe. These hopes were dashed when the Allied advance in Italy bogged down in the face of German resistance, and when the plans for invasion in the Balkans which Churchill had proposed at Teheran failed to materialize. Thus it was not the Western armies, as Kállay and others had hoped, but the Red Army, which was moving toward Central Europe. From Hitler's point of view, of course, it made no difference which enemy threatened the Nazi redoubt in the center of Europe. In March 1944, therefore, in order to protect the hinterland of the eastern front, which was rapidly being pushed westward, Hitler ordered the occupation of Hungary. Kállay was overthrown, and, with eager cooperation from Hitler's Hungarian followers, the Germans got the reliable satellite government in Hungary that they needed.

Even had the Western Allies approached Central Europe from the south, the Germans, supported by their numerous pro-Nazi Hungarian devotees, could at any time have carried out this coup anyway. Therefore the claim Kállay made in his memoirs that the failure of "Anglo-Hungarian collaboration" was an essential cause of the tragedy of half of Europe was extraordinary. According to Kállay, had this Anglo-Hungarian collaboration developed, Churchill could not have been voted down at the Teheran conference over the question of attacking in the Balkans, and British and American influence would today prevail in the Balkans and on the Danube.[2] Kállay's commentary on the failure of his policy was just another exhibit of that traditional delusion of grandeur which always, throughout central and eastern Europe, led the small nations to seek exalted roles of partnership with the Great Powers and which was the fundamental reason for the failure of these small nations to work together.

But, though the failure of Kállay's policy was not instrumental in the ruin of half of Europe's chance to be liberated by the West, still his failure certainly crushed the Horthy regime's chance to perform the triple miracle of saving itself and of saving Hungary from both the German and the Russian occupation. Up until Kállay's overthrow, Hungary had managed to remain, in spite of several incidents and measures of the Nazi type, a relative "island of freedom" in Hitler's Europe. Kállay's successor as premier was a pro-German Hungarian general under whose government Nazi terror engulfed the country. Hundreds of thousands of Hungarian Jews were now added to the millions murdered by the German Nazis. Nevertheless Regent Horthy, who stayed in office after the Nazi coup in March 1944, did not give up hope of saving Hungary from total defeat. The elements favoring a separate peace regrouped around him, and in the confusion of great German defeats, he was able in August to appoint to the premiership an anti-Nazi Hungarian general who was ready to negotiate with the Russians, rather than, like Premier Kállay, exclusively with the Western Allies.

Meanwhile in Romania and Bulgaria also, the break with Germany was in preparation behind the scenes. Even in the two satellite states that owed their very existence to Hitler, Croatia and Slovakia, plans for defection were laid. The foreign minister of satellite Croatia paid with his life for an unsuccessful attempt to bring his country over from Pavelić's Fascists to the Allied side. And the initial success of the partisan rising in satellite Slovakia, in the summer of 1944, owed at least something to the connivance of some people in the Tiso regime, in the army in particular.

The Hitler era was drawing to a close in Eastern Europe. But what would the Soviet liberation be like? What would the liberators and the liberated do? The active or potential anti-German forces which looked forward to liberation were split into numerous mutually suspicious or even openly hostile factions. In many of the underground movements, loose "popular fronts" did unite different resistance groups, sometimes even conservatives with Communists. But the fratricidal struggle in Yugoslavia between the two partisan leaders, the Communist Tito and the anti-Communist Mihailović, was a warning of what could happen elsewhere, with the stage set for similar conflicts. Suppressed nationalist rivalries in the Danube Valley were threatening to erupt. Old ruling classes were trying to save themselves, and great social revolutionary forces were preparing for the day of reckoning.

Who would "take the lead," who would be "playing the hand" in these affairs? How could order be brought out of chaos? These were the questions that weighed heavily upon Churchill's mind in the spring of 1944.[3]

As the difficulties of cooperation with the Russians increased, Churchill renewed his plea for an Allied thrust from Italy toward Vienna, this time with the explicit intention to "forestall the Russians in certain areas of Central Europe."[4] In view of the stubborn German resistance, it is uncertain whether much of Central Europe could have been liberated by the Western Allies ahead of the Red Army. The crossing of the Alps would have been a tremendous task, even had the Allied forces in Italy not been stripped of their offensive power by the landing in southern France. In any case, the military power was not available for Churchill's plans, so he resorted to power politics to meet the unsettled problems of Central Europe and the Balkans. He himself considered his controversial deals with Stalin as "wartime arrangements," stressing in his memoirs that "all larger questions were reserved on both sides for what we then hoped would be a peace table when the war was won."[5] Nevertheless they were unquestionably sphere-of-influence arrangements.

On May 17, 1944, Eden suggested to the Soviet Ambassador in London that the Soviets "should temporarily regard Rumanian affairs as mainly their concern under war conditions," while leaving Greece to the British. The Russians agreed, but wanted to know if the United States had been consulted. On May 31 Churchill notified Roosevelt of the plan. The American reaction was cool. Cordell Hull was of the view that "any creation of zones of influence would inevitably sow the seeds of future conflict." On June 8 Churchill urged acceptance, and added Bulgaria to the list of countries where the Russians would be taking the lead. On June 11, Roosevelt rejected the plan, advising instead the setting up of "consultative machinery" which would "restrain the tendency towards the development of exclusive spheres." Churchill replied on the same day and again strongly urged acceptance, suggesting that the arrangement should have a trial of three months. On June 13 Roosevelt, without consulting Cordell Hull, agreed to this proposal, adding, "We must be careful to make it clear that we are not establishing any post-war spheres of influence." The Soviet government was notified accordingly on June 19, but actually no final agreement was reached. Stalin, on July 15, noting that "the American Government have some doubts regarding this question," proposed "to revert to the matter." However, no further discussions followed.[6]

In the middle of August, Churchill, driven by his desire to bring "order out of chaos," met Tito in Naples, where he succeeded in paving the way for an agreement of cooperation between Tito and Šubašić, the Premier of the Yugoslav exiles. But the assurance which Tito gave Churchill that he had "no desire to introduce the communist system into Yugoslavia,"[7] was probably not the same assurance that he gave Stalin a few weeks later when he left his British-protected stronghold on the Adriatic island of Vis for a secret trip to Moscow.

The Russian summer campaign was driving the Germans westward with irresistible force, and the need for East-West agreement on post-liberation policies was greater than ever. Most disturbing was the Soviet behavior during the heroic Warsaw uprising against the Germans in August. Not only was no help rendered by the Red Army, which was within easy reach of the city, but even the use of Soviet airfields was denied to the West, anxious to bring relief to the Warsaw Poles who paid allegiance to the London government in exile. Soviet charges that some of the Poles in the London government were reactionaries and enemies of Russia were not without foundation. On the other hand, Premier Stanisław Mikołajczyk was an agrarian democrat and a sincere advocate of reconciliation and cooperation with Russia. The popular Western assumption that cooperation with the Russians was a matter of a liberal and progressive partnership was a delusion. It greatly impeded any realistic interpretation of Soviet policies, even in such a case as Poland, where the Russians made little effort to hide their imperialistic designs.

The Russians took the lead in dictating armistice terms to Romania, when on August 23 the country followed King Michael to a man and overthrew the pro-German regime. They were again in the lead in signing an armistice with Finland after fighting stopped on September 4. Without even consulting the Western Allies, the Russians declared war on September 5 against Bulgaria. (Bulgaria, alone among Hitler's satellites, and although at war with the Western Powers, had maintained diplomatic relations throughout the war with Soviet Russia.) The Russo-Bulgarian "war" lasted four days and enabled Russia to treat Bulgaria as a defeated German satellite.

Where Hitler's tyranny ended, Stalin's began, in the Danube Valley. Only in Hungary were the Nazis able to solidify their rule for a little longer. Horthy's coup against the Germans on October 15 was a complete failure. The Hungarians did not follow their regent to a man as the Romanians had followed their king. While Horthy was engaged in the immensely difficult task of bringing over German-occupied Hungary to the Allied side, the Germans had the much easier job of passing the government of Hungary over to a group of Nazi extremists whom they had held in reserve for the eventuality of Horthy's defection.

This was the inglorious end of Admiral Horthy's counterrevolutionary regime. Or, in the more kindly words of C. A. Macartney (the most understanding chronicler among the Western historians of the Horthy era), this was "the end of a world."[8] The conservative wing of the Horthy regime was clever enough to foresee Hitler's doom. But the indoctrination — anti-Semitic, chauvinistic, pro-German — of Hungarian public opinion under Horthy's regency was responsible for the hope which so many Hungarians blindly shared, for Hitler's victory. Horthy's Nazi successors posed as defenders of Christianity and national rights, while at the same time distinguishing themselves as Hitler's ablest disciples in committing crimes against humanity. As part of their propaganda they denounced the horrors of impending Bolshevik rule and the sinister plans of the Allies to reimpose on Hungary the unjust terms of the Trianon Treaty. This propaganda unfortunately proved true. However, the Hungarian Nazis' fanatical faith in Hitler's final victory was proved wrong. Their brief period of power under the "leadership" of Major Ferenc Szálasi marked the all-time low point in Hungary's history.

Threatened by the advancing Russians from the north, the Germans began to withdraw from the Balkans. A critical situation arose in Greece, where the greater part of the country was held by the Communist ELAS guerrilla bands. Although, in the so-called Caserta agreement, ELAS had recognized the authority of the Greek government in exile, and although according to the British-Soviet June agreements, Britain was supposed to take the lead in Greece, the restoration of the legal government to power in Athens constituted a grave problem in view of the mounting disorder.

With growing concern Churchill watched "the upsurge of Communist influence" in Eastern Europe (a fact which according to him the United States "were very slow in realizing"), but his concern, at least for the time being, was limited to certain countries. He felt that Britain's past relations with Romania and Bulgaria did not call for any special sacrifices; but, he said, "the fate of Poland and Greece struck us keenly. For Poland we had entered the war; for Greece we had made painful efforts."[9]

On October 9, Churchill and Eden arrived in Moscow for another round of conferences, which were conducted in the same spirit in which the "temporary arrangements" had been made in June. On the first day of the Moscow conference it was agreed that Russia should have 90 percent "predominance" in Romania, 75 percent in Bulgaria; Britain should have 90 percent of Greece; while Russia and Britain should go fifty-fifty in Yugoslavia and Hungary.[10] On the subject of Poland, protracted negotiations, to which the Lublin Poles and Mikołajczyk were also invited, produced meager results. The percentage system, this newly discovered basis of East-West agreements, failed to bridge the gulf between the Lublin Poles and Mikołajczyk. Bolesław Bierut, head of the Lublin Committee, contended that "if Mikołajczyk were Premier he [Bierut] must have 75 percent of the Cabinet." Churchill backed up Mikołajczyk with a proposal of "fifty-fifty plus himself" (that is, Mikołajczyk as Premier). As to the other burning issue, the Russo-Polish frontier, Mikołajczyk was "going to urge upon his London colleagues the Curzon Line, including Lvov, for the Russians." Nevertheless Churchill was hopeful that a final settlement would be reached soon.[11]

Churchill's optimism was sustained by events in Greece. When it came to an armed showdown with the Greek Communists, the Russians kept their hands off and let the British act. In other words, the Moscow percentage agreements worked beautifully in Greece. The course of events in Poland, however, contributed only to pessimism. Mikołajczyk resigned after his failure to make his London colleagues accept the Curzon Line. The deadlock between Moscow and the Polish government in exile became complete when, on January 1, 1945, Moscow recognized the Lublin Committee as the provisional government of Poland.

The United States never subscribed to Churchill's percentage diplomacy. Roosevelt and his advisers opposed these special arrangements because they were anxious to avoid the creation of zones of influence. The United States government believed as strongly as the British government that the Soviet Union was entitled to full security along her western borders, and that the countries in Eastern Europe should have governments friendly to the Soviet Union. But Roosevelt believed, in the words of Edward R. Stettinius, Jr., Hull's successor at the head of the State Department, that "a strong world organization, created before the end of the war . . . would help the world to deal with the inevitable difficulties that would arise over the control of liberated territories and would make spheres of influence of less importance than in the past."[12]

On the eve of Yalta the difference between Churchill's attitude and

Roosevelt's seemed to be this: Roosevelt was hopeful that a strong United Nations organization might prevent the partition of Europe into spheres of influence; whereas Churchill, recognizing Europe's partition as an accomplished fact, sought to ease its consequences by bargaining with the Russians.

12 *Yalta: Hopes and Lessons*

The year 1945, which brought victory for the Grand Alliance over Nazi Germany, began on the battlefields under the auspices of Allied unity. The German Christmas offensive in the Ardennes, contrary to Hitler's expectations, strengthened the ties of East-West alliance and pushed Western hatred of Germany to a new pitch of emotionalism. The Führer was greatly mistaken when he thought that military setbacks would make the Western Allies alive to the threat of Soviet domination in Europe. The crisis on the western front, instead of forcing the Western Allies to seek a compromise peace with Nazi Germany, made them even more anxious to seek cooperation with Soviet Russia. And the hardships the Western armies had encountered on the battlefields of Europe strengthened the conviction of American strategists that Soviet participation in the war against Japan was highly desirable, too.

Anxious to know whether the Russians could do anything from their side to take off some of the German pressure against the West, Churchill inquired in Moscow whether the Western Powers could "count on a major Russian offensive on the Vistula front, or elsewhere, during January." Stalin promptly replied that, taking into account the position of the Western Allies, the Red Army, regardless of weather, would commence large-scale offensive operations not later than the second half of January.[1]

Churchill was impressed with this "thrilling message." The Soviet winter offensive began shortly after, and at the time the Big Three were on their way to Yalta, the Soviet armies were already scoring their great victories — which allegedly was exactly what Stalin had planned as a backdrop to the conference in order to strengthen his bargaining position. The Western leaders were unaware of such a plan, if it existed; and Churchill, who had asked for the Soviet offensive, could hardly have suspected ulterior motives behind the timing. He was "distressed," however, on the eve of the Yalta meeting, which took place between

February 4 and 12, because of the deadlock in the negotiations which were going on at the same time over the future of the Polish government. In a message to Roosevelt, he expressed his feeling that "the end of this war may well prove to be more disappointing than was the last."[2] But by the time he reached Yalta, as Secretary of State Stettinius observed, most of this pessimism seemed to have left him,[3] and Churchill's own record of the Yalta conference is proof of the general optimism with which the Western leaders viewed the results of their meeting with Marshal Stalin.

The protocol of proceedings which summarized the agreements reached at the conference reflected the optimistic One-World mood with its initial announcement that a new universal organization would be created soon. Because Big Three unity seemed to be assured as the foundation of this new world instrument for peace, called the United Nations, the fulfillment of everything else that had been agreed upon was anticipated with hope and confidence. And insofar as the Western leaders considered some of the other agreements less satisfactory than the one on the United Nations, they looked upon the world organization, and Soviet Russia's participation in it, as the best means for remedying them. Consequently, especially to President Roosevelt, Soviet agreement to participate in the United Nations seemed so important that it justified concessions on what, at the time of Yalta, seemed less important points.

The protocol listed thirteen other agreements, among which first in line was the famous Declaration on Liberated Europe. It was introduced by President Roosevelt toward the end of the conference and was accepted with only a few minor changes and without much discussion. In this document Marshal Stalin, Prime Minister Churchill and President Roosevelt jointly declared "their mutual agreement to concert, during the temporary period of instability in liberated Europe, the policies of their three governments in assisting the peoples of the former Axis satellite states of Europe to solve by democratic means their pressing political and economic problems." Furthermore they pledged that "the three governments will jointly assist the people in any European liberated state or former Axis satellite state in Europe . . . to form interim governmental authorities, broadly representative of all democratic elements in the population and pledged to the earliest possible establishment, through free elections, of governments responsive to the will of the people." In conclusion the Big Three reaffirmed their faith in the principles of the Atlantic Charter, their pledge in the Declaration of the United Nations, and their determination to build, in cooperation with other peace-loving nations, world order under law, dedicated to peace, security, freedom and the general well-being of all mankind.

This document, prepared by the American State Department, was originally an integral part of a proposal for the establishment of a European High Commission composed of Britain, the Soviet Union, France and the United States. The European High Commission was planned to assist in establishing popular governments and in facilitating the solution of emergency economic problems in the former occupied and satellite states of Europe. (The European High Commission was to have no responsibilities in regard to the conduct of the war or the post-war control of Germany. Questions regarding Germany were to be left to the European Advisory Commission which had been created at the Moscow conference in October 1943.) President Roosevelt, however, decided against presenting the proposal for a European High Commission to the Yalta conference.[4] Thus was missed an opportunity to ensure, in some form at least, *direct* participation of the Western Powers in assisting the East European nations to establish popular governments.

The Declaration on Liberated Europe, as approved by the conference, provided no *direct* guarantees for, or *direct* assistance to, the formation of democratic governments in the Russian-occupied areas. It envisaged merely that the Three Powers would "concert" their policies, that they would "jointly assist" the liberated peoples, and would "consult together on the measures necessary to discharge the joint responsibilities set forth in this declaration." The Three Powers also expressed their hope that France might be associated with them in these procedures. Big Three unity, then, was the *indirect* guarantee and assistance which the Western Powers offered the nations of Eastern Europe in those nations' efforts to establish for themselves democratic regimes; otherwise those nations were left to themselves in their assigned task of "getting along with Russia," which was the frequently repeated advice the West offered at that time to nations under Soviet occupation.

Special arrangements of some sort were made concerning Poland, but only in the form of implementing, in very general terms, the phraseology of the agreements of the Declaration on Liberated Europe. This special provision "authorized as a commission" Soviet Foreign Minister Molotov, and the two Western ambassadors at Moscow, Averell Harriman and Sir A. Clark Kerr, "to consult" with the Poles in regard to forming a government "on a broader democratic basis." The acceptance of this special Declaration on Poland was much less smooth than the agreement that the Big Three reached on the general Declaration on Liberated Europe. As Churchill reported in his memoirs, Poland was discussed at no fewer than seven out of eight plenary meetings of the Yalta conference.[5] Finally it was agreed that the Polish provisional government, which had been set up and recognized by the Soviet Union, should be reorganized with the inclusion of democratic leaders from Poland itself and from Poles abroad. This new government should then be called the Polish Provisional Government of National Unity, and should be pledged to the holding of "free and unfettered elections as soon as possible on the basis of universal suffrage and the secret ballot." But again, apart from the Molotov-Harriman-Kerr commission's authorization "to consult," nothing but the good faith of Soviet Russia and the unity of the Big Three served to guarantee that this provision would be carried out.

A special agreement was reached also on Yugoslavia; but this was even more vague than the one on Poland. The Big Three agreed merely "to recommend" to Marshal Tito and to Dr. Šubašić that their pact concluded in December 1944, which had not yet been carried out, should immediately be put into effect and that a new broader government, uniting the exiles with Tito's partisans, should be formed on the basis of that pact.

The Big Three sounded the note of unity again in concluding the protocol of the conference, when they announced that permanent machinery would be set up for consultation between the foreign ministers of the Three Powers, and that these meetings should be held as often as necessary, probably about every three or four months.

The only secret agreement of the conference was made with reference to Japan. It was agreed that in two or three months after Germany had surrendered and the war in Europe had terminated, the Soviet Union would enter the war against Japan on the side of the Allies. In return for Russia's willingness to break her non-aggression treaty with Japan and enter the war in the Far East, important strategic islands and other concessions were promised to Stalin.

It was often said that in Europe too it was due to military considerations that the Western leaders made concessions to Stalin. No doubt the Western leaders were anxious (or, as it appears in retrospect, unduly anxious) to keep Russia in the war against Germany and to bring her into the war against Japan. However, it would be wrong to assume that the Western leaders adhered to the Yalta agreements under the compulsion of military necessity only. Military necessity was of course paramount — most of the territory under consideration was already occupied or about to be occupied by the Red Army; nevertheless the agreements concerning Eastern Europe were very much in line also with the Western views on the future of that area. It was a Western axiom that the primary task of the Eastern European nations was to establish friendly cooperation with Soviet Russia: and the Yalta agreements on Eastern Europe were designed to achieve just that.

Both Britain and the United States readily acknowledged the special interests Russia claimed to have in this area from the point of view of her security. They did not intend to let Eastern Europe become an exclusive Soviet sphere of influence; nevertheless Churchill, in his percentage agreements with Stalin, had indicated the limits of British interest in Eastern Europe, and he seemed now to adhere to these earlier agreements, although the Yalta Declaration on Liberated Europe provided free and unfettered elections for every liberated country and obviously superseded all previous arrangements. Thus, immediately after Yalta, when the Big Three agreement was being trampled down in Romania, Churchill still felt, for some time at least, bound by the percentage agreements. "We were hampered in our protests," he explained in his memoirs, "because Eden and I during our October visit to Moscow had recognized that Russia should have a largely predominant voice in Rumania and Bulgaria, while we took the lead in Greece."[6]

The United States, although never a party to any sphere of influence agreement, indicated its generally limited interest in Europe when Roosevelt, at the first plenary meeting in Yalta, said "the United States would take all reasonable steps to preserve peace, but not at the expense of keeping a large army in Europe. . . . The American occupation would therefore be limited to two years."[7] And when the Soviet violation of the Yalta agreements became quite apparent, the withdrawal of American troops from Europe still continued according to schedule. In fact, after Yalta the American policy, more rigidly than the British, remained committed to the Yalta principle that the East European nations must try to get along with Russia — and U.S. policy adhered to this principle, in spite of the rapid deterioration of conditions, which in any case had never been favorable for its fulfillment.[8] Starting, it seems, from the broad assumption that peace and freedom in Eastern Europe depended on Big Three unity, the Western leaders were anxious, first of all, to cement this unity. Thus, at Yalta, for fear of impairing Big Three unity, they pressed only lightly their ideas for guarantees, no matter what these guarantees could have been. Then, after Yalta, the vicious circle continued. The Big Three agreements were trampled down by Russia, but the West seemed to be more concerned with preserving Big Three unity than in taking measures against Soviet violations of the Big Three agreements.

During the Yalta conference, it was only in the case of Poland that the Western representatives insisted, for a while, upon Allied supervision of the forthcoming elections. The Western proposition provided for the American, British and Soviet ambassadors in Warsaw to watch the polls and report whether the elections were really free and unfettered; the Soviet negotiators on the other hand maintained hypocritically that such supervision would "offend the Poles." After some wrangling, the Soviet arguments prevailed, and the idea of supervision was dropped.

Among Central and Eastern Europe's many territorial problems, again only those pertaining to Poland were discussed in Yalta by the Big Three. The Curzon Line was recognized as Poland's eastern frontier and it was agreed that she must receive "substantial accessions of territory in the north and west." Final delimitation of Poland's western frontier was to await the peace conference. Both Roosevelt and Churchill agreed, however, that Poland should receive compensation up to the line of the Oder; but they favored the eastern rather than the western Neisse as a continuation of the new Polish frontiers southward from the Oder. They also agreed in principle that the German population should be expelled from the newly acquired Polish territories, as they had agreed earlier with Beneš's demands that the non-Slav minorities should be expelled from Czechoslovakia.[9]

The mutual problems of the smaller nations of Central Europe, whose quarrels in the past had contributed so much to their undoing, did not figure at all on the agenda of the Yalta conference. The restoration of the pre-war national states was taken for granted. Their better future was deemed to be assured by the election of democratic governments, by friendly cooperation with Soviet Russia, and by Big Three unity in the United Nations organization. The road to happiness for the nations of the Middle Zone was described by Churchill, when in the House of Commons on February 27 he said regarding Poland: "The Poles will have their future in their own hands, with the single limitation that they must honestly follow, in harmony with their allies, a policy friendly to Russia." And he continued: "The impression I brought back from the Crimea . . . is that Marshal Stalin and the Soviet leaders wish to live in honorable friendship and equality with the Western democracies. I feel that their word is their bond. . . . I decline absolutely to embark here on a discussion about Russian good faith."

President Roosevelt expressed a similar point of view in his message to Congress on March 1: "I think," he said, "the Crimea conference . . . spells, and it ought to spell, the end of the system of unilateral action, exclusive alliances, and spheres of influence, and balances of power and all the other expedients which have been tried for centuries and have always failed. . . . I am sure that, under the agreement reached at Yalta, there will be a more stable political Europe than ever before."

Unfortunately, both Churchill and Roosevelt were wrong: both were as wrong as Neville Chamberlain had been when he spoke of "peace with honor" and "peace in our time," after his return from another crucial international meeting of the twentieth century.

To sum up: The Yalta agreements were based on several broad principles upon which the peace of Europe was supposed to rest. First of all, peace in Europe was to be guaranteed by the global cooperation of the United States, Britain and Russia within the framework of the United Nations. Furthermore there were three specific policies according to which the peaceful reorganization of Europe was to proceed: friendship with Russia, hostility to Germany, restoration of the pre-war nation-state system. Or at least, Western diplomacy took for granted that these would be the principles of European peacemaking. As far as Soviet Russia went, if tactics are distinguished from policy, it is obvious in retrospect that Soviet diplomacy had never emancipated itself from the fundamental principle of Bolshevik foreign policy: hostility to the West.

Since the breakdown of the Yalta agreements, several theories have been advanced to explain the causes of the failure. The most popular among them was perhaps the one least instructive. This was what Henry Steele Commager aptly called the "conspiracy theory of Yalta."[10] According to this theory President Roosevelt, naive and senile, sold out half of Europe to Stalin at Yalta as a result of some Communist, or leftist, conspiratorial work in the State Department. The "conspiracy theory" was popularized by Senator Joseph R. McCarthy, chief promoter of the "Red Scare" in the United States after the Second World War. But post-war American party struggles also added much fuel to the demagogic interpretation of the Yalta agreements. The Republicans, who had been out of power for almost a generation, indulged in some irresponsible criticism of Yalta in order to discredit both the foreign and the domestic policies of the Democratic administration.

Following General Eisenhower's electoral victory in 1952, the Republican-administered State Department made public (March 1955) the American documents concerning the Big Three agreements (*The Conference at Malta and Yalta, 1945*). The release added little or nothing to what was already known about Yalta. The Yalta Papers paid special attention to Alger Hiss, former State Department official, target of the advocates of the "conspiracy theory," who was convicted of perjury for denying that he had passed official documents to a confessed Soviet spy. But it was clear from the documents that Hiss participated in the Yalta negotiations as a reporter rather than as a policymaker. This fact did not prevent Republican Senator Karl Mundt, for instance, from contending after the publication of the Yalta Papers that the Russians were able to obtain concessions from the United States at the Yalta conference because "at that time Alger Hiss was acting in an espionage capacity."[11] The conspiracy theory was far from dead ten years after Yalta.

This theory was as unrealistic as the once flourishing leftist suspicion which sensed some reactionary conspiracy precipitated by Roosevelt's death in April 1945, behind the breakdown of the East-West alliance. After the war, many Western liberals believed unity between the Western Powers and Soviet Russia broke down because one of its chief architects and a leading Western liberal, President Roosevelt, died. This belief was echoed by the President's son, Elliot, in the mythical suggestion that "Franklin Roosevelt's ideals and statesmanship would have been sufficient to keep the unity a vital entity during the postwar period. . . ."[12] And long after Roosevelt's death, the belief lingered on among liberals that East-West cooperation had broken down mainly because of reactionary intrigues. So, for instance, Rexford G. Tugwell, one-time member of President Roosevelt's Brain Trust, in a book published in 1957 hinted at "a reversal of the dead President's intentions" and "the intransigence towards Russia of the reactionaries in the Cabinet, the Department of State and the embassies everywhere," as having been the cause of the cold war.[13] The theory of reactionary conspiracy, it seems, had its diehard believers as did the theory of leftist conspiracy.

Pro-Soviet sympathies of the Left were, no doubt, responsible to a great extent for the naive Western views on Russia and communism, but much more conducive to Western friendliness for the Soviet Union was the fact that East and West were united in a life and death struggle against a common enemy, Hitler's Germany. Many Western progressives committed a grave mistake by portraying Communists as essentially "social reformers." But their influence in shaping the West's pro-Russian policy was greatly exaggerated and their motives grossly distorted.

The pro-Soviet Left in the West during the war advocated friendship with the Soviet Union primarily for military reasons, as did everybody else. As a rule, they favored cooperation with the Soviet Union in the interest of their respective nations, rather than in the interest of Russia or communism. The worst they did was to make cooperation with the Russians an ideological issue, hailing East-West unity as a triumph for liberalism and suspecting as reactionaries all who did not commit themselves wholly to friendship with the Soviet Union. Prominent in their thinking was the shame of Munich. They fostered what Beneš liked to call the West's "bad conscience" regarding Munich. This could have been a real service, had they not also, in the meantime, spread the naive belief that cooperation with Russia would undo past crimes and mistakes and introduce a new millennium. They thus weakened the sense of realism that the West so greatly needed. But in no way did they make Western policy, either at Yalta or at any other place where the crucial decisions were made. The "conspiracy theory" just did not fit the facts.

Another theory, propounded most elaborately by Chester Wilmot in his book *The Struggle for Europe,* explained Yalta mainly in terms of alleged Anglo-American antagonism. In order to represent Americans as entertaining strong anti-British and pro-Russian biases, Wilmot quoted statements by General Eisenhower and others, such as: "The ordinary Russian seems to me to bear a marked similarity to what we call an 'average American,'" "special bond between the U.S.A. and the U.S.S.R.," "unbroken friendship [with the U.S.S.R.] that dated back to the birth of the United States," "both were free from the stigma of colonial empire building by force" — only to come to the following conclusion: "This belief was implicit in Roosevelt's approach to the problems which were to be discussed at Yalta. In his eyes, Britain was an imperial power, bearing the 'colonial stigma'; Russia was not. That assessment of his allies was a decisive factor in Roosevelt's readiness to make concessions to the Soviet Union both in Europe and in Asia in order to ensure Stalin's entry in the Pacific War."[14]

The consequence of this alleged anti-British and pro-Russian bias was that the Americans opposed Churchill's strategy. Regarding Churchill's strategy — and motives — Wilmot claimed that in 1943 Churchill favored military operations in the Balkans in order to achieve "the restoration of democratic influence in Central and South-Eastern Europe." As Arthur Schlesinger, Jr., pointed out while refuting these theories: "Not a fragment of evidence is presented to support the confident assertion that Churchill ever had these political motives at that time. . . ."[15] But it is easier to start than to stop a myth.

Believers in the Balkan invasion myth pretended to know that, at the Teheran meeting of the Big Three in 1943, the aim of Churchill's strategy was the defense of Europe against communism. Furthermore they were convinced that had Churchill's plan been carried out the post-war bolshevization of Eastern Europe could have been prevented. That such political motives, if they had existed and shaped Allied strategy, could have ruined East-West cooperation and could even have led to a separate peace between Germany and Russia, did not bother the makers of this myth. Nor did they care to explore the military complications of such strategy, automatically taking its success for granted. And of course they disregarded the simple fact that Churchill in 1943 did not advocate Balkan invasion plans on the scale or with the motives that the believers of the myth said he did.

In his memoirs, Churchill clearly stated the nature and motives of his Balkan invasion plans of 1943. Said he, in defense against the makers of myths: "It has become a legend in America that I strove to prevent the Cross-Channel enterprise called 'Overlord,' and that I tried vainly to lure the Allies into some mass invasion of the Balkans, or a large-scale campaign in the eastern Mediterranean, which would effectively kill it. Much of this nonsense has already in previous chapters been exposed and refuted."[16] Especially refuted in Churchill's memoirs is the contention that the strategy which he urged in 1943 in the Balkans and the eastern Mediterranean had something to do with efforts alleged against him to forestall the Red Army in Central Europe. It is clear from Churchill's narrative that what he sought was to speed up the common victory. He was eager to employ the large forces already assembled in the Mediterranean most efficiently, and wanted "to use otherwise unemployable forces to bring Turkey into the war."[17] "The object," he wrote, "of all the operations in the Mediterranean which I had contemplated was to take the weight off Russia and give the best possible chance to 'Overlord.'"[18]

It is true that in 1944 — but assuredly not in 1943, as Wilmot claimed — Churchill became suspicious of Russia's intentions and tried at that time "to forestall the Russians in certain areas of Central Europe."[19] However, at Yalta he seemed to regain his confidence in Russia, and it was only afterwards, in the spring of 1945, when the Soviets trampled down indiscriminately (not only in Romania and Bulgaria) the Big Three Yalta agreements, that he definitely lost that confidence, and began to advocate both diplomatic and military resistance.

During the spring of 1945 Churchill's views on Soviet Russia began to differ fundamentally from those maintained by the American State Department, and in the light of subsequent events it is clear that Churchill was right and the United States policy-makers were wrong. Wilmot's "colonial stigma" theory may perhaps partly explain why at this particular juncture the United States brushed aside Churchill's prophetic warnings.[20] The American policy-makers suspected an anti-Communist bias in Churchill; and in some instances they acted as if they were more fearful of the bogey of British imperialism than aware of the obvious facts of Soviet imperialism. However, there is no evidence that at any time during the early phases of the war, any anti-British sentiments could have been "a decisive factor" in the pro-Russian policy of the United States.

Certainly Roosevelt was especially anxious to dispel the suspicion of the Russians that they were facing an Anglo-American front, and he therefore often played the role of mediator between Stalin and Churchill. But this was a tactical position, which cannot prove that Roosevelt sought the friendship of Soviet Russia more ardently than did Churchill. Both Western leaders sought it, although, apart from their common conviction that the friendship of Russia was essential in winning the war and in building the peace, their underlying motives may have been somewhat different.

Roosevelt had a better grasp than Churchill of the forces propelling the modern world toward social change; also, he was in sympathy with them. He was convinced that capitalism and communism, by different methods, could both serve human progress. Or at least, Roosevelt seemed to hold this conviction during the period of East-West cooperation. He did not believe this in 1940, at the time of the Russo-Finnish war, when he told an American Youth Congress that the Soviet dictatorship was "as absolute as any other dictatorship in the world." A highly pragmatic man, he adopted, tried and discarded many hypotheses in his life. Had he lived after the Second World War, doubtless he would have been able to change his views on the democratic potentialities of Soviet tyranny. During the war, at any rate, fashionable leftist doctrines about the synthesis of democracy and communism made a greater impression on Roosevelt than on Churchill, although the Conservative Churchill was not entirely immune to them. In a letter of October 11, 1944, which he never dispatched but did publish in his memoirs, Churchill wrote to Stalin: "We feel we were right in interpreting your dissolution of the Comintern as a decision by the Soviet Government not to interfere in the internal political affairs of other countries. . . . We have the feeling that, viewed from afar and on a grand scale, the differences between our systems will tend to get smaller. . . ."[21]

Such ideological speculations did not impress Churchill too deeply. On the other hand, up until the spring of 1945, he was more ready than Roosevelt to accept the Soviet Union as a partner in power politics; his percentage agreements with Stalin clearly proved this. Churchill viewed the post-war world more in the perspective of balance of power, whereas Roosevelt viewed it more in the perspective of global cooperation; nevertheless, both Churchill and Roosevelt seemed to assume that after Germany's defeat the Western democracies, by recognizing Russia's legitimate security interest in Eastern Europe, would be able to cooperate successfully and to coexist peacefully with the Soviet Union.

The critics of Yalta were particularly prone to forget what the military situation had been at the time of the Crimean conference. The defenders of Yalta therefore were anxious to stress that, under the then existing military situation, the Yalta agreements were the very best the Western negotiators could obtain from the Russians. This argument was forcefully stated by Secretary of State Stettinius. He reminded the critics of Yalta that "while President Roosevelt was meeting with Prime Minister Winston Churchill and Marshal Stalin in the Crimea, American and British troops had just recovered the ground lost by the Battle of the Bulge. The Allies had not yet bridged the Rhine. In Italy our advance had bogged down in the Apennines. Soviet troops, on the other hand, had just swept through almost all of Poland and East Prussia, and at some points had reached the Oder River in Germany. Most of Hungary had been captured, and the Yugoslav Partisans had recaptured Belgrade in November 1944. By February 1945, therefore, Poland and all of Eastern Europe, except for most of Czechoslovakia, was in the hands of the Red Army. As a result of this military situation, it was not a question of what Great Britain and the United States would permit Russia to do . . . but what the two countries could persuade the Soviet Union to accept."[22]

And at a time when, in the McCarthyite phase of post-war American politics, Yalta became the symbol of "treason," George F. Kennan helped to set the record straight by pointing out: "The establishment of Soviet military power in Eastern Europe . . . was not the result of these talks; it was the result of the military operations during the concluding phases of the war. There was nothing the western democracies could have done to prevent the Russians from entering those areas except to get there first, and this they were not in a position to do."[23]

Several military analysts questioned the inevitability of Eastern Europe's control by the Red Army. Their arguments, however, were far from convincing. They either maintained without benefit of evidence, like Chester Wilmot, that no heed had been given to the right military counsel which allegedly had been available; or else, in hindsight counsel, they recommended such moves as would seem, even today, of doubtful military value for achieving victory over Nazi Germany. Opinion in the latter category was voiced by Hanson W. Baldwin, who suggested it was a great mistake not to let Hitler and Stalin fight each other "to a frazzle," because it would have placed the democracies in supreme power in the world, instead of elevating one totalitarianism at the expense of another and of the democracies.[24]

It cannot be denied that supreme world power for the democracies would have been the ideal result of the war. Past experience should prove, however, that to attempt to achieve this by pitting Germany against Russia can more easily create a bond of union between those powers (as, for example, at Rapallo and in the Nazi-Soviet pact) than secure a Western victory over both. The defenders of Yalta profited by the experiences of the past to the extent of recognizing Big Three unity as the indispensable prerequisite of military victory. On the other hand their political arguments in support of the Yalta agreements were less than convincing. They put all the blame for failure to carry out the Yalta agreements on the Russians. They claimed in effect that the agreements were good, if the Russians had only kept them. This was also the essence of a most elaborate defensive thesis presented by W. Averell Harriman, one of President Roosevelt's advisers at Yalta, before the United States Senate Committee on Foreign Relations on July 13, 1951. In brief, this defensive thesis maintained that not only did the West not sell out East Europe to the Communists, as reckless critics of Yalta charged, but on the contrary Yalta provided for the liberated nations of Eastern Europe to have democratic governments, established through free elections.

This argument was sound inasmuch as the Kremlin was to be called to task for violating the Yalta agreements. On the other hand, it is questionable whether Soviet readiness to cooperate in holding "free and unfettered" elections in the countries of Eastern Europe was ever considered to be as much of a possibility as was later claimed, rather naively, by the defenders of Yalta. After all, Soviet Russia's poor record, as well as the Middle Zone countries', in practising free elections was well known. Moreover, the Western Powers never pressed too hard the issue of supervising the elections in the Soviet sphere. From the Yalta agreements the conclusion could have been drawn, above all by the Russians, that some allowance had been made for the Russian interpretation of "free" elections — though of course not as much allowance as the Russians themselves took the liberty of making.

The text of the Yalta agreements, while quoted verbatim by its defenders, did not reveal the true meaning of the policy the Western Allies were pursuing in Europe in general, and in Eastern Europe in particular. For, whatever was said in the Yalta agreements, it was also assumed that Soviet Russia would have a predominant influence over Eastern Europe. A kind of friendly partition of Europe between East and West corresponded with the spirit of Allied policy. Hostility to Germany was the principal motivation of this policy. Lest the common enemy put the torch to the world once more, the Soviet Union with her Slavic allies was to stand guard over vanquished Germany in the east, while the democratic powers stood guard in the west.

The West had relied on the Slavs against Germany ever since the beginning of the conflict with the Germans which culminated in the First World War. The anti-German alliance between Russia and the West was broken up in 1917 by the Bolshevik revolution. After the First World

War, French policy built up out of the nation-states in the predominantly Slavic Middle Zone between Germany and Russia a cordon sanitaire which, though primarily anti-German, was anti-Russian as well. During the Second World War, the West discarded the anti-Russian purpose of the cordon sanitaire, while retaining its anti-German function. Henceforth the nation-states of the Middle Zone were to cooperate with Russia, forming a great Slavic counterpoise to Germany within the framework of East-West cooperation.

This scheme was certainly meant to avoid the mistakes of the bankrupt French cordon-sanitaire policy in Central Europe. But the deeper cause of Europe's tragedy, namely the insane competition of reckless nationalism, was not taken to heart at all. The bankruptcy of the European nation-state system which precipitated the outbreak of the Second World War, and the aberrations of nationalism which culminated in the incredible inhumanities of Hitlerism, failed to drive home the lesson that the entire political fabric of Europe, based on sovereign nation-states, sorely needed revision.

The restoration of the pre-war European nation-state system was carried out so completely that it was even, contrary to earlier plans, applied to defeated Germany. At Yalta "the study of the procedure for the dismemberment of Germany" was referred to a three-power committee. Six months later, at the Potsdam conference, principles governing the treatment of Germany were agreed upon which already looked for the eventual restoration of a German nation-state. It was agreed that "for the time being" no central German government should be established, but nevertheless "certain essential central German administrative departments" were to be created without delay, and during the period of occupation Germany was to be treated as a "single economic unit."

These plans concerning Germany, like all the other East-West agreements, were not carried out in the way agreed upon. The point however is that even the solution of the German problem was envisaged according to the old nation-state pattern. The treatment of Germany as a "unit" was of course far better policy than "dismemberment"; the latter was likely only to incite nationalist passions into seeking reunification. Yet restoration of Germany, even in the "decentralized" form envisaged by the Potsdam agreement, was a nationalist solution and therefore fraught with all the dangers pertaining to it. Only a federated Germany in a federated Europe could be conducive, if anything could, to ending the disastrous conflict between Europe and the Germans.

During the war Churchill had toyed with the idea of European federalism, but he failed to arouse Roosevelt's interest in any special European organization. And in any case Churchill's program itself was only, as Hajo Holborn called it, "a study project rather than an accepted policy." In the West generally, and not only by American policy-makers, it was believed that "the various nations of Europe would revive after the defeat of Germany and be able to exist in relative independence if Germany were kept disarmed and demilitarized. . . . This pattern . . . involved the rebirth of the old independent national states." In short, the Western world was confident that "somehow the old Europe would ultimately reemerge."[25]

It could be well argued that the Western Powers could have done nothing, even had they wanted, to promote federalism in Soviet-occupied Eastern Europe, inasmuch as the Russians were opposed to it. This, however, cannot exonerate the West from its share of the blame for cooperating in the restoration of the old system of national states in Central and Eastern Europe in a new and particularly vicious form. The Western Powers became accomplices in the genocide plans of those Slavs, Communist and non-Communist, who, bewitched by the totalitarian magic of homogeneous national states, decided to expel millions from their homelands. Furthermore, in forsaking the principle of federalism, the Western democracies failed to create unity of their own where Soviet Russia could not have interfered.

Paul-Henri Spaak, one of the few truly federalist European statesmen, exclaimed in 1952: "What a pity Europe was not 'created' in 1945—a great chance was lost . . . ruins lay everywhere . . . everything had to be begun again, everything could have been begun on a new basis. Instead, Russia was left to consolidate her conquest and organize Eastern Europe, while Western Europe was going to work again in the old way, resuming outdated traditions."[26]

The "great debate" on Yalta may still flare up from time to time, and military and political analysts may continue their debate on the great mistakes of Western strategy and diplomacy. However, as regards the lessons to be learned from past mistakes, no further evidence is needed to prove it was a capital error not to know the true nature and aims of Soviet communism.

According to Hugh Seton-Watson, the fact that "leaders and the public in Britain and America took an optimistic view of their Soviet co-belligerents" was due to "the general ignorance of the nature and aims of communism, for which the main responsibility must fall on those who ruled the democracies between 1917 and 1939."[27] While this is true, it should be remembered that there was also general ignorance regarding the nature of the inner crisis that plagued the nations of the Western world. Had this crisis, caused by intense nationalism and the obsolete system of nation-states, been understood by leaders of the Western world, they would not even have considered the restoration of "old Europe," however ignorant they might have been as to the nature and aims of communism. And had they understood the historical necessity of federalization, Soviet imperialism could hardly have destroyed so easily the fruits of Western victory in the Second World War.

Cooperation with the Russians was bound to be the West's first choice, as Wallace Carroll concluded in a profound analysis of wartime policy, but the mistake lay in failure to prepare an alternative policy in the event that the Russians refused their cooperation. "The nature of the alternative course of action," said Carroll, "was clear enough, and it was one of those happy alternatives which could have been prepared without endangering the success of the primary policy. It was, in effect, to create under American leadership a kind of peace federation of like-minded nations whose material strength and moral authority were so great that no one nation would long have dared to run counter to their will."[28] This "happy alternative" was proposed in its most radical form during the war by Clarence K. Streit, who in his famous book *Union Now* laid down the scheme of a transatlantic federation of the United States and Canada with the democracies of the European continent.

Of course, had the Western nations been capable of working out such a "happy alternative," they also could have made it into a happy correlative of their policy of cooperation with the Soviet Union. Unfortunately, the war did not forge the Western democracies into a dynamic, progressive, international force. The Soviet Union not only dared to run counter to their will, but was probably even tempted to aggression by the Western show of irresolute weakness.

13 *Stalin's Triumph*

In the spring of 1945 Churchill saw the Soviet menace clearly and definitely. Not even Churchill, however, could foresee the extent of Communist post-war expansion or the slowness of Western reaction to it. Two years were to pass before Russia was confronted with the slowly awakening Western will to resist Soviet aggression in Europe. By that time the Soviet conquest of Eastern Europe was nearing completion, while in Asia the final phase of communism's triumph had just begun. And, in the worldwide struggle between communism and democracy, the communization of China, completed in 1949, was a gain of even greater political importance than the Soviet conquest of Eastern Europe.

Stalin's actions did not indicate that he had any "revolutionary master plan" for the Communist conquest of Eastern Europe. Indeed, as Isaac Deutscher pointed out, if he anticipated Communist domination of Poland, why did he not let the Poles keep Lvov? — what difference would it have made whether Lvov was in Soviet Poland or the Soviet Ukraine? Or, if Stalin planned to establish Communist dictatorships over all Eastern Europe, including Eastern Germany as the nucleus of a Communist Germany, why did he champion expulsion of the Germans, and why did he insist upon the unpopular reparation demands from the former enemy states? Such actions could not fail to have a damaging effect on the Communist cause in those countries.[1]

But, improvised and incoherent as Stalin's actions seemed to be in the early phases of Soviet policy in Eastern Europe, he did not take long to replace improvization with a coherent plan for Soviet subjugation. The plan called for the creation of "people's democracies." It was a flexible plan, but the final aim of seizing power by a tyrannical oligarchy was never compromised. The "coalition governments" of the post-war era figured in the Soviet plan as legal tools by which the power of the democratic parties participating in the coalitions could be reduced by stages. Hugh Seton-Watson, in describing these stages, labelled the types of government operating in Eastern Europe during the period of Communist seizure of power as, first, "genuine coalitions," which then changed into "bogus coalitions," and finally gave way to what the Communists called "monolithic" unity.[2]

Sometimes stages were skipped, and sometimes they had different durations; but the appearance of legality was preserved. The model for turning the Central and Eastern European countries into Soviet satellites was not the Russian civil war, but the "peaceful revolution" by which Mussolini and Hitler had seized power. H. R. Trevor-Roper aptly called this method "a policy of learning from the success of fascism."[3] But Stalin's triumph did not depend solely upon methods by which local opposition to Soviet aims could be liquidated. Even more important in the Communist scheme was the exclusion of Western influence from Eastern Europe.

From the beginning there was a great consistency in the Soviet determination to act unilaterally, rather than, as the Yalta agreements stipulated, "jointly" with the Western Powers, in the liberated countries. Military occupation was of course the primary source of strength that enabled the Russians to act unilaterally. But there were other factors which also played into their hands.

First of all, the Western Powers, in the spirit of the Yalta program, willingly recognized Russia's special interests in Eastern Europe. This Western disengagement from Eastern Europe was conceived in good faith; partly as a recognition of the claim that Soviet security required the establishment of "friendly" governments in the countries along Russia's western boundaries; and partly as a concession to secure Russia's cooperation in building a new world order within the organization of the United Nations. The cooperative attitude of the Western Powers was not, however, reciprocated by the Russians. Western concessions did not induce the Soviet Union to follow the agreed course of Allied policy, nor did Western protests deter the Soviet Union from violating treaty obligations. Western demobilization, especially the withdrawal of American troops from Europe, contributed immensely to Stalin's feeling of security as he plotted to convert Eastern Europe into an exclusive sphere of Soviet influence without running the risk of retaliation.

There must also have been a feeling of insecurity, however, which counselled Stalin to convert the Middle Zone countries into Soviet satellites. For how could he afford to let these countries have "free elections" if the peoples of the Soviet Union themselves did not enjoy such democratic privileges? And what assurance could he have that these "freely elected governments" would promote friendship toward the Soviet Union? Stalin, at Potsdam, was said to have expressed the view that "a freely elected government in any of these countries would be anti-Soviet, and that we cannot allow."[4] And then, too, the safest way to protect Russia against Germany was to seize control of the territory lying between the two countries, especially since this territory was actually in Soviet hands as a result of the victorious war.

The establishment of Soviet satellites in the Middle Zone jeopardized, of course, the friendly relations between Russia and the Western Powers. But the Soviet leaders, by the very nature of the regime they had created in Russia, must have preferred solutions attained by force to arrangements secured by the organization of the United Nations. The Western leaders were not quite unaware of these dangers, but they believed, as Stettinius said in discussing Roosevelt's views, that they "could do much through firmness, patience, and understanding, over a period of time, in dealing with the Soviet Union to influence its evolution away from dictatorship and tyranny in the direction of a free, tolerant and peaceful society."[5]

Unfortunately, Western patience toward the Soviet Union was not coupled with understanding of the Soviet goals, and Western firmness was both late and insufficient to halt Soviet aggression in Eastern Europe. Western policy was still based on the wartime idea of "getting along with Russia," whereas post-war Soviet policy already gave ample evidence of its undisguised hostility to the democracies. Western ingenuity was very slow indeed in inventing means by which to try to sway Soviet Russia's evolution *away* from dictatorship and tyranny. Nor did the West exert itself within the Soviet zone of influence, where the political trend was moving *toward* Communist dictatorship and Soviet tyranny. From the point of view of democratic interests, Western influence on the post-war policies of the Middle Zone nations was just as ineffective as was Western influence on the evolution of Soviet Russia's policy. What type of guidance the Western democracies, as liberators, would have extended to these peoples in Central and Eastern Europe after the Second World War can never be known. Soviet occupation blocked free contact with the West. But such political guidance as the democratic leaders in the Soviet orbit did receive from the West was mainly in the form of encouragement to get along with Russia and the

Communists — while the Communists were bent upon destruction of these democratic elements.

The Czech democrats did not even need Western encouragement to get along with Russia. They were the pioneers of Soviet friendship in the Middle Zone. The bitter memory of Munich lay heavily on their minds and they were prepared to stake their future security on the Soviet orientation in any case. In Yugoslavia, the former partisans, who formed the core of the new regime headed by Tito, were of course devoted Communists, and as yet loyal admirers of the Soviet Union. But in all the other former Nazi-occupied countries too, political alliances between democrats and Communists in post-war coalition governments were considered, by many democrats at least, as the logical outcome of the common struggle against the Germans and their Nazi accomplices. Moreover, common revolutionary objectives in the post-war reconstruction era gave to cooperation between democrats and Communists an impetus similar to that which had encouraged their cooperation against the Nazi foe during the war.

The old social order was either completely destroyed or seriously dislocated when the war ended. Revolutions were bound to sweep across Eastern Europe, not only because liberation by the Red Army was an invitation to social revolution, but also because the oppressed and humiliated masses, resentful of the past, were overwhelmingly in favor of radical change. In this revolutionary excitement, a great many democrats who considered themselves loyal to the Western ideals of democracy found themselves nevertheless in agreement with the social and economic reforms advocated by the Communists; they also favored swift revolutionary solutions because of fear that any delay would endanger the success of reforms. On the other hand, reactionary opponents of such popular demands as agrarian reform, nationalization of big industry, mining and banking, sprang to the defense of "democratic processes" and appealed to the West for support. Thus situations arose in which to a great many people, social reaction seemed to be supported by the West, while progressive aspirations seemed to be backed by the Soviet Union.

Another popular sentiment which aided the Soviet cause in Central and Eastern Europe was Slavic nationalism. With the exception mainly of the Romanians and Hungarians, the population of the territories liberated from the Nazi-German yoke by the Red Army was Slavic. The degree of Russian and Communist sympathy among the Slavs varied considerably; it was highest, perhaps, among the Czechs and lowest among the Poles. But more than ever before, all of the Slavs responded to the wartime slogans of Slavic solidarity, propagated from Moscow, and all of them hailed the defeat of Nazi Germany as the beginning of a glorious "age of the Slavs."

Nazi cruelties and inhumanities incited the Slavs to hatred and desire for revenge — and also to retribution in kind. Communist disregard for the laws of humanity only added further impetus to an already well advanced process of demoralization. The wild outburst of Slavic nationalism at the war's end was sad evidence of Central and Eastern Europe's dehumanization. Reckless national aspirations were popular with both Communists and non-Communists. In fact, the program to expel the non-Slavs from Czechoslovakia was originated by President Beneš, who was not a Communist.[6] And the anti-Communist Polish émigré government in London was as much in favor of the Oder-Neisse frontier, including the expulsion of millions of Germans living east of this frontier, as was the Soviet-sponsored Polish government in Warsaw.

In Poland's case, to be sure, the desire for revenge was coupled with an undeniable — though exaggerated — claim for territorial compensation. The territories taken by Poland from Germany in the west were in compensation for the territories Russia took from Poland in the east. The Czech scheme for expulsion, on the other hand, was one of Slav revenge pure and simple.

In December 1946, the first post-war Slav Congress met in Belgrade. This congress turned out to be also the last occasion when the delegates of all the Slavic nations gathered to celebrate their triumph and brotherhood. Slav solidarity remained a slogan of Soviet policy, but the organization of the "people's democracies" in Eastern Europe became for Moscow a more urgent task than the organization of Slav congresses. And the "people's democracies" of the Soviet satellites caused bitter disappointment to the Slav nationalists as well as to the progressive democrats who had believed they could work with the Communists to obtain social reforms and improved conditions for the working masses. At the end of the long line of Russia's disappointed friends in Eastern Europe stood the not-so-few native Communists, who discovered that the Soviet sphere of influence was a dangerous place to live in — even for Communists.

From the beginning, Soviet conduct in Central and Eastern Europe was such that it took a great deal of optimism to have faith in Russian cooperation. The Red Army's atrocities, their looting and raping, far exceeded anything that could be explained by the dehumanizing effects of war. However, optimism was sustained by those pacifist sentiments that arose naturally as an emotional reaction to the sufferings of war. Also, preoccupation with social reforms and self-centered nationalism, as a rule, made the victims of Communist aggression themselves fully aware of their danger only when their turn came. Many reform-minded non-Communists were ready to believe that only reactionaries had to fear the Communists, who were clearing the way for radical social reforms. And those who suffered little from Soviet interference were not particularly impressed by the alarming progress Communist tyranny was making in their neighborhood. As previously in the era of Hitler's aggression, there was at the time of Stalin's aggression no move toward united action in opposition. One by one, and by stages, the countries of Central and Eastern Europe were brought under the rule of Soviet tyranny. In fact, Czechoslovakia, the first among the victims of Hitler's aggression and the last among those of Stalin, was the most optimistic in believing that she would succeed, although those around her failed, in cooperating with Russia. And for that matter the West became really aware of the Soviet menace only after the Communist coup in Czechoslovakia in February 1948, when already the Western nations felt themselves directly exposed to the danger of Soviet aggression.

Yet even at the time of the Yalta conference (February 1945), when the chances of cooperation with Russia were viewed with the greatest optimism, Communist aggressiveness was apparent in all the countries liberated by the Red Army. In addition to the chronically grave crisis in Poland, there was trouble in Romania, where the Russians were greatly dissatisfied with the government headed by General Râdescu. The charges against the Râdescu government as reactionary were not without foundation, nor was the complaint wholly unjustified that the government was unable to maintain order in the rear of the Red Army. For example, Soviet reports about Romanian nationalists massacring Hungarians in Transylvania might have been exaggerated, but it was true that order was restored only when the Soviet authorities took over the administration. In any case, the actions which the Russians took against the Râdescu government were neither democratic nor in line with the Yalta provisions.

Early in March 1945, Soviet troops disarmed the Romanian troops in Bucharest, and Soviet Deputy Foreign Minister Andrei Vyshinsky, after an ultimatum, ordered King Michael to appoint a new government headed by the pro-Communist Petru Groza. With the appointment of the Groza government on March 9, only a month after Yalta, a regime was already safely established in Romania which could efficiently carry out the bolshevization of the country, while ruthlessly exterminating the anti-Communist opposition. The Communist coup in Romania was cleverly accompanied by concessions granted to the new Romanian government in the administration of multinational Transylvania. The Russians did not lack the talent for exploiting ethnic rivalries in the Danube Valley according to the old devices of "divide and conquer."

At the time of Romania's defection from the Axis in the summer of 1944, the Russians, in agreement with the Western Powers, were already capitalizing on the rivalry between Romania and Hungary by promising Transylvania, "or the greater part thereof," to the Romanians as a reward for their defection. After the Communist coup, Russia, without consulting the West, transferred the administration of the whole of Transylvania to the Groza government. The Romanians therefore felt confident that the peace conference too would award the whole of Transylvania to them. Thus Groza brought Transylvania as a dowry to the Romanians, and thereby he considerably strengthened the popularity of his regime.

In the meantime, Moscow's agents in the Hungarian provisional government intimated that Transylvania might not be lost yet — if only Hungary could catch up with Romania's progress toward a people's democracy. Thus, old feuds between the Danubian nations and nationalist passions were harnessed to promote sympathy for Soviet Russia.

The Communists in Czechoslovakia were in a specially favorable position to appeal to nationalist passions. They could remind their compatriots that Russia, in addition to restoring Czechoslovak sovereignty over territories inhabited by alien populations, supported also the expulsion of alien peoples therefrom. This gain seemed so valuable that the Czechoslovaks even forgave Russia for taking away Ruthenia. Moreover the cession of Ruthenia to Russia, effected by the Czechoslovak-Soviet treaty of June 29, 1945, was interpreted as a fulfillment of T. G. Masaryk's program; for in 1918, when the Czechs took Ruthenia from Hungary, Masaryk had declared that Czechoslovakia would hold it only as a trustee for Russia. And for that matter, by ceding Ruthenia to the Russians, the Czechs and Slovaks did not surrender their own co-nationals. The population of the ceded territory, which had twice changed hands between Hungary and Czechoslovakia since 1918, consisted of over half a million Ruthenes and over 100,000 Hungarians.

To the Bulgarians, in the meantime, the Communists pointed out that Soviet justice and respect for the principle of ethnic freedom had enabled them to keep Southern Dobrudja, a territory which they had gained from Romania under Nazi auspices. This ostensible appeal to high principles cloaked a rapidly extended bolshevization of Bulgaria. There, the decisive moment in the Communists' taking over the government had already arrived before Yalta. In September 1944, the Muraviev government, which represented the democratic elements, was swept aside after one week in office. Although the new government was headed by a non-Communist, Kimon Georgiev, Communist power expanded rapidly. Communist aggressiveness against the democratic elements precipitated a major crisis in January 1945, when the Western-oriented Dr. G. M. Dimitrov was forced to resign as General Secretary of the Agrarian Union. Thereafter it was only a question of time until the other Dimitrov — the famous Communist Georgi Dimitrov, former secretary of the Comintern — should take over as premier.

In Yugoslavia, the special Yalta agreement, envisaging a coalition between Communists and Western-oriented democrats, was carried out inasmuch as Tito became premier and Šubašić foreign minister in the government formed on March 7, 1945. But those democrats, including Šubašić, who tried to cooperate with the Yugoslav Communists were soon either in jail or in exile. The democrats, who were anxious to equip Yugoslavia with free institutions on the Western model, were on the losing side, as well as the exiled King Peter II and his reactionary clique, who were dreaming of restoring the dynasty and Serbian hegemony. Tito, as leader of the Communist revolution in post-war Yugoslavia, showed no greater respect than Stalin for the democratic Yalta principles. However, the Western Powers, although critical of Tito's dictatorial practices, reluctantly recognized his regime; for, in Churchill's words, addressed to the disillusioned Peter II, the West was "unable to prevent" the events which had disappointed their "best hopes."[7] Tito won recognition by a political *fait accompli* which followed from his military victory in the war. So too did the Communist Enver Hoxha, who was in control of Albania when the war ended.

Disputes over recognition of post-war governments in Eastern Europe opened the chasm between East and West shortly after Yalta. The sole exception was Czechoslovakia, where Beneš and his Czechs, after returning from London *via* Moscow, seemed to settle down to a happy marriage with the Communists. On the other hand, the great crisis was caused over Poland, where freedom remained in eclipse after Yalta as before, even though, as Churchill was wont to say, "it was for this that we had gone to war against Germany."

At Yalta it was agreed that the Polish government, which had been formed from the Lublin Committee of Soviet puppets, should be *reorganized* on a broader democratic basis, and that this *new* government should be pledged to the holding of free and unfettered elections. Averell Harriman and Sir Archibald Clark Kerr, respectively the American and British ambassadors in Moscow, were to join with Soviet Foreign Minister Molotov in a commission to assist the Poles in forming a truly representative government. This commission, however, made no progress of any kind in implementing the Yalta agreement. The ambiguities of the Yalta text itself were exploited by the Russians to dispute the Western interpretation of the agreement. Whereas the Western negotiators wanted to replace the Soviet puppet government by a Polish government of all the democratic parties, the Russians "defended" Polish sovereignty against Western "interference"; meanwhile they tightened their octopus-like grip over the country.

Under the impact mainly of the Polish crisis, Churchill began to sound the alarm in inter-Allied communications early in March 1945. He was disturbed by Soviet actions elsewhere too, especially by what was going on in Romania and Bulgaria. However, since Stalin did not interfere with British actions in Greece, Churchill chose to respect the pre-Yalta agreements he had made with Stalin concerning Soviet "predominance" in the two Balkan countries; moreover, he "did not want to do anything . . . which might harm the prospect of a Polish settlement." For Churchill felt that Poland was, in general, the "test case" between the Western Powers and the Russians, in relation to the meaning of such terms as "democracy, sovereignty, independence, representative government, and free and unfettered elections."[8]

On March 8, in a message to President Roosevelt, Churchill expressed his deep concern about the Polish situation. He informed the President of his plan to send a personal message to Stalin, urging "an early settlement on the basis of the Yalta decision," and he also expressed his hope that the President would do his "utmost to bring this about."[9]

Thus Churchill began the series of messages, propositions and pleas which he made public in the last volume (*Triumph and Tragedy*) of his memoirs, and which proved conclusively that in the spring of 1945 he grew fully aware of the Soviet menace and was also ready to take action against it. Unfortunately the American government did not sense the danger as early as Churchill did. And Churchill noted sadly: "We could make no progress without American aid. . . ."[10] For, even before the war had ended, it was evident that the future of Europe would depend upon two extra-European Great Powers, the United States of America and the Soviet Union.

Roosevelt agreed with Churchill's objectives, but fearing lest the Polish issue aggravate the East-West chasm, he disagreed with Churchill's tactics. As far as the objective of implementing the Yalta decisions on Poland was concerned, Churchill's tactical proposal was modest indeed: he wanted Mikołajczyk, ex-premier of the London Poles, to attend the negotiations on the reorganization of the Lublin government. But it was only after repeated urging that Roosevelt, on March 29, agreed to address Stalin directly in support of Churchill's proposal. Stalin promised to use his influence with the Lublin Poles to make them withdraw their objections to inviting Mikołajczyk. Meanwhile, however, other incidents had intensified the strain: the Russians refused to let Foreign Minister Molotov attend the founding conference of the United Nations in San Francisco unless the Lublin Poles were admitted to represent Poland; fifteen leaders of the Polish anti-Nazi underground movement disappeared mysteriously after a meeting with Soviet representatives; and, most serious for the East-West alliance in the closing days of the war, Stalin accused the Western Powers, in the so-called Berne affair in early April, of negotiating secretly with the Germans in the Swiss capital.

The Western Powers rejected Stalin's accusation; President Roosevelt, in his reply to Stalin, used especially strong language, expressing his "feeling of bitter resentment" over the "vile misrepresentations." The affair was closed with Stalin's explanation of the Soviet point of view which Churchill thought came "as near as they can get to an apology." On April 12, the day of his death, President Roosevelt summed up his views of the Soviet problem. He cabled to Churchill: "These problems, in one form or another, seem to arise every day, and most of them straighten out, as in the case of the Berne meeting. We must be firm, however, and our course thus far is correct."[11]

After Roosevelt's death, President Truman without delay took up the still unsettled Polish question. Within two days, he proposed to Stalin that Mikołajczyk and two other Polish leaders from London should be invited to Moscow at once. Truman also rejected the Soviet contention that the position of the Lublin Poles was similar to that of Tito's Yugoslavs. Therefore the Western recognition of Tito's government was not a precedent which could be applied to Poland.

But the East-West deadlock over Poland continued, and toward the end of May Truman sent Harry Hopkins to Moscow. Hopkins spoke about America's concern for certain fundamental democratic rights, while Stalin assured him that "the Soviet system is not exportable."[12] Hopkins' mission was considered a success because Mikołajczyk and two of his émigré colleagues finally went to Moscow to join the discussions on the reorganization of the Polish government. Churchill himself persuaded Mikołajczyk to go, telling him in parting: "We are responsible for your journey. If something should happen to you we shall start fighting." Mikołajczyk decided to go in a last desperate attempt to save whatever he could of Poland's freedom. Gloom prevailed over the words of Tomasz Arciszewski, Socialist premier of the doomed Polish government in exile, when he said in his farewell to Mikołajczyk: "In your hands lies the future of Poland."[13]

The compromise reached at Moscow was hardly a guarantee of Poland's future as an independent nation. Mikołajczyk, as leader of the Peasant party, became Second Deputy Premier of the new so-called Provisional Government of National Unity, headed by one of the Lublin Poles, Osóbka-Morawski, a pro-Soviet Socialist. The First Deputy Premier was the Communist Władysław Gomułka. Fourteen of the twenty-one members of the government were Lublin Poles, while Moscow's trusted stooge, Bierut, continued to function as President of the Polish Republic.

The Polish government was recognized by both Britain and the United States on July 5, at Truman's request. The recognition was one of the first acts of the new American Secretary of State, James F. Byrnes, who took office on July 3. As Churchill saw it, all the Polish parties, except Stalin's Communist puppets, were in a hopeless minority in the Polish coalition government which the Western Powers had recognized. However, he resigned himself to this act of appeasement — though only after all his efforts during the spring of 1945 had failed to create a partnership with the United States for what he called "an early and speedy showdown and settlement with Russia."[14]

In the spring of 1945 Churchill had reached the conclusion that Soviet Russia had become a "mortal danger." He saw "a great failure and an utter breakdown of what was settled at Yalta." He urged "dogged pressure and persistence," because otherwise "Eastern Europe will be shown to be excluded from the terms of the Declaration on Liberated Europe," and the West "shall be excluded from any jot of influence in that area." He spoke already of an "iron curtain" drawn upon the Soviet front. He was convinced that "a new front must be immediately created" against the Soviet onward sweep. He urged that the Western armies should meet the Russians "as far east as possible," that they should take Berlin and Prague — though Vienna, another of Churchill's objectives, had already been lost to the Russians. When because of American objections he was unable to change Allied strategy in the last days of the war, he wanted to maintain the Western armies, because he was convinced that above all "a settlement must be reached on all major issues between the West and the East in Europe *before the armies of democracy melted,* or the Western allies yielded any part of the German territories. . . ."[15]

Almost ten years later, in November 1954, Churchill revealed in a speech to his constituents at Woodford that in the spring of 1945 he had ordered Field-Marshal Montgomery to stack the arms of surrendered German troops for possible reissue if the Russians advanced too far west. It is debatable whether the order, and especially its disclosure, was wise or unwise. In any case, the order itself was further evidence of Churchill's prompt reaction to the Soviet Union's treacherous behavior in the spring of 1945.

Following the German surrender on May 8, Churchill urged Truman several times not to withdraw the American armies from the western borderland of Czechoslovakia and from the areas in Germany which were assigned to the Soviet zone of occupation. The withdrawal, he argued, should be made only when accompanied by "the settlement of many great things which would be the true foundation of world peace." Truman and his advisers thought, however, this would harm relations with the Russians. All Western troops began withdrawing on June 21 from an area four hundred miles long and one hundred and twenty miles at its greatest depth.[16]

It was of course not only the size of the area abandoned to the Russians that mattered. Churchill opposed the withdrawal of troops because he saw that "the Soviet menace . . . had already replaced the Nazi foe." He realized that only the military might of the West, if anything, could force the Russians to respect the Yalta agreements. But he was unable to gain American support for his new policy. The American policy-makers seemed to regard the East-West conflict in Europe as a dispute mainly between Britain and Russia. They felt the United States could stand between Russia and Britain as a "friendly mediator, or even arbiter."[17] They were anxious to concentrate American forces — and to engage Russia's help — in the unfinished war against Japan. Under these circumstances, Churchill's last hope was that his meeting with President Truman and Generalissimo Stalin, the new Big Three conference which was scheduled to take place in Potsdam, might save the situation.

Churchill attended only the first half of the Potsdam conference, which began on July 17. On July 25, he returned to London to learn the result of the elections. The Conservative party's defeat at the polls ended Churchill's premiership and his attendance at the Potsdam conference. In his memoirs, however, Churchill disclosed that he had planned a "showdown" with the Russians, or even a "public break," at the end of the conference. He pointed out especially that neither he nor Eden would ever have agreed to the Western Neisse as the frontier of Poland.[18]

Even more weighty reasons, for that matter, than the problem of Poland's western frontiers called for a showdown. The entire East European situation was in fact grave enough to call for a drastic reappraisal of the West's policy toward Soviet Russia. But whatever the basis, it is hard to imagine how Churchill could have carried out his "showdown" plan, with Western public opinion so overwhelmingly friendly toward Soviet Russia. Nor would it seem that Roosevelt's death contributed materially to the failure of the new policy which Churchill was advocating behind the scenes, although Churchill himself referred to the "deadly hiatus" and the "melancholy void" which existed "between the fading of President Roosevelt's strength and the growth of President Truman's grip of the vast world problem."[19]

The real "deadly hiatus" which cost the West the fruits of victory resulted from the failure of the Western Powers to integrate the democracies into a socially progressive and spiritually dynamic international force. At the war's end, the Western democracies stood, with their atomic bomb which forced Japan into surrender (August 15), with their armies stronger than the world had ever seen, not knowing how to use their power effectively in the service of democracy and peace. There was no lack of willingness in the West to help the war-torn world. The United States, with its tremendous wealth and economy unscathed by war, stood ready to help needy peoples with food and supplies; for some time, American aid even continued to flow into countries which had developed strongly anti-Western attitudes under Communist governments. In 1945–46, American-supported UNRRA shipped more than a billion dollars' worth of aid to the Central and Eastern European countries in the Soviet orbit; Poland received 481 millions, Yugoslavia 420, Czechoslovakia 270, Albania 24 millions; Hungary, one of the worst devastated countries, as well as Romania and Bulgaria, also received some Western aid, although as former enemy states they were not eligible for UNRRA aid.

Unfortunately, Western willingness to aid the world economically was not matched with ability to act politically. The Western nations were very slow to comprehend the swiftly changing international situation. Individual domestic problems absorbed their attention as soon as the great struggle was over. They demobilized much too soon, hopeful that the world's peace would be assured by the United Nations. In Europe, the Western victors concentrated on what at that time were believed to be the basic provisions for peace — namely, punishing Germany and establishing friendly relations between Soviet Russia and the Middle Zone nations. And although Russia's behavior was anything but cooperative, the Western democracies, as if gripped by a deadly inertia, kept repeating to themselves, and to those who were looking to them for guidance, the old wartime slogan, "Get along with Russia!" — a slogan now shorn of its one-time realism and signifying nothing but appeasement of the new aggressor.

14 From Potsdam to Prague

The Potsdam conference of the Big Three was held from July 17 to August 2, 1945. President Truman and Generalissimo Stalin, with their foreign ministers, Byrnes and Molotov, led the American and Russian delegations respectively. Because of the British Labour party's electoral victory (July 25), the places of Churchill and Eden were taken during the second half of the conference by the new Prime Minister, Clement R. Attlee, and his Foreign Secretary, Ernest Bevin.

One of the major objectives of the Potsdam conference, as stated by Secretary of State Byrnes, was to reach agreement on "plans for carrying out the Yalta Declaration on Liberated Europe, with the hope of ending the constant friction which had prevailed over Russian policy in Eastern Europe since the Crimea Conference." The American delegation (and for that matter the British delegation headed by Attlee) contemplated no "showdown" with Russia such as Churchill had planned. On the contrary, as Byrnes put it, in words true for Britain and Western public opinion at large as well as for America: "The Soviet Union then had in the United States a deposit of good will as great, if not greater, than that of any other country."[1]

With this good will toward Russia, hardly justifiable by Russian behavior between Yalta and Potsdam, the conference reached a series of agreements. The principal agreement concerned the establishment of a Council of Foreign Ministers. The task of the council was to prepare treaties of peace with the European enemy states, first with Italy, Bulgaria, Romania, Hungary and Finland, and then with Austria and Germany. Thus the Western Powers, instead of facing the Soviet menace directly, decided upon a new round of gambling with the Russians. It was the West's hope that an early peace settlement in Europe, accompanied by the withdrawal of Soviet occupation forces, would ultimately result in an effective carrying out of the Yalta Declaration on Liberated Europe. Apart from this distant hope, the conference produced nothing that could restrain Soviet aggressiveness.

Western complaints against Russian policy in the liberated countries were indignantly rejected by Stalin. He was "against sovietization of any of those countries," Stalin assured Churchill while reminding him once again that Russia was not meddling in Greek affairs. Bierut, the Communist President of Poland, went even further in his promises than Stalin. He told Churchill: "Poland will develop on the principles of Western democracy."[2] It was written into the protocol of the conference that Poland would hold "free and unfettered elections as soon as possible on the basis of universal suffrage and the secret ballot." The Big Three agreed also to improve the work of the Allied Control Commissions in Romania, Bulgaria and Hungary. But the value of all these agreements, like those of Yalta, depended upon Soviet good faith.

In the case of the reparation agreements reached by the conference, the Western Powers were evidently not aware of the concessions they were granting to the Russians. It was agreed that Russia's reparation claims should be met from, among other things, "German external assets" in eastern Austria, Hungary, Romania and Bulgaria. The Western experts did not foresee, however, that since the rights and properties seized by the Nazis in these countries were enormous the Soviets would claim to be the owners of a considerable part of the Danubian economy. The Russians thereupon, with a display of false generosity, offered these "assets" as their contribution to the establishment of "jointly owned" nationalized companies in the occupied countries, thus effectively laying the economic foundations of the Soviet colonial empire in the Danube Valley.

The case of Poland was as always the main point of East-West disagreement during the Potsdam conference. Confronted with a *fait accompli,* the Western Powers reluctantly agreed to the German territories east of the Oder-Neisse line remaining under Polish administration, while the final delimination of the Polish-German frontiers should await the peace settlement. The Soviet annexation of Königsberg and the adjacent area (half of East Prussia) was also approved. Finally the Western Powers gave their consent to the expulsion of the Germans from Czechoslovakia and Poland, including the territories under Polish administration, with the provision that the transfers should be effected "in an orderly and humane manner," as if such acts, however orderly in execution, could ever be humane. The Poles from the provinces lost to Russia in the east were to be resettled to the west and take the place of the expelled Germans. The land of the Germans in Czechoslovakia, on the other hand, was a net gain for the Czechs. The Western Powers also approved the expulsion of the Germans from Hungary. However, it was not mentioned at the time of the Potsdam conference that the expulsion of the Germans of Hungary was tied in with a Czech plan to expel the Hungarians of Czechoslovakia — that is to say, the Germans to be expelled from Hungary were to make room for the Hungarians marked for expulsion from Czechoslovakia.

In Potsdam both Stalin and the Communist Poles pretended that the number of Germans marked for expulsion from Poland would be insignificant. "The German population had retreated westward with the German armies. Only the Poles remained," said Stalin.[3] In fact, over five million Germans were expelled by the Poles — in a rather disorderly manner — after Potsdam. In somewhat more orderly fashion, though replete with atrocities, the Czechs expelled, according to their own statistics, 2.6 million Germans. But they did not succeed in expelling all the Hungarians from Czechoslovakia, because Western objections were raised at the Paris Peace Conference in the summer of 1946. Before then, about 100,000 Hungarians were forced to leave Czechoslovakia, most of them on the basis of a bilateral Hungaro-Slovak population exchange agreement, concluded in February 1946; for the approximately 500,000 Hungarians remaining in Czechoslovakia, the Slovaks made life miserable.

Soviet-occupied Hungary and Romania, and Tito's Yugoslavia, deported their German minorities according to Communist directives, either to Germany or Russia — although Romania and Yugoslavia were not authorized at all by the Potsdam conference to expel their Germans. However, most of the Saxons of Transylvania escaped expulsion.

The Council of Foreign Ministers, Potsdam's hopeful creation, first met in London in September 1945. The meeting was a complete failure. Western strategy to resolve East-West differences by a speedy conclusion of the peace treaties clashed with Soviet delaying tactics.

The chief obstacle blocking the conference was Soviet Foreign Minister Molotov's insistence that the Western Powers recognize *all* of the East European governments. He suspected the Western Powers of hostility toward the Soviet Union. Referring to the Romanian government, for instance, he asked: "Should we overthrow it because it is not liked by the United States Government, and set up a government that would be unfriendly to the Soviet Union?" Secretary of State Byrnes in turn suspected that East-West "friendship" would require the West to let the Soviet Union establish "complete suzerainty" over the Eastern European states. But the "deposit of good will" the Soviet Union had in the United States gave Byrnes other ideas too. He was "impressed" by the Soviet statements that Russia "sought security" against Germany. He proposed therefore a twenty-five-year treaty between the four principal powers for the demilitarization of Germany. The American proposal, however, failed to impress Molotov.[4]

The Western Powers were particularly disgusted with the governments of Romania and Bulgaria, where the Russians so brazenly flouted the Yalta agreements. But in order to demonstrate their friendliness and fairness, both the United States and Britain extended recognition to the governments of Austria and Hungary, where the Soviet behavior was less disappointing. In fact, the Hungarian general election on November 4 was the only "free and unfettered" election that took place in the countries *under Soviet occupation.* It was not, of course, entirely free from Soviet interference; but at least it was a democratic election which could not have been held under Hungary's pre-war reactionary rulers. Czechoslovakia, too, had a free election, but it took place in May 1946 after the Soviet troops had evacuated the country.

It can only be surmised that Western firmness could have stopped Soviet aggressiveness. It is certain, however, that Western softness ruined whatever chances existed for saving Eastern Europe from complete Soviet domination. The West's appeasement policy toward Russia was led by the United States. Critics of the Secretary of State, James F. Byrnes, have often pointed out his inexperience in foreign affairs. Sumner Welles, for instance, spoke of Byrnes's profound ignorance of even the rudimentary facts of international life.[5] Whatever his shortcomings, however, it seems that Byrnes's conduct of American foreign policy was in harmony with the public opinion then prevailing in the West, and even in accordance with the fundamental meaning of the Yalta agreements — namely, that friendship between Russia and her western neighbors should be the cornerstone of peace in Europe.

Surely there was no secret about what Russia's interpretation of "friendship" was. Western appeasement of Russia was nevertheless continued on the assumption of Byrnes's slogan that "peace breeds peace," and in the wishful thought that the Yalta principles pledging democracy and freedom to the liberated countries of Europe might with a general peace settlement somehow prevail.

Byrnes, after his return from the unsuccessful London meeting of the Council of Foreign Ministers, in a speech delivered on October 31, at the New York *Herald Tribune* Forum, outlined the American attitude toward Eastern Europe in these words: "Far from opposing, we have sympathized with . . . the effort of the Soviet Union to draw into closer and more friendly association with her Central and Eastern European neighbors. We are fully aware of her special security interests in the arrangements made for the occupation and control of the former enemy states." Echoing Byrnes's ideas, Under-Secretary Dean Acheson, speaking at a rally sponsored by the National Council of American-Soviet Friendship in New York on November 14, said: "We understand and agree with them [the Soviet Union] that to have friendly governments along her borders is essential both for the security of the Soviet Union and for the peace of the world."

In this spirit, a further act of appeasement was committed when the Big Three Foreign Ministers (Byrnes, Bevin, Molotov) met again in Moscow in December. In order to end the East-West impasse over recognition of the governments in the Soviet sphere, and thus clear the way for the peace negotiations, the conditions under which the West was ready to recognize Russia's satellites were now greatly reduced. It was agreed that in each of the still contested countries, Romania and Bulgaria, two of that country's opposition representatives should enter the government. In Romania a Soviet-British-American Three-Power Commission was appointed to act as consultant; but in Bulgaria the Soviet authorities alone were entrusted with assisting the political parties to reach agreement.

In Romania, the Three-Power Commission, which consisted of Vyshinsky and the British and American Ambassadors in Moscow, Clark Kerr and Harriman, agreed on the two representatives of the National Peasant and Liberal parties, whereupon recognition was promptly granted to the "new" government. But in Bulgaria, where Vyshinsky alone assisted, the negotiations with the opposition Agrarian and Socialist party representatives ended in failure. Thus Bulgaria remained the only country in Eastern Europe where the government was unable to meet even the greatly reduced conditions required for Western recognition. In spite of that, however, the Bulgarian government was soon recognized; the West pressed no further the controversy over recognition, turning its attention instead to the work of drafting the peace treaties.

The Moscow agreements of the Big Three Foreign Ministers on Romania and Bulgaria made a mockery of the Yalta agreements. They were something like, or even worse than, Churchill's notorious percentage arrangements of 1944. But Churchill himself had long recognized the futility of his dealings with Stalin, and, when the Western governments were reluctant even to mention publicly their difficulties with the Russians, Churchill became the chief critic of the appeasement policy.

In his famous address at Westminster College in Fulton, Missouri, on March 5, 1946, the British ex-Premier described the "iron curtain" which had been spread across Europe from Stettin to Trieste. To halt the "expansive and proselytizing tendencies" of the Soviet Union, he urged a "fraternal association," leading eventually to common citizenship, between the United States and the British Empire. And, although Churchill did not think that Russia desired war, he warned that Russia admired nothing so much as strength. Union of the democracies and firmness toward Russia: these were indeed the essentials of the policy needed for the West's defense. But Churchill as opposition leader in the House of Commons was no more successful than he had been during the last months of his premiership, in stopping the West's appeasement of Russia.

With American demobilization the West's military strength, which was the asset Russia admired above all, melted away from Europe as Churchill had feared, while the West now focused its policy on the drafting of the first five peace treaties with former enemy states, Italy, Bulgaria, Romania, Hungary and Finland. The irony of this period of peacemaking was that while the Western Powers were anxious to speed up work on the peace treaties in the hope that termination of the state of war and withdrawal of occupation forces would reduce Russian influence, the Russians were rapidly extending their grip over the whole of Eastern Europe, including former allied as well as former enemy countries. In two of the former enemy states, Bulgaria and Romania, sovietization made great headway behind the facade of the "National Front" coalition governments. In Hungary, where alone of the Soviet-occupied countries a promising start had been made toward democracy, with the free elections of 1945, the chief aim of Soviet tactics was to destroy the Smallholders' party which represented the majority of the electorate (57 percent) in the coalition government.

Communist strategy to seize power by infiltration, terror and the splitting up of anti-Communist forces ("polarization" of the enemy, as Communist jargon called it) was not confined to the former enemy states. The pattern was basically the same everywhere: the Communists seized control of the "levers of power," in particular the security police, the army general staff and the publicity machine.[6] They wiped out the independent Socialist workers' organizations by "uniting" them with the Communist parties. They crushed peasant resistance to communism by destroying the independent agrarian parties.

In Poland the target of Soviet attacks was Mikołajczyk's agrarian Polish People's party, a suppressed minority in the coalition government, but representative of the majority of the Polish people. Meanwhile, in Yugoslavia no Soviet interference was needed to promote communism: Tito was both determined and sufficiently strong to extirpate the oppponents of his Communist dictatorship. The dramatic climax of Tito's unscrupulous drive against his enemies was the execution of Draža Mihailović, his rival in the partisans' war against Germany.

Only in Czechoslovakia did Communists and non-Communists continue to cooperate more or less successfully. There the governmental coalition was built on more solid foundations than elsewhere in Central and Eastern Europe, because Communists and non-Communists were in agreement on basic points of national policy: to make Czechoslovakia into a homogeneous Slav state, and to carry out radical socialistic reforms. This agreement was enhanced by the fact that potential opposition to the government had already been suppressed prior to the formation of the coalition. The Czechoslovak Agrarian party, once the strongest in the country, was suppressed after liberation for its guilt of collaboration with the Germans, although the party as a whole was certainly not guilty. Thus, the political force of the Agrarians — the party of the peasants that is, which everywhere else in Central and Eastern Europe was the chief antagonist of the Communists in the coalition governments — was eliminated from the Czechoslovak political scene.

The cohesion of the Prague coalition was strengthened especially by agreement on the expulsion of the non-Slavs from Czechoslovakia (about one-quarter of the country's post-war population). The expulsion of Germans and Hungarians was a most popular program of exalted nationalism; a great many Czech and Slovak nationalists, who found themselves in agreement with the Communists on this issue, were prone to overlook basic differences separating them from the Communists. Likewise, the Czech nationalists were further encouraged to trust the Communists on the strength of a common position with regard to the Slovak question.

When troubles with the Communists began in Slovakia's politics — prior even to similar occurrences in the Czech lands, stronghold of the Communist party — these troubles were explained by the Prague government as being merely the result of reactionary influences among the Slovaks. There were such influences, no doubt. But a great many Czechs were also disposed to accept such sweeping explanations mainly because they were irritated by feuds over the scope of Slovakia's autonomy, intertwined as these feuds were with the old dispute as to whether the Czechs and Slovaks were one nation or two. The Communists themselves followed opportunistic tactics concerning this delicate issue. Courting the favors of the Slovaks after liberation in 1945, they stood for greater Slovak autonomy in a revision of Czech-Slovak relations along the lines of a federal union, which was a program popular with masses of Slovaks hostile to the recreation of old, Czech-dominated Czechoslovakia. Following the 1946 elections, however, the Communists changed tactics when their popular rivals in Slovakia, the Democratic party — a creation chiefly of former Agrarians opposed to communism — took the lead as champions of Slovak autonomy. The change of tactics consisted of switching Communist support to the Czech nationalists, favoring centralism and less autonomy for the Slovaks in line with Beneš's conception of a single Czechoslovak nation. This change of tactics, in turn, may well have strengthened the Czechs' confidence in Communist loyalty. Thus Czech-Slovak rivalry brought grist only to the Communist mill.[7]

In accordance with their divide-and-conquer tactics, the Communists evidently did not mind if tension developed between Czechs and Slovaks. And tension reached a high point in 1947 with the hanging of Tiso, former president of "independent" Slovakia, the capital punishment being favored mainly by the Czech nationalists and by the Communists who were setting the pace in executing war criminals everywhere. Many, but not all, of these sentences will be upheld before the bar of history.

While the Communists were leading the campaign of retribution for crimes committed during the Hitler era, they were themselves perpetrating criminal acts. In spite of official tact toward Soviet Russia, the Western governments could not help but notice violations of the Yalta agreements in the Soviet sphere of influence. Western protests against rigged elections, arbitrary arrests, unfair trials, coercion, intimidation, violence and disregard of international obligations in the Soviet satellites soon became a matter of Western diplomatic routine. The battle of diplomatic notes was on, while the Big Four Foreign Ministers worked on the first five peace treaties.

The peace conference convened in Paris on July 29, 1946. The Big Four made all the decisions, both before and during the conference. The peace terms were dictated, very much as after the First World War, although the vanquished were invited to attend the conference, and allowed to state their case.

The first five peace treaties did not tackle the central problem of Europe, which was Germany. They did not even deal fully with the problem of the smaller nations of Central Europe, inasmuch as Austria was not included in the peace settlement. The chief causes of past enmity between the Danubian countries, the territorial disputes between Hungary and the former Little Entente, were, however, partly covered by the conference. The Hungarian peace delegation made a modest attempt to achieve territorial revision of the unjust Trianon Treaty, but was lucky to get off with no more punishment than the loss of some more Hungarian territory, the so-called Bratislava bridgehead, which Czechoslovakia coveted.

The transfer to Czechoslovakia of the Bratislava bridgehead, Hungarian-populated as it was, violated the ethnic principle; moreover the incorporation of additional Hungarians into Czechoslovakia lacked logic, since simultaneously the Czechs were pressing for the expulsion of those Hungarians who had already been incorporated into Czechoslovakia after the First World War. The Hungarians fought desperately against expulsion. If the Czechs wanted to expel the Hungarians — so Hungary's peace delegation argued — they should also return the land on which those half a million or so Hungarians (mostly peasants) had lived from time immemorial. But the Czech Foreign Minister, Jan Masaryk, retorted haughtily: "Who won the war, the United Nations, or Hungary?"[8] The Western Powers went to the rescue of the Hungarians, and the Soviet-supported Czech proposal to expel the Hungarians from Czechoslovakia was finally defeated.

There was a brief flare-up of the old Hungaro-Romanian controversy over the ownership of Transylvania and the future of the close to two million Hungarians under Romanian rule. The armistice of 1944 had pledged Transylvania, "or the greater part thereof," to Romania, and the Hungarians were trying to get at least part of it. But the Russians backed up the Romanians, with the result that the Hungarian claims were ruled out. The Hungarians kept silent about their half a million co-nationals in Yugoslavia — in deference to Tito, who was then thought of as Stalin's formidable Balkan lieutenant. Nor was mention made, of course, of the 100,000 Hungarians living in the former Czechoslovak Ruthenia, who since 1945 had been subjects of Stalin's Russia. Thus the Paris Peace Conference, with Soviet Russia present, confirmed essentially the territorial provisions of the Trianon Treaty which the Western Powers had drawn up after the First World War in Soviet Russia's absence. Then, in the name of international justice, the Communists had denounced the treaty as a work of bourgeois imperialism. Now, in a frenzy of Pan-Slav nationalism, the Russian Stalinists and their Slavic satellites believed the provisions to be too good for the non-Slav Hungarians.

Vanquished Bulgaria was luckier than Hungary. She was allowed to retain Southern Dobrudja, a territory which she had obtained from Romania with Hitler's aid. Bulgaria's right to Southern Dobrudja, based on the ethnic principle, was no stronger than Hungary's territorial demands. But Hungary could only appeal to the sense of justice of the peace conference, while Bulgaria had more realizable assets to call upon. She was a Slavic country, her regime was already firmly under Communist control, and therefore she enjoyed the support of Soviet Russia. Moreover, the former owner of Southern Dobrudja, Romania, did not question Bulgaria's right to that territory. Romania was satisfied with the whole of Transylvania, which she had regained from Hungary. The transfer of Transylvania was to compensate Romania also for the loss of Bessarabia, which, since the First World War, had changed hands four times between Romania and Russia.

Thus, Hungary alone, among Hitler's former Danubian satellites, bore the consequences of defeat without any mitigation: but then, Hungary, unlike the other Nazi satellites, had had no chance to escape the opprobrium of her association with Germany. Slovakia and Croatia could hide their Nazi record behind the victory-facade of resuscitated Czechoslovakia and Yugoslavia; Romania and Bulgaria could invoke their participation in the last phase of the war against Hitler; but

Hungary had been stigmatized as the last fighting ally of Nazi Germany, and was dealt with accordingly.

Among the Danubian victors Yugoslavia, with her annexation of Venezia Giulia, made the most significant territorial gain. The Italo-Yugoslav battle for Trieste, however, ended in a tie. Trieste was proclaimed a "free territory" — a very sound status for a city whose port is the natural outlet to the sea for all the landlocked Central European countries, notably Austria, Hungary and Czechoslovakia. Under the prevailing post-war circumstances, however, Trieste could not fulfill her natural role as a "free territory." And she held her potentially sound status only until 1954, when she was returned to Italy by virtue of an Italo-Yugoslav agreement, with the blessing of the Western Powers.

The peace treaties were signed in Paris on February 10, 1947, but the expectation that they would be instrumental in reducing Soviet influence in Central Europe proved entirely unrealistic. In Hungary and Romania, even the peace treaties entitled the Russians to keep military units to maintain "lines of communication" to their zone of occupation in Austria. But no treaties, however perfect, could have forced the Russians out of the Danube Valley anyway. The Communists, far from withdrawing, were stepping up their offensive throughout Central and Eastern Europe.

The Western Powers themselves began to realize the futility of their policy of appeasement. In January 1947, General George C. Marshall succeeded Byrnes, and under the new Secretary of State American foreign policy began to change from appeasement to containment. On March 12, 1947, the Truman Doctrine was announced, which pledged aid to Greece and Turkey in particular, and support to free peoples in general "who are resisting attempted subjugation by armed minorities or by outside pressure." Secretary Marshall's Harvard address on June 5 set in motion the European economy recovery program known as the Marshall Plan. Theoretically the Marshall Plan extended American economic aid to all European nations. Its avowed purpose, however, was "the revival of a working economy in the world so as to permit the emergence of political and social conditions in which free institutions can exist." This was a direct challenge to the Soviet purpose of destroying what the West called "free institutions," and it was small wonder that the Soviet Union neither participated herself, nor allowed her satellites to participate, in the American aid program.

The East European countries did not benefit from the slowly changing

Western policy. On the contrary, as the East-West tension mounted, Soviet Russia rushed through what remained to be done to complete the conquest of Eastern Europe.

True, American aid saved Greece, where revival of civil war in 1946, with support rendered to the Communist guerrillas by the three northern neighbors (Albania, Yugoslavia and Bulgaria), had created a critical situation. American aid also strengthened Turkey's power of resistance against Soviet Russia. Elsewhere, however, Western aid against Communist aggression was as a rule limited to notes of protest.

In Hungary the decisive moment, portending the end of the democratic prelude to Communist dictatorship, came in February 1947, when Béla Kovács, general secretary of the Smallholders' party, was arrested by the Soviet authorities on charges of reactionary conspiracy. Toward the end of May a Communist coup overthrew the government of the Smallholders' premier, Ferenc Nagy, who was also accused by the Communists of being involved in this alleged conspiracy. But in fact, the Smallholders' party was not involved in any conspiracy, and the accusation against it by the Communists was a blow against democratic elements. For though the party was not altogether immune to reactionary influences, its bulk was made up of peasants who were stalwart supporters of agrarian reform, the backbone of Hungarian democracy in the making. Premier Nagy was vacationing in Switzerland at the time of the coup and he was called to return in order to clear himself of the Communist charges. With the choice of becoming a martyr or an exile, he chose the latter. His successor was an obscure figure of his own party. But the country's real boss was now Mátyás Rákosi, one of the outstanding figures of international communism and a self-confessed practitioner of so-called "salami tactics," which consisted of slicing up the opposition piece by piece until all opposition was destroyed.

Following the Communist coup in Hungary, new elections were held in the summer of 1947. In spite of intimidation and fraud, the Communist party gained only 22 percent of the votes (as against 17 percent in 1945), while the *ad hoc* organized opposition, lucky to have survived the pre-election terror, the Independence party and the Catholic Democratic People's party, received 30 percent. The remaining votes went to the Smallholders and the National Peasants, who, purged of their democratic leaders, became mere tools of the Communists in the "coalition." Soon all the opposition parties, harassed by the Communists, were disbanded, and their leaders fled to the West.

In August–September 1947, the spotlight was turned on the rule of terror in Bulgaria, when the peasant leader, Nikola Petkov, was tried and executed. Dimitrov, the country's Communist dictator, later declared he could not pardon Petkov because the Western Powers had intervened in his behalf, and this constituted interference with Bulgaria's sovereignty. Implied in Dimitrov's statement was the warning that Western protests would not deter the Communists from their chosen path — quite the contrary.

The next step in Communist strategy was announced on October 5, with the formation of a Communist Information Bureau (Cominform). One of Stalin's right-hand men, Andrei Zhdanov, was secretary general of the new organization; and the members included not only the Communist parties of the Eastern bloc — Soviet Russia, Poland, Czechoslovakia, Hungary, Yugoslavia, Romania and Bulgaria — but also those of France and Italy. Thus did the Communist International (Comintern), which had been disbanded during the Second World War, reappear under a new name. The establishment of the Cominform indicated also the vanishing importance of the Slav Committee; the accent in Moscow's policy was shifting from Slav solidarity to Communist solidarity.

In October the aged leader of the Romanian Peasant party, Iuliu Maniu, was put on trial, to be sentenced to life imprisonment. In the same month Mikołajczyk was accused by the Communists of being an "agent of Western imperialists" and he fled from Poland. In December, Michael, King of Romania, then a figurehead only, abdicated and left the country. Thus the last of the kingdoms in the Soviet orbit fell. (The British saved, in Greece, one of the five pre-war Balkan kingdoms.) Romania, proclaimed a republic, followed the example of Yugoslavia, Bulgaria, Albania — and Hungary, which had been a kingdom without a king ever since 1919. But republicanism, the cherished ideal of so many democrats in these former monarchies, did not expand the rule of democracy. Communist control over the satellites of the Soviet sphere of influence was being drawn tighter and tighter. Only one country, Czechoslovakia, seemed to be able to get along with Russia without succumbing to Soviet domination, as had once been hoped for all the countries of Central and Eastern Europe.

There is no evidence to show that the Russians chose Czechoslovakia for tactical reasons to be the last on their timetable of conquest. The fact, however, that Czechoslovakia was conquered last gave Russia all the tactical advantages of a brilliant strategy. Of all the countries in the post-war Soviet sphere of influence, Czechoslovakia, with her reputation for democracy, enjoyed the greatest popularity in the West. The apparent success of the Czech democrats in cooperating with both native and Russian Communists gave, therefore, many Western observers the false impression that the Czechs succeeded where others failed precisely because they were democratic. Conversely, in countries with reactionary and Fascist records, the failure of non-Communists to work in harmony with the Soviet Union was attributed to continued reactionary influence.

The Czech democrats themselves were not quite innocent of spreading false impressions. They made great efforts in the West to keep alive Czechoslovakia's reputation as a "bastion of democracy and peace," though, in cooperation with the Communists, they were guilty of some of the worst crimes ever committed against democracy in Central Europe. With the persecution and expulsion of the non-Slav ethnic minorities, post-war Czechoslovakia obliterated T. G. Masaryk's humanistic traditions. The Czechs did not worry unnecessarily, either, over the tragic destiny of their fellow democrats in neighboring countries; instead, they continued to propagate optimism concerning cooperation with Soviet Russia. They seemed to believe that the Czech Communists were not like other Communists, and that the Soviet Union had no reason to behave toward their country as she did toward others, because Czechoslovakia was a sincere friend and ally of the Soviet Union.

Czechoslovakia had a Communist premier in the person of Klement Gottwald, and, in proportion to the country's population, the strongest Communist party in the non-Communist world. In 1946 the Communists won the greatest success ever recorded in free elections: 38 percent of the total poll — 40 percent in the Czech lands, and 30 percent in Slovakia. From the summer of 1947 on, however, both the Czechoslovak Communists and the Soviet Union began to behave toward Czechoslovakia as they had elsewhere. The crisis started when Czechoslovakia first accepted, then, under Soviet pressure, turned down, the invitation to a preliminary conference in Paris on the Marshall Plan. Soon an alleged reactionary conspiracy was discovered in Slovakia. The Communists, realizing the decline of their popularity, began to pack the police department in anticipation of the new elections due in the summer of 1948. The crisis reached its climax in February 1948, with the Communists prepared for a showdown, while the non-Communists were confused and paralysed.

On February 21, the non-Communist members of the Prague government, with the exception of the Social Democrats, resigned in protest against the Communist seizure of the police department. The Communists swung into action, without concealing their determination to seize power by force if necessary. In an atmosphere of imminent civil war, on February 25, President Beneš appointed a new Gottwald government which satisfied the Communists. Beneš's choice lay between yielding and civil war. He knew that in case of civil war the Russians would not hesitate to interfere if, as seemed probable, Communist success were in jeopardy. On the other hand, from the West Beneš could expect hardly more help than diplomatic notes. In fact, after the Prague coup, the Western Powers not only protested individually, but also issued a joint American-British-French declaration, the first of this type, branding the events in Czechoslovakia as placing "in jeopardy the very existence of the principles of liberty."

Jan Masaryk remained foreign minister until March 10, when the free world was shocked to learn of his suicide. Rumor reported him murdered by the Communists. Rumors of the same type had been heard when Count Paul Teleki, the wartime premier of Hungary, committed suicide; at that time the Nazis were suspected of murder. The fact of Masaryk's suicide, unlike that of Teleki's, has never been proven to everybody's satisfaction. Yet the assassination theory can be discounted. It can safely be assumed that both Masaryk and Teleki ended their own lives, in utter exhaustion and desperation, when they realized the complete failure of their respective policies.[9]

The failure of the Czech democrats' pro-Soviet policy, which took the life of Jan Masaryk, also felled Eduard Beneš, who was the architect of that policy. Broken and sick, President Beneš vanished shortly after the February surrender. He resigned the presidency on June 7, and died the following September 3. "His passing symbolized the end of Czechoslovak democracy," Western comment said.[10] Actually, the Czech democracy which the West had learned to respect and admire had not been revived since the Second World War. It was a victim of the war.

"We made no mistake," said the Czech democrats after the Prague coup. "In the last resort it was two factors which we could not control which decided the fate of our country: the increasing tension between the U.S.S.R. and the Western Powers, and the dynamism of Soviet imperialism."[11] In substantial agreement with this analysis, some observers thought that Russia acted to bring Czechoslovakia into line with her other satellites under pressure of the gathering crisis between Tito's Yugoslavia and the Soviet Union. Soviet control of Czechoslovakia, it was said, had to be secured before the showdown with Tito.

The Tito affair broke into the open only on June 28, 1948, when it was announced that the Yugoslav Communist party had been expelled from the Cominform; earlier serious clashes between Tito and the Russians had, however, as we know now, coincided with the Czech crisis.[12] Tito had displayed impatience with Stalin's tutelage, and the Soviet dictator was determined to cure his Balkan disciple of his ambitions for independence. The Tito affair may well have influenced the timing of the Czech coup. Or possibly Stalin's expectation, in the winter of 1947–48, that the cold war between East and West might become hot may have impelled him to believe that a showdown with both Yugoslavia and Czechoslovakia was urgent. In any event, if the Russians could not stand a Communist independent Yugoslavia in their sphere of influence, they could tolerate even less a non-Communist independent Czechoslovakia, however friendly and cooperative.

The blindness of Czech democrats to the approaching catastrophe, despite the series of Communist seizures of power around them, was caused mainly by their great faith in Slav cooperation. Hubert Ripka, for instance, one of the leading Czech democrats, on November 7, 1947, just before the Communist coup, expressed his faith in Soviet Russia's respect for the "independent Slav nations administering their own affairs in their own way, according to their own law and their own national tradition." He paid the customary tributes to the Soviet revolution and the Soviet regime, declaring that the Czechoslovaks were "as equally convinced Russophiles as Sovietophiles. . . ."[13] After the Communist coup, Ripka stated in apology: "If the democrats of our country had allowed themselves to be drawn into an anti-Soviet policy . . . such a policy would never have been approved by the population. . . . The people did turn against Russia . . . only after they had seen for themselves that Moscow, in spite of the friendship of which we had given her so many proofs, had decided to put an end to our independence."[14]

It is true that the war had fired to unprecedented intensity the traditional pro-Russian sentiment of the Czechs. But their democratic leaders, too, were whipping up these feelings of Slav friendship for Soviet Russia. And most painful of all, their aspirations and motivations were not firmly anchored in the ideals of democracy. Of that, Beneš's Russian policy was a case in point.

15 *Beneš and the Russians*

During the Second World War Eduard Beneš, the exile, reached the zenith of his long political career. The contempt which so many of his countrymen had felt for him after Munich, when they considered him the gravedigger of Czechoslovakia and bankrupt as a statesman, had given way to the greatest popularity he had ever enjoyed. He embodied his people's hopes for liberation from Nazi tyranny. Beneš achieved also the greatest possible recognition by all the nations, East and West, allied in the struggle against Hitler.

He occupied, in fact, a unique position among members of the Grand Alliance. He represented a country whose democracy was highly respected in the West, and whose betrayal at Munich had become the symbol of past mistakes. He represented a country on whose behalf he was cooperating most successfully with Soviet Russia, an achievement which was then considered the symbol of victory and future peace.

During the period of Nazi-Soviet cooperation, Beneš did not join the Western chorus of indignation against Russia, nor did he share the disappointment which so many Western friends of the Soviet Union experienced. Rather he viewed the Nazi-Soviet cooperation as a temporary, though indeed ugly, consequence of Munich. Moscow had broken off diplomatic relations with the Czech exiles, while recognizing the pro-Nazi Slovak government in Bratislava. The Czech Communists, at that time, denounced Beneš as a "bourgeois chauvinist" and an "agent of Anglo-American capitalism" who sought to bring about "tragic clashes between the Czech nation and the German revolutionary working class."[1] Nevertheless Beneš did not lose hope that ultimately Soviet Russia would become an ally in the war against Nazi Germany.

When Hitler attacked Russia, and Russia became an ally of the West in the war against Hitler, Western pro-Soviet sentiment began to fall in line with that of Beneš. The motivations, too, were similar, such as a belief in the changing nature of communism and the need for a Slavic counterpoise to the Germans in Europe. On the other hand, Czech national aspirations gave to Beneš's Russian policy very distinct characteristics which were only vaguely understood in the West.

Beneš often said that repudiation of Munich by the Great Powers was "the sole remaining aim" of his life; but actually he wanted much more than the mere repudiation of Munich. He aimed, by expelling the Germans and Hungarians, who comprised over 30 percent of pre-war Czechoslovakia's population, to make the country into a "homogeneous" Slav national state. This was a program of territorial expansion, in disguised form, since the land made available by expulsion of Germans and Hungarians was to be colonized by Czechs and Slovaks.

With his ability to get along with both East and West, an aim cherished by many but attained by few, Beneš was successful in gaining both Eastern and Western support for Czechoslovakia's two chief post-war objectives: restoration of the pre-war frontiers and expulsion of the minorities.[2] The avowed aim of his policy was to establish post-war Czechoslovakia as a "bridge" between Western democracy and Eastern communism. But his main concern was to make Czechoslovakia safe from German aggression. He was convinced that no Munich could have occurred had the Western Powers and the Soviet Union been friends and allies. Moreover it was his conviction that should East-West cooperation fail after the Second World War "the world would race towards a new catastrophe, or rather, we should face another Munich and then the world would be plunged into another catastrophe." Therefore he believed "our main task is to bring about lasting understanding between the Anglo-Saxons and the Soviet Union."[3]

Beneš was proud of his contribution to the successful conclusion of the British-Soviet treaty in 1942.[4] He was eager to follow up the British-Soviet treaty with a Czechoslovak-Soviet treaty, which he accomplished in December 1943. And he rejoiced when General Charles de Gaulle's provisional government concluded a twenty-year French-Soviet treaty of alliance and mutual assistance in December 1944, patterned after the British-Soviet treaty.

In addition to working as a diplomat and politician for East-West cooperation, Beneš distinguished himself also as an ideologist of East-West rapprochement. In the enlarged edition of his wartime book *Democracy Today and Tomorrow,* he developed a program which foresaw the progressive disappearance of the differences between a democratic and a Communist state. If a democracy turned "left," that is to say if it nationalized its basic industries and expanded social reform, then it would achieve, economically, that progress which he thought had been made in Soviet Russia. On the other hand, he argued, the Soviet regime ought to develop and expand the sphere of political and cultural liberty, thereby turning, as he expressed it, "to the right."[5] Along the same lines of East-West synthesis, in his essays on *New Slav Policy,* he reached the conclusion that the two most important factors favoring the liberty of the Slavs were the ideas of the American democracy, in the form of President Wilson's program of national self-determination which had liberated the Slavs after the First World War, and the social ideas of the Soviet revolution.[6]

However, notwithstanding his hopes and theories about East-West unity, and his views on Czechoslovakia's role as a "bridge" between East and West, Beneš's policy was "east" of the center of the "bridge." He not only foresaw, but welcomed, Soviet Russia's dominant position in post-war Eastern Europe. To be sure, he also saw the Western Powers' disengagement from the affairs of the Middle Zone. But he did not merely adjust his policy to an inevitable situation; Beneš was the advocate of a policy which was Russian-oriented in any case. He hailed the rebirth of Russian nationalism. Slav solidarity, he believed, would be the leading tenet in Soviet post-war policy. Under Russia's protection, he thought, the Slavs would be safe forever from German aggression, from whose threat the Western Powers in the past had been either unable or unwilling to protect Eastern Europe. Moreover "the new Slavism," as Beneš liked to call the new age of Slavic policy, promised a fulfillment of Czechoslovakia's future, the transformation of pre-war heterogeneous, multinational Czechoslovakia into a homogeneous Slav national state. The United States and Britain had also approved Beneš's plan to expel Czechoslovakia's non-Slav nationalities. But they did it rather reluctantly and in vague terms. Beneš was bound to know that this plan, so obviously a violation of all rules of democratic state-making, could be carried out, if at all, only with the full support of Soviet Russia. Indeed Beneš's ideas about the revival of Czechoslovakia were poles apart from the Western democratic ideas which had inspired the founding of the state under Thomas G. Masaryk.

The Czech democrats, like many progressive democrats the world over, believed in the democratic potentialities of Soviet tyranny. But it was extreme nationalism, above all else, that drove Beneš and his followers into the arms of Soviet Russia. Had they not found their extreme nationalistic aspirations so perfectly in harmony with the new Slav course of Soviet policy, they probably would have been much more cautious.

Instead of being cautious, however, Beneš went ahead tirelessly to propagate the goodness of Russia's intentions. Apparently, having so successfully cemented friendly relations between his own country and the Soviet Union, he minimized the troubles which others (especially the Poles) were having with the Soviets. Those troubles, if carefully scrutinized, could have served to warn him of the dangers Czechoslovakia too might eventually face. But as Otto Friedman, a Czech democrat who did not come under the spell of Beneš's uncritical Russophilism, said: "He [Beneš] kept on persuading others, including President Roosevelt, that Russian interference need not be feared. . . . Thus, instead of warning others of the dangers that his country was likely to face, he was one of those who inspired that credulity towards the Russians which is mainly responsible for the post-war crisis in Europe."[7]

Beneš seemed to believe he could set the pattern of post-war cooperation between Soviet Russia and the countries of Eastern Europe. With this idea in mind, he went to Moscow in the winter of 1943–44, signing there a treaty of friendship, mutual assistance and post-war cooperation between Czechoslovakia and the Soviet Union. The plan of the treaty was only reluctantly approved by the United States and Great Britain. The Western Powers saw in it a return to the pre-war system of bilateral agreements, and a deviation from the global security system to be achieved through the United Nations. The British Foreign Office was especially critical lest the Czech-Soviet treaty isolate the Poles. The Polish government in exile shared this fear. The Poles opposed the Czech plan because, as Beneš admitted in his memoirs, they saw in it the end of their plans for a Central European federation. Nevertheless, Beneš, although a partner to the earlier Polish-Czechoslovak federation treaty, did not hesitate to supersede it with a Soviet-Czechoslovak treaty, believing that "if we are able to achieve complete accord with the Soviet Union, we shall be able to use this as an example. I expected that this would bring the Great Allies closer, that it would lessen and dispel the groundless suspicions. . . ."[8]

The Soviet-Czechoslovak treaty, signed on December 12, 1943, contained a so-called "Polish clause," which anticipated that similar treaties would be concluded between the Soviet Union and Poland on the one hand, and between Czechoslovakia and Poland on the other. These treaties and many more, between Soviet Russia and the countries of the Soviet orbit, were signed later; but instead of guaranteeing national independence as Beneš hoped, they were only instruments in the cynical game Soviet diplomacy was playing in Eastern Europe.

Hans Kohn saw the Czechoslovak-Soviet treaty in its proper historical perspective when he called it another Munich. The "justification" for both Munichs lay in the strategic situation; in 1938, at the time of the first Munich, Hitler was in as favorable a position in Central Europe as was Stalin later, when Beneš became partner to another Munich. Moreover, as Kohn pointed out, "the Czech liberals trusted, as Neville Chamberlain had in 1938, in the case of Hitler, that Stalin would keep the agreement and that the collaboration between communists and liberals was possible"; whereas, of course, the Communists stood as little by their agreements as Hitler had stood by his.[9]

However, those who trusted respectively the Fascist and Communist dictators also gave evidence of a remarkable degree of nationalist blindness. In the autumn of 1938, for instance, the Hungarians and Poles, unaware of the true meaning of the Munich tragedy, in a triumphant nationalist mood carved out from Czechoslovakia territories which they considered their rightful share. Likewise, in the winter of 1943–44, Beneš was in high spirits because his agreements with the Russians satisfied all his aspirations, including the ultra-nationalistic demand that the Germans and Hungarians be expelled from Czechoslovakia.

"We came to a complete agreement about everything!" — these were Beneš's words, recorded by his secretary, after his return from the final talks with Stalin.[10] Among the agreements was of course the Soviet pledge not to interfere in Czechoslovakia's internal affairs. And Beneš was especially hopeful that his agreements with Stalin would pave the way to a Soviet-Polish understanding. But when Czech-Soviet cooperation did not help to improve the relations between Russia and the other nations of Central and Eastern Europe, and when Soviet interference had blotted out one by one the independence of these nations, Beneš and the Czech democrats continued to hope for Soviet Russia's good intentions toward them. This hopefulness was not just a naive trust on the part of liberals, but was derived rather from the blindness of self-centered nationalists.

The great celebrations of Slav brotherhood which accompanied the signing of the Czech-Soviet treaty, inspired Beneš to make new declarations of faith in Soviet Russia's evolution toward democracy. For instance in a message to Jan Masaryk he said: "The ideological development since 1935 [when Beneš visited Moscow], and especially since the war, is great, genuine, and final. It would be a fundamental error to consider the dissolution of the Comintern, the new attitude towards religion, cooperation with the West, Slav policy, etc., merely as tactical moves. A new, definitive development is undeniable: it points towards a new Soviet empire which will be decentralized and will give each nation in the Soviet Union its firm place in the spirit of a new peoples' democracy. Out of the war a new Soviet Union will emerge, which will maintain the economic and social structure of the Soviet system, but will be completely new politically: it will be the leader of the Slavs and thereby a new place in the world will be secured both for the Soviet Union and for the Slavs. . . . They consider the treaty with us as the beginning of a new, very important political phase, and it may well serve as a pattern for all the Slavs."[11]

On his way back to London from Moscow, Beneš remarked to his secretary: "T. G. Masaryk persistently refused to believe that the Soviet regime would last. I wonder what he would say now?"[12] T. G. Masaryk would surely have been impressed by Soviet Russia's heroism and power of resistance during the Second World War, as was every true foe of fascism. But it is impossible to imagine President Masaryk in Beneš's role as a totalitarian Slav nationalist. True, Masaryk too, as a Slav and Czech nationalist, believed that a Slavic Central Europe, allied with Russia, would serve as a counterpoise to Germany. Before the Russian revolution he thought that "a Russian dynasty, in whatever form, would be most popular" in Bohemia; and even after the Bolshevik revolution, in his book *New Europe: The Slavic Point of View,* he wrote in 1918: "Europe, humanity, needs Russia, a free and strong Russia."[13] But he had never mistaken the Soviet Union for a free Russia. As a humanist and democrat, he never changed the opinion he had originally formulated as an eyewitness of the Bolshevik revolution. He thought of the Bolsheviks as Cicero thought of Caesar's murderers. They killed the Tsar, Masaryk once said, paraphrasing Cicero's famous saying on tyrannicide, but they did not kill tsarism.[14]

The resurrection of Czechoslovakia in 1945 under President Beneš's totalitarian nationalism differed considerably from the founding of the state in 1918 under President Masaryk's liberal-nationalist leadership. This difference represented the shocking degeneration of Central European nationalism under the impact of inter-war rivalries, nazism, the new war, and finally communism. But the greatest shock after the Second World War was that of all people the Czech democrats should take the lead in inciting the orgies of chauvinism.

President Masaryk too had believed in the nation-state, but more as a step toward a higher union among nations than as exclusively an aim in itself. After the First World War, Masaryk preached moderation as he led the return of the exiles from the West to the liberated homeland. He was determined to make Czechoslovakia into a model state, avoiding the errors of old Austria. Although in mapping out the boundaries of Czechoslovakia Masaryk too fell victim to nationalist excesses, nevertheless within the boundaries of the new state he condemned chauvinism and ethnic oppression.

President Beneš on the other hand, when he led the exiles back from the West after the Second World War, instead of acting as a moderator, headed and supported the instigators of national hatred in liberated Czechoslovakia. He made common cause with the Communists who were the leading force behind the gruesome atrocities committed in the German borderlands of Bohemia. In a frenzy of Czech nationalist fraternization with the Communists, Beneš did not suspect that Communist cruelty against the Germans would soon be turned against himself and his Czech democrats.

There was of course plenty of genuine and justifiable hatred against the Nazi German oppressors and their accomplices. However, the persecution of the minorities, aiming at their complete liquidation, was not a spontaneous outburst of bitterness. It was the result of a carefully prepared policy of vengeance carried out by the government. It was directed against both the Germans and the Hungarians. Both nationalities were treated as collectively guilty of fascism and complicity in the destruction of the state in 1938–39. The charge of collective guilt levelled against the defeated was as absurd as the title of collective innocence to which the victors were laying claim. The case of the Slovaks against the Hungarians was especially without foundation, because in 1938–39 Slovak resentment against the Czechs was one of the causes of Czechoslovakia's dissolution, and afterwards the Slovaks set up a Fascist state of their own.

Incited to violence by the government's program for an ethnically pure Slav Czechoslovakia, the Czechs and Slovaks outdid each other in acts of terrorism against the Germans and Hungarians. These atrocities led to such excesses that the Russian authorities interfered several times in order to stop them. The Czech democrats, while invoking the "humanitarian ideals of Masaryk," simultaneously incited the spirit of intolerance. President Beneš himself, at the height of the terror, delivered inflammatory speeches (for instance in Bratislava on May 9, and in Lidice on June 10, 1945), demanding that the country be cleared of minorities. The Czechs and Slovaks, he said, wished no longer to live in the same state with Germans and Hungarians. His notorious "presidential decrees," depriving the Germans and Hungarians of their citizenship rights, outlined the strategy by which Czechoslovakia was to be made into a "homogeneous" national state.[15]

While after the First World War Masaryk tried to avoid the errors of the Habsburgs, Beneš after the Second World War chose forms of vengeance akin to Hitler's methods. Czechoslovakia had travelled a long road from Masaryk's ideals by 1945, when a British observer, F. A. Voigt, made this sad commentary on the state of Czech democracy: ". . . The Czechs, who were amongst the most submissive of all the nations under German rule, have developed an unbridled nationalism. They have accepted a racial doctrine akin to Hitler's (with the Slavs, instead of the Germans, as the "master race") and methods that are hardly distinguishable from those of fascism. They have, in fact, become Slav National Socialists."[16] This censure of post-war Czechoslovakia was rather an isolated one, however. Millions of citizens were being expelled and their properties confiscated without compensation, thousands being confined to concentration camps, the schools of the minorities closed, and the use of their languages forbidden on the street and in the church; yet the press of the West continued to bill Czechoslovakia as a democratic country, or indeed as the only democratic country of the Soviet orbit.

When Oscar Jászi, an exiled democrat from Horthy's Hungary, and a friend of Masaryk's Czechoslovakia, revisited the Danubian countries in 1947, he was appalled by the "wholesale destruction, both physical and moral" of the national minorities in Czechoslovakia to which the enlightened public opinion of the world gave scarcely any attention. "Just forty years ago," Jászi wrote reminiscently, "R. W. Seton-Watson, the eminent English historian, published his book *Racial Problems in Hungary,* in which he denounced the sins of Hungarian feudalism against the national minorities of the country. This book became one of the strongest arguments for the dismemberment of Hungary in 1918.... Yet today one hears only the feeble voice of the persecuted, which is easily silenced. No book is written today by an influential foreign authority on 'Racial Problems in Czechoslovakia.'"[17] Professor Jászi, recalling his intimate personal contact with T. G. Masaryk, whom he deemed "the greatest man" of the First World War period, experienced his "greatest shock" after the Second World War in finding that the "successors of Masaryk . . . had adopted the philosophy of Hitler and Stalin."[18]

The Communist coup in February 1948 ended the short marriage between Czech democrats and Communists. The Czechs who fled abroad accused Stalin of treachery. The apologists of Beneš's Russian policy developed the theory of a double betrayal, according to which Beneš was driven into the arms of the Russians by the West's betrayal at Munich, only to be again betrayed by Stalin.[19] Few Czechs had the moral courage to confess the betrayal committed by the Czechs themselves; few Czechs seemed to realize that their unusually successful cooperation with the Communists, while it worked, worked mainly because they had turned their backs on democracy.

What made them do this? National chauvinism, which wiped out their sense of justice — such was the diagnosis arrived at by a Czech exile who remained true to Masaryk's critical thinking. And he added: "Injustice is the common denominator of communism and national chauvinism."[20]

Eduard Beneš played a role unique in Central Europe's tragic history from the monarchy of the Habsburgs to the tyranny of the Soviets. Out of the failure of evolution which frustrated attempts to transform the Habsburg Empire into a democratic federal union of equal nations, Beneš emerged as a leader of national revolution in Central Europe. For three decades he remained a dominant figure in European politics. He triumphed over the Habsburgs, the dynasty with the longest record of uninterrupted rule in European history.He took vengeance on Hitler, who destroyed national independence in Central Europe in an insane bid for Continental hegemony and German world domination. But Beneš's triumph was subverted by Stalin, who subjected the nations of Central Europe to his triumphant tyranny, while carrying out the old plans of Russian imperialism on the one hand, and making a new bid for Communist world domination on the other. The irony of the tragic end of Beneš's career lay in the great trust which he placed during the last years of his life in Stalin's Russia. Certainly this trust was interspersed with occasional doubts: but Beneš's trust in Russia was not shaken until it was too late to escape the consequences of his credulity.[21]

The deeper cause of Beneš's failure lay in the fundamentally false pattern of his policy. This pattern was not of his invention. It was the product of the age of nationalism. Its aim was the nation-state, an aim which sooner or later had mesmerized all the nations of the Habsburg Empire. It was an impossible aim, so far as being a solution of the problem of Central Europe was concerned, because it denied the principle of equality among nations, therefore tending to sharpen and perpetuate their rivalries instead of paving the way for peaceful cooperation among them. The greatly inflated dreams of the nation-states appeared to be possible, however, when the smaller nations of Central Europe had allied themselves with superior powers against their rivals.

This pattern of policy was first applied successfully by the Hungarians. By allying themselves with the Germans of Austria in the Compromise of 1867, the Hungarians assured their own supremacy over rival nationalities. This arrangement was supported by the ascendant power of imperial Germany until its defeat in 1918. Between the two world wars, Czech supremacy in Central Europe was maintained by an alliance system which Beneš's foreign policy built and manipulated; this system collapsed, however, when its cornerstone, France, failed to live up to her assigned role. After the Second World War, Beneš hoped, by substituting Russia for France, that he had found the perfect security for the Czech nation-state. Hence his daring advocacy of the expulsion of the Sudeten Germans, for he was not afraid that the German nation, though almost ten times bigger than the Czech, would ever be in a position to take revenge. He seemed to believe both in the lasting paralysis of defeated Germany and in Czechoslovakia's permanent protection under the wings of the powerful Soviet ally.

Although Beneš's policy toward the minorities differed fundamentally from President Masaryk's liberal program, Beneš's ideas concerning the security of Czechoslovakia were not altogether different from those advocated by the President Liberator. When Masaryk, during the First World War, arrived at the conclusion that an independent Czech national state could become viable, he based his optimistic views about Czechoslovakia's security on assumptions similar to Beneš's during the Second World War. Rejecting the idea of preserving the Habsburg

Empire in any form, and arguing against the objection that small nations cannot protect and support themselves, Masaryk anticipated a general diminishing of "military spirit and oppressive propensities" among the European nations; he hoped for a "longer time of peace" during which Czechoslovakia could "easily be consolidated"; and above all, he was confident that the new state could get its necessary protection "from alliances."[22]

What distinguished Czech nationalism up to the Second World War from that of the other nations of Central Europe was its democratic character — rooted, incidentally, in the petty-bourgeois Czech social traditions of the much disparaged Habsburg era. Admittedly the Czechs never acknowledged their rivals' equal rights to national self-determination; but the democratic environment of Czechoslovakia after the First World War ensured for the nationalities under Czech rule at least some measure of fair treatment. After the Second World War, led by Beneš and allied to the Communists, the Czech democrats earned for themselves a very different type of distinction. They were the authors of the perverted idea of the homogeneous nation-state, to be achieved by the totalitarian method of population expulsion.

Czech democracy was a unique product of the Habsburg era of Czech history. Its decline proved what havoc nationalism can create. Its collapse revealed the depth of disintegration, both political and moral, which the two world wars of the twentieth century had produced in Central Europe.

Part Three: The Aftermath — Eastern Europe since 1948

The Iron Curtain
since 1945
Petsamo
Murmansk
Archangel
NORWAY
SWEDEN
FINLAND
Oslo
Stockholm
Helsinki
Porkkala
Leningrad
Tallin
ESTONIA
Baltic Sea
SOVIET
UNION
Riga
LATVIA
Moscow
DENMARK
LITHUANIA
Kaunas
EAST
Berlin
GERMANY
R. Oder
Warsaw
POLAND
NETH.
Bonn
BELGIUM
WEST
GERMANY
Prague
CZECHOSLOVAKIA
FRANCE
R. Danube
CARPATHO-RUTHENIA
N. BUKOVINA
Vienna
Bratislava
SWITZERLAND
AUSTRIA
Budapest
BESSARABIA
HUNGARY
TRANSYLVANIA
Trieste
VENEZIA GIULIA
RUMANIA
Belgrade
Bucharest
Adriatic Sea
YUGOSLAVIA
S. DOBRUDJA
Black Sea
BULGARIA
Sofia
ITALY
Rome
Tirana
ALBANIA
Ankara
TURKEY
GREECE
Athens
Aegean Sea

Epilogue One: The Unfinished Struggle for Independence

With the Communist coup in Czechoslovakia, in February 1948, the westward expansion of Soviet power reached its full scope. The power-vacuum left in Central Europe by Germany's defeat in the Second World War had been filled. It was replaced by Soviet power. Pre-war independent Central Europe became Communist Eastern Europe with Soviet Russia as the overlord.

The East-West alliance which had defeated Hitler lay in ruins; likewise ruined were the Yalta agreements, with their expectation that the governments of the Middle Zone nations would be independent of, while friendly toward, the Soviet Union. In a series of cleverly manipulated moves, through deceit as well as force, the Soviets helped to hoist Communist dictatorships to power in Romania, Bulgaria, Hungary, Poland, and finally Czechoslovakia. Thus, while independent in name, these countries with a total population of about 70 million people became colonies, or so-called satellites, of the Soviet-Russian empire. The architect of this policy, Marshal Stalin, could take no little pride in his achievement. He had led Russia to victory in the greatest struggle of her history; he had moved Russia's frontiers westward into East Prussia and across the Carpathians into former Czechoslovak Ruthenia; he had extended Russian power, and with it the Communist revolution, across the satellites and the occupation zone of Germany, deep into the heart of the European continent.

But 1948 was not exclusively a year of triumph for Stalin's imperial communism. In June of that year, the Communist world was shaken by Yugoslavia's expulsion from the Cominform. Although called "expulsion," Yugoslavia's case was actually one of preventive "self-liberation" to forestall Russian domination. Tito's position was strong enough; he needed no Soviet support to maintain himself in power; he could afford to resist Soviet infiltration. And, although the overwhelming majority of Yugoslavia's 16 million people were not Communist, the country stood behind Tito in his bid for freedom from Soviet interference. The Tito affair struck a heavy blow at Soviet Russia's post-war policy of expansion. In a most drastic manner, it gave the lie to the Russians' contention that the so-called people's democracies were one happy family of Communist nations. Now even Tito, most prominent among Eastern Europe's Communist leaders, was to testify to Soviet Russia's oppression and exploitation of these nations. The Stalin-Tito break revealed the grave conflict which existed even on the Communist level between the people's democracies and Soviet Russia. It foreshadowed the struggles for independence to come against Soviet imperialism in the Communist-dominated nations.

And then too, 1948 witnessed the closing of ranks among the Western nations to forestall further Soviet expansion. The Marshall Plan, that great economic recovery program, was followed up now by a series of political and military moves. The Western nations were forging ahead, more resolutely than ever before, toward unity. They formed unprecedented alliances, like NATO, the first military alliance in peacetime between the United States and Europe. They also revived old ideas of federal union among the strife-torn European nations. Rather as in the Second World War, it was Churchill again who raised the banner of a United States of Europe. In the so-called cold war against the threat of Communist world domination, the terms "Western Union" and "Atlantic Community" became the popular watchwords of the free world. In actually repelling Communist militarism, too, the strength of Western unity made itself felt, in both Europe and Asia. The Soviet attempt to force the Western Powers from occupied Berlin by blockading the city (June 1948–May 1949) ended in failure. The Communist aggression in Korea (June 1950) met with collective resistance organized under the aegis of the United Nations. Thus Stalin's aggressive post-war policy produced something he was least eager to promote: a search for new forms of cooperation and unity among the nations of the West.

Mainly the Soviet aggression in Eastern Europe prompted the Western nations to unite. But the Russians' European satellites were not the main issue within the great East-West struggle led by the two superpowers of the post-war world, Russia and the United States. True, the West denounced the Russians for depriving these nations of their independence and for subjecting them to a rule of ruthless terror. Also, a heavy propaganda barrage was directed toward the satellites from the West, especially from the United States, on the principle of keeping the hope of freedom alive in the captive lands. But it was primarily a protective barrage in the interest of Western security. For the more the Russians were hampered in consolidating their puppet regimes, the less Eastern Europe could serve them as a base for aggression against the West. In addition, generous American military and economic aid was given to Tito: it was intended partly to back him up in his feud with the Russians, a feud which prompted him to adopt a somewhat less authoritarian form of Communist dictatorship; partly the aid was given in the hope of causing more trouble to the Soviet Union by encouraging, through Tito's example and his reward, the latent forces of "Titoism" in the satellites. Following the American election campaign of 1952, which was waged at the height of an anti-Communist propaganda crusade, the slogan for liberation of the satellites was frequently heard. But all the multiple expressions of Western sympathy for the satellites could hardly conceal the fact that both the chief concern of the West's policy and also the chief points of the East-West conflict lay elsewhere. They lay in the former colonial areas of Asia and Africa, where, as many distinguished Western experts believed, the global struggle between communism and democracy was bound to be decided. And as far as Europe was concerned, it was clear beyond doubt that there the cold war was being fought essentially for the control of Germany.

With the collapse of East-West cooperation the conditions envisaged for a German peace settlement had been invalidated. Consequently the original joint punitive policy toward Germany, which rested on the assumption of East-West cooperation, was abandoned. It gave way to rival policies, each aiming to enlist Germany in the power bloc of either the East or the West. The Western zones of occupation were formed into the Federal Republic of Germany, and integrated gradually into the West's economic, political and military organizations. Simultaneously the Soviet zone of occupation was accorded Soviet-style sovereignty, and membership in the Soviet satellite empire, under the name of the German Democratic Republic. Thus Germany remained divided, with over 50 million of Europe's 70 million Germans living in the western Federal Republic. Both East and West advocated reunification of divided Germany, but under mutually unacceptable conditions. The Western program of free elections was unacceptable to the Russians because it spelled certain defeat for the Communists. The Soviet program of an East-West German coalition government was unacceptable to the West because it smacked of the Soviet tactics of seizing power.

The East-West deadlock over Germany was of course no obstacle to the Russians in carrying out communization of the eastern half of Europe. On the contrary this deadlock suited Stalin's intention well: for only in a Europe partitioned, with the eastern half hermetically sealed off by the Iron Curtain from the western half, could Stalin's rule of terror operate in high gear. But no sooner had the Iron Curtain sealed off the satellites from the West than Tito's defection made Stalin aware of a danger threatening him from within the Communist orbit. Thus during the Stalinist rule of terror the heresy of Titoism, or national communism, was persecuted in the satellites with no less brutality than all other crimes purportedly of Western origin. From 1948 to 1952, many Communists suspected of Titoist sympathies found that their way led to the gallows, prisons and concentration camps, in company with other victims of the Stalinist terror. Whether less brutality would not better have served the Communist cause was something for Stalin's successors to ponder. At any rate, the rule of terror achieved at least one object of the Communist revolution: it completed the destruction of the old social and economic order in the satellites.

The new society, on the other hand, was a far cry from what the happy slogans of Communist propaganda pretended. The Communists spoke of a "free and classless" society. But in reality the new society was the victim of "the most refined tyranny and the most brutal exploitation," as described by Milovan Djilas, a disenchanted Yugoslav Communist. And the power of the "new ruling and exploiting class" was, to quote Djilas again, "more complete than the power of any other class in history. . . ."[1] Political power was monopolized by the Communist party, property was concentrated in the hands of the new regime, the regimented society was under the surveillance of the ubiquitous secret police. Moreover, in the Soviet satellites — unlike in Tito's Yugoslavia — the tyranny of the "new class" was doubled by the tyranny of the Soviet Union. For the rule of terror in the satellites was not solely of their own making. It was engineered and directed from Moscow, where Stalin, aging tyrant of the Kremlin, presided over this hierarchy of violence.

But great as was the corruption of the revolutionary cause, the countries of Central and Eastern Europe under Communist tyranny were nevertheless undergoing truly revolutionary changes. The new society consisted of more than merely the "new class" of opportunists and exploiters, stooges of the Kremlin and brutal thugs of the secret police. Behind the facade of the corrupted revolution, and beneath the apathy and cynicism of the terrorized and demoralized masses, the vision of a new freedom was kept alive. It was alive among the peasants and the workers as well as among the new intelligentsia of proletarian origin. Communist tyranny deprived the people of the fruits of the hard work spent in rebuilding their war-ravaged countries — it preached social justice on the one hand and made mockery of it on the other; nevertheless it was instrumental in generating a new social consciousness.

The peasants resisted Communist collectivization as firmly as they hated the memory of the defunct latifundia. The workers (their number swollen under forced industrialization) despised Communist work norms as deeply as they scorned the old capitalist owners' class. And the new intelligentsia of proletarian origin, in spite of totalitarian indoctrination and isolation, nurtured instinctive sympathies for the democratic traditions of political radicalism. Moreover, the oppressed masses of the new society shared with the scattered members of the disintegrated old society their general suffering and humiliation. Hurt national feelings and persecuted religious beliefs increased the spirit of social solidarity. This suspicion-ridden, corrupt and exploited new society was living in a state of fear and frustration. Nevertheless it was carrying in itself the promise of a new social order as different from the Communist present (with regard to civil rights) as from the capitalist past (with regard to property rights).

Stalin's death, in March 1953, marked the opening of a new era in the history of the Soviet satellites. The new Soviet "collective" leadership (headed first by Premier Georgi M. Malenkov and later by Marshal Nikolai A. Bulganin, but concentrated increasingly in the hands of the Communist party's first secretary, Nikita S. Khrushchev) was indeed no less determined than Stalin to keep the Soviet satellite empire intact. Russia's security together with the service of the Communist cause committed the new Soviet leaders to a policy of sustaining Stalin's conquests. But they were also aware of the critical state of their legacy. They seemed to realize that the terror and violence by which Stalin had built the Soviet satellite empire were no suitable instruments for maintaining it.

Two new instruments were devised by Stalin's successors to maintain the status quo. One was liberalization in the satellites, the other peaceful coexistence with the West. The object was clear enough. The new policy sought broader popular support for the satellite regimes in order to assuage widespread discontent. The Russians were out to prove that the satellites were independent, sovereign nations who of their own free will followed a policy of close cooperation with Soviet Russia; logically therefore it should appear that communism in the satellites presented no obstacle to peaceful coexistence between East and West. The "thaw," "new look," or "new course," as this new Communist policy was called, affected the satellite dictatorships in different ways. They began to display more distinctly than before characteristics of their own. Inasmuch as this was in line with the Leninist principle of "different roads to socialism," the Soviet leaders began to cite it in support of their new policy.

The "different roads," to be sure, were still to lead to the Kremlin. Nevertheless an important concession was made by the new leaders of Soviet Russia in their lifting of the anathema issued by Stalin against Tito. This reconciliation between the Kremlin and Tito, in June 1955, was supplemented in the satellites by the release of the imprisoned, and the rehabilitation of the executed so-called "Titoists." The concessions made to Titoism were calculated also to impress Western public opinion. And the Kremlin could take no little pleasure in observing a marked tendency in the West to accept some form of national communism as the best attainable solution of the satellites' problem. This optimistic appraisal of the new Soviet regime's conduct was strengthened by Russia's surprising decision to withdraw her occupation forces from Austria. When with the signing of a peace treaty in May 1955 Austria emerged as a neutral free nation, hopes began to rise that the long East-West deadlock on the German peace treaty might also be broken. In addition, Russia's success in catching up with the West in the thermonuclear arms race contributed a sense of urgency about ending the cold war. The hopeful mood of the peaceful coexistence era culminated in the Big Four meeting at Geneva of July 1955, only to be followed by disappointment when the subsequent meeting of the foreign ministers again reached a deadlock on the German question. Nor was this disappointment eased by Russia's magnanimity in evacuating the Finnish naval base of Porkkala, thereby restoring full sovereignty to her western neighbor in the north.

The German question kept the cold war in Europe alive. The satellites' situation, on the other hand, disturbed East-West relations relatively little. Naturally, pronouncements were heard from time to time expressing hope in the captive peoples' liberation, and a private American organization, the National Committee for Free Europe, gave support to the liberation propaganda of the exiles from Communist lands; but President Eisenhower and Secretary of State John Foster Dulles began to speak more guardedly on the theme of "peaceful liberation" than they had during the election campaign of 1952. Official American pronouncements came to favor "self-liberation" rather than "liberation." Such an ambiguous expression could of course have several meanings. For one, it could seem to mean that the captive nations would soon regain freedom, with or without Western help, because the Communist system in the satellites was heading toward collapse. For another, it could seem to mean, especially to listeners behind the Iron Curtain, that America was encouraging the captive peoples to strike for freedom. All that a realistic appraisal of Western policy could fairly conclude, however, was that the West took the position of an interested observer of the satellites' struggles and wished them well. And as far as the fermentation of the post-Stalin era in the satellites was concerned, the utmost one could realistically hope for was that the captive nations might succeed in regaining some measure of independence from Moscow, somewhere between the satellite status and Titoist independence.

The Soviets labelled the "satellites problem" an invention of Western propaganda. A Soviet press communiqué of June 14, 1955, for instance, sharply attacked Secretary of State Dulles's intention of bringing up "the problem of the countries of Eastern Europe" at the forthcoming Geneva conference. "It should be clear to all," said the Soviet communiqué, "that no 'problem of the countries of Eastern Europe' exists. The peoples of these countries, having overthrown the rule of the exploiters, have established in their countries a people's democratic government and will not allow anyone to interfere with their domestic affairs." Previously, the Soviets had branded even such serious outbreaks of discontent as the East Berlin workers' riots and the Pilsen strike of Czech workers, in June 1953, as the work of Western provocation. Yet obviously the very policy by which Stalin's heirs sought to improve the critical conditions within the satellites belied the Soviet contention that no problem of the satellite states existed. And for that matter, no Western provocation could have stirred up greater confusion in the satellites than did Khrushchev himself with the de-Stalinization campaign that he launched at the Twentieth Congress of the Soviet Communist party in February 1956.

The events of 1956 proved, if proof were needed, that the satellites problem did indeed exist. Moreover these events proved that that problem, far from being invented by Western propaganda, was capable of an explosion that could take both the Russians and the West completely by surprise. The confusion reigning in the ranks of the Western allies, who had let their cold war unity melt away in the relaxed mood of the era of peaceful coexistence, was of great help to the Russians in surviving the 1956 crisis. But the Russians' other good luck was that the confusion stirred up by Khrushchev's de-Stalinization campaign did not engulf the entire satellite empire. The Balkan satellites, Romania and Bulgaria, not to speak of Albania, were barely awakening from the apathy of the Stalinist rule of terror. East Germany was under massive Soviet military occupation and was given very little chance to participate in the benefits of the liberalization policy. Czechoslovakia, though not under Soviet occupation, was held in bondage by her efficient domestic Communists. Post-Stalin fermentation of the Czech Communists was cautious, while the people were disenchanted with Pan-Slav friendship for Russia and thoroughly frightened over the German revival in the West. Czechoslovakia's passivity under Communist tyranny was a fact which embarrassed anti-Communist exiles as well as puzzled Western liberals who remained remarkably faithful to the memory of democratic Czechoslovakia but seemed to know little about the Czechs' talent for passive resistance as a means to national survival.[2]

National characteristics were not necessarily the decisive factor in determining the satellites' behavior under communism. But independence-mindedness and traditional anti-Russian feelings could at least partly explain why the Soviet liberalization policy got out of hand in Poland and Hungary. Both the Polish and Hungarian Communists, who took their cue from Khrushchev in criticizing the Stalinist past, went much further than the Soviet liberalization policy intended them to go. They did not stop at uncovering the crimes committed against their fellow Communists. They did not simply restore "socialist legality" to strengthen the Soviet loyalty of the satellite regimes, as Khrushchev expected them to do. They criticized ever more boldly the corruptness and bankruptcy of the entire Soviet system which had betrayed the promise of a socialist society and had deprived the nations of their independence. The attacks against the existing regime were led by writers and students — in fact, by the élite of the new society. And the liberty which the Communists themselves took in criticizing their own system awakened the masses of people from the apathy into which they had sunk under the rule of terror.

In Poland the people manifested their regained vigor in the uprising of the Poznań workers in July 1956. The Soviet leaders tried to blame the Poznań revolt on "imperialist agents" and warned the Polish Communist party against the dangers of "democratization." But the party group which advocated democratization (and which fortunately included Party Secretary Edward Ochab) forged ahead. It won a victory on October 21 when Władysław Gomułka, imprisoned under the Stalinist rule of terror as a national Communist, was elected the new First Secretary. The top Russian Communist leadership hastily arrived in Warsaw, but could not stop the rebellion. Khrushchev's threat to use Soviet troops was countered by Gomułka's threat to appeal to the nation.

Following Gomułka's victory the Soviet troops remained stationed in Poland and the country also kept her membership in the Soviet military alliance system set up by the Warsaw Treaty of 1955; but the military rights of the Russians were now regulated by new accords. Agreement on Polish-Soviet military cooperation, in defense of Poland's territorial integrity, against Germany, was favored by the Poles themselves. This was no surprise, since Poland's western frontiers, along the Oder-Neisse line, were recognized as final only by the Soviet bloc nations. Politically, on the other hand, the new Polish Communist regime won freedom from Soviet interference. The Polish coup thus achieved, if not the Tito-type, but a kind of Communist self-liberation from Russian domination.

Events in Hungary had a different ending. There the Communist advocates of democratization regarded Imre Nagy, the new-course Premier from July 1953 to March 1955, as their leader. But Nagy was not given a chance to play the Gomułka role in Hungary. When the Russians removed the country's hated Stalinist, Mátyás Rákosi, as Party Secretary in July 1956, it was only to replace him with his hated *alter ego,* Ernő Gerő. And when Imre Nagy was finally recalled to power, it was too late.

In Budapest on October 23 a peaceful demonstration was staged in sympathy for Gomułka's victory in Poland. This demonstration was rapidly transformed into a nationwide insurrection when the secret police fired at the demonstrators and when (in the early morning of October 24) Soviet troops intervened. At this juncture Imre Nagy was made Premier, in the thick of a revolution he neither wished for nor knew how to stop. He could scarcely be blamed for not being able to work out a compromise with Russia on the Polish model, for from the very beginning the course of the revolution was different from the Polish. And then too the status of Hungary as a Soviet satellite was unique. None of the other satellites experienced such deep humiliation, under leaders so "foreign" and "alien" to the people (as Imre Nagy himself accurately characterized them) as did Hungary under the tyranny of the Muscovites.[3] Furthermore, following the Second World War, Soviet Russia supported all the Middle Zone nations' claims for territorial compensation except those of Hungary.[4] Poland and Czechoslovakia in particular depended upon Russia for the security of their territorial status quo against Germany. And even the rebel Tito was prone to fall in line with Moscow's policy toward Germany, irrespective of fluctuations in Yugoslav-Soviet relations. The Hungarians on the other hand were not afraid of Germany, and therefore sought no protection against her from Russia; moreover they regarded themselves as victims both of Communist tyranny and of Pan-Slav imperialism. In addition to everything else, these were factors in the revolution. The fighting spirit of the Hungarian insurgents could hardly be explained without taking these special circumstances into consideration.

Nagy knew that socialism could never be a success in Hungary by way of "denationalization" and "national nihilism" under leaders who opposed "the ideal of national independence, sovereignty, and equality, as well as Hungarian national feeling and progressive traditions." He wished for the leadership of those "who spring from the people and are of the people, and fight for them."[5] And he wished for a peaceful evolution toward this end. But once the revolution broke loose, Nagy had no choice save to identify himself with it. Nor was there essentially anything in this spectacular, spontaneous insurrection of which he, as an honest patriot and Communist, could not approve. What the revolution in essence demanded was the withdrawal of Soviet troops and the establishment of a truly free socialist society to replace the corrupt Communist society which overnight had collapsed like a pack of cards.

The principal forces of the revolution were the industrial workers and the new intelligentsia of proletarian origin. The revolution was the work of the new, not of the old, Hungarian society — a fact which some Western liberals, with leftist suspicion of all things Hungarian on account of the country's past reactionary record, were slow in recognizing. A mistaken view was also taken by those who were misled by conservative and Catholic propaganda and saw the imprisoned Cardinal Joseph Mindszenty's spiritual inspiration as the principal force behind the revolution. The cardinal, as a matter of fact, was freed only on the eighth day of the revolution. He returned to Budapest in triumph, and no doubt rightist elements, both at home and in exile, would gladly have exploited the popularity of the martyred cardinal for their special political purposes. But it is unlikely that any survivors of Hungary's chequered past could have changed the course of the workers' victorious democratic revolution had the Russians allowed that revolution to stabilize itself.[6]

The revolution seemed to be victorious on the fifth day, at which time the Russians decided to withdraw from Budapest. The Communist Premier, Imre Nagy, formed a coalition government with those democratic parties which had been suppressed under the Stalinist rule of terror, the Social Democrats, the Smallholders and the Peasants. But the consolidation of the new regime, and of the revolution which produced it, proved a tragic failure.

A Soviet statement, on October 30, acknowledged that "the further presence of Soviet Army units in Hungary can serve as a cause for an even greater deterioration of the situation," and it also expressed the Soviet government's willingness to enter into negotiations "on the question of the presence of Soviet troops on the territory of Hungary." Meanwhile, however, Soviet reinforcements poured into the country. Thereupon Premier Nagy, yielding to the pressure of revolutionary groups and in a desperate effort to save the revolution, repudiated Hungary's membership in the Warsaw Treaty, proclaimed the country's neutrality, and appealed to the United Nations for help. The chronological sequence of these moves was significant. For it showed that, contrary to widely held opinion, Nagy's renunciation of the Warsaw Treaty was not the cause of Soviet aggression but rather the result of it.

The Russians responded with a sinister game of duplicity; while negotiating with the Hungarian government for the withdrawal of troops, they were preparing for a scond armed intervention. On November 4 they launched a general offensive and suppressed the Hungarian revolution in a merciless bloodbath.

Upon reconquering Hungary, the Soviets installed a puppet government under János Kádár, a renegade national Communist, and reinstituted a rule of terror reminiscent of the Stalinist era. To justify their bloody deed, the Soviet leaders branded the Hungarian revolution as a "counterrevolution" launched by "Western imperialist circles" and led by "Horthyite Fascists and aristocrats." But great as was the Soviet effort to keep alive the unsavory memory of the Horthy era, Hungary's revolution and martyrdom actually cleansed her, in the eyes of the world, of the Fascist stigma of her past.

The United Nations, verbose but impotent, was capable of nothing more than condemnation of the Russian aggression.[7] Furthermore, its attention was diverted just then by the Suez crisis, which broke loose when Israeli forces invaded Egypt on October 29 and when an Anglo-French attack followed two days later. The Suez crisis was accompanied by a deep crisis in the Western alliance, since the United States condemned its allies, Britain and France, and Israel, for their aggression.

It was for the historian to ponder the connection between the aggression of the Suez crisis and the Soviet aggression in Hungary. The European historian with a broader sense of history was bound to notice the coincidence that the two simultaneous crises exploded in the areas of two defunct empires (the Habsburg in Central Europe and the Ottoman in the Middle East) where disintegration of the old order was followed by nationalist revolutions. But most Western historians, upset by Allied disunity, were in no mood to draw parallels of any sort. They preferred to ignore in fact any connection between the two crises. However, even the historian who was as "absolutely convinced" as Max Beloff that the Soviet suppression of the Hungarian revolution was "the result of calculations about the future of the Soviet empire in Europe and had little to do with the affairs of the Middle East," had to admit that the outcry against the Anglo-French action in the Middle East "showed that the West was too deeply divided to react" against the Russian action in Hungary.[8]

Indignation over the brutal Russian suppression of the Hungarian revolution was very great, even among Communists. It also affected

Afro-Asian nationalists, who were primarily upset over the Western invasion of Egypt, and who were prone to regard Soviet Russia as their potential ally against "Western imperialism." But the worldwide indignation was not the equal of that great stir of human mind which was the Hungarian revolution. The challenge to the world of that revolution evoked no correspondingly heroic response. Naturally the failure of the free world to back up Hungary's bid for freedom troubled the West's conscience, but her worst pangs were soon over: they penetrated less deeply than did her shame during the Second World War over the Munich betrayal, and there was no great public controversy such as in the Yalta debates of the post-war era.

Western self-criticism was cut short by self-placating arguments which maintained that any attempt to save Hungary would have led to a a third world war. There was no need to deny that action involved the risk of war. However, it was far from certain that Russia would have run the risk of a third world war if the Western Powers had shown a firm resolve to defend Hungary's independence as guaranteed in the Charter of the United Nations. Furthermore, there was much reason to doubt whether the Western Powers had exhausted all means of help short of war. It should be noted that the Hungarian situation was brought before the United Nations Security Council on October 28 — that is to say, four days before Premier Nagy's first call for help, and one week before the final Soviet assault — but no action of any sort was even proposed. Meanwhile, on October 27, Secretary of State Dulles in a speech made with White House approval said that the United States had "no ulterior purpose" in desiring the independence of the satellite countries. "We do not look upon these nations as potential military allies," he said. "We are confident that their independence, if promptly accorded, will contribute immensely to stabilize peace throughout all of Europe, West and East." Thus, while the United States reassured the Russians of non-intervention, Western help to Hungary was limited *a priori* to an appeal to Russia's good will and to an assurance that there was no peril to her security in making concessions.

Indeed, the Western statesmen who claimed to have saved the world from war by not intervening in Hungary had no claim to greatness or gratitude. The less so, because, while their caution allegedly kept mankind from the risk of war in Hungary, their prudence failed to forestall the international anarchy that produced war in the Middle East; and that war in the Middle East unquestionably had fatal consequences for the situation in Hungary. In the autumn of 1956 the Russians were more sensitive than ever to world opinion. They had already proved in Poland how eager they were to avoid violence. True, Russian troops intervened in Budapest on October 24. Furthermore, the massing of fresh Soviet troops in Hungary began before the Middle East crisis erupted. But if the Russians had used their military might immediately after October 24 as unscrupulously as they eventually did on November 4, they could have crushed the revolution at the time of their first intervention. The crucial fact seems to be that just on the eve of the Middle East explosion, on October 27, the Russians had ordered their troops out of Budapest. Had the Western Powers by their Suez action not produced a precedent for making war, and had the war in the Middle East not diverted the world's and the United Nations' attention from Hungary, the Russians might have shied away from resorting to war in Central Europe. They might have used their military presence as a pressure, but they might well have chosen to settle the Hungarian situation by essentially political rather than purely military means.

At any rate, the Hungarian tragedy gave fresh evidence of Western "disengagement" from Eastern Europe.[9] This was especially painful in view of the Anglo-French action in the Middle East; for the British and French governments took their action without any apparent concern over the effects the invasion of Egypt might have on the Hungarian situation. There was painful irony in the fact that the British action in Suez took place under the premiership of Anthony Eden, who had once endeared himself to democrats in Central Europe through his opposition to Neville Chamberlain's appeasement policy; and the American disengagement was no less painful, in view of the long years of liberation propaganda. The American disengagement attitude was carefully phrased by Secretary of State Dulles at his news conference on December 18, 1956. The American government, he said, would be satisfied if the Soviet Union itself negotiated a settlement with the nations of Eastern Europe, a settlement based on the principle of national freedom — as in Austria, Finland, or Poland — and on some form of neutralization.

Western disengagement from the Middle Zone was of course nothing new. Ever since the Munich surrender in 1938 — or, more exactly, since the collapse of Poland in September 1939 — the Western Powers had eschewed commitments and involvements in the far-away Middle Zone. Yet it was a tragedy that events like those in Hungary were needed to reveal anew the true state of Western policy toward Eastern Europe. The attitude of the Western governments during the crisis of 1956 was essentially the same as at the time of the Yalta episode. First, there was hope that Russia if assured of non-intervention in Eastern Europe might follow a liberal course in her sphere of influence. Then came the furious but helpless outburst of indignation over Soviet treachery and brutality. Western policy, it appeared, was invaribly based on the assumption that nothing tangible could be done on behalf of freedom within the Soviet sphere of influence.

Cold war propaganda was instrumental in concealing the true state of Western policy. The American election campaign of 1952 in particular gave false impressions by popularizing the slogan of "liberation." Even during the election campaign of 1956, Vice-President Nixon, on October 29, spoke of what then appeared to be a Soviet defeat in both Poland and Hungary as a triumph of the American "liberation position." But even if President Eisenhower, or Secretary of State Dulles, or Radio Free Europe, had never said a word about liberation of the Soviet satellites, the free world's prestige would have suffered a humiliating defeat in 1956. Indeed, it boded ill for the cause of liberty that the Western democracies were incapable of drawing any benefit from the crisis of Soviet tyranny which began with Stalin's death in 1953 and culminated in the Hungarian revolution of 1956.

The tragic autumn of 1956 had at least one favorable consequence for the cause of freedom. Suez and Hungary reminded the Western nations of the sorry state of their unity. With a new sense of urgency they resumed work on European federalization. And they also started to mend NATO's fences.

In the autumn of 1956, Soviet power had seemed to be crumbling under the impact of revolutionary upheavals in satellite Poland and Hungary. In the autumn of 1957, the Russians successfully launched the first earth satellite and their power seemed to stand firmer than ever. In reality, however, the crisis which culminated in the Hungarian revolution was not so grave (even if Hungary had succeeded in liberating herself) as to threaten the Soviet satellite empire with total disintegration. Hungary, surrounded by rival nations, was not the country to lead a general Danubian uprising. Rather, a Communist Little Entente against Hungary made its appearance when all three neighbors — satellite Czechoslovakia and Romania as well as Titoist Yugoslavia — alarmed as they were by the collapse of the Communist regime in Hungary, closed ranks with the Russians.

Nor, on the other hand, was the consolidation of Soviet power which followed the crisis so stable as to make Russian domination permanently safe against the oppressed peoples' craving for liberty. National independence was a specter haunting Khrushchev as he charted the course of Soviet policy in Eastern Europe between the Scylla of re-Stalinization and the Charybdis of de-Stalinization. Tito's independent Yugoslavia, unwilling to yield to Soviet dictates, became again the chief target of Moscow's ire against national communism (now preferably labelled, in concert with Peking, as one of the crimes of "revisionism"). Gomułka's semi-independent Poland, a moderate example of Communist self-liberation, was living in a state of uneasy truce within the Soviet satellite empire. And from Hungary, defeated in her struggle for independence, came, with the execution of Premier Imre Nagy and General Pál Maléter in June 1958, a new brutal warning to all Eastern Europe that Khrushchev's Russia was determined to keep what Stalin's Russia had conquered.

The Nagy executions shocked the world as no other Soviet crime since November 4, 1956. But once again, as in 1956, the world's attention was diverted by crisis in the Middle East, with American troop landings in Lebanon and British in Jordan. The subsequent debate in the United Nations offered a truly grotesque spectacle as both the Soviet Union — defiant of the 1956 UN order to withdraw the Russian troops from Hungary — and the United States — silent about its failure to help Hungary — outdid each other in championing the small nations' rights to freedom and independence.

Those who gave serious thought to the problem of the Russians' European satellites came to realize more strongly than ever that any progress toward freeing the eastern half of Europe from Soviet domination hinged on the solution of the German question. George F. Kennan, in his Reith Lectures in the autumn of 1957, suggested that the deadlock over Germany could be resolved if the whole area of Central and Eastern Europe could be isolated from East-West rivalry. In order to get the Soviet army out of Central Europe, he argued, the Western Powers should withdraw from Germany. But even the sympathetic Western critics of Kennan's ideas were skeptical about the success of this particular brand of "disengagement." For, as one critic reasoned: "As things stand, the Russians cannot withdraw their troops from eastern Europe unless they are prepared to accept the disintegration, either gradually or explosively, of their satellite empire. Since they now clearly believe that the cards are stacked more heavily in their favor than ever before, there is no reason to suppose that they would be willing to consider a retreat."[10]

How and when the Russians would be willing to consider a retreat, no one could foretell. One thing, however, seemed almost certain — namely that if anything could induce the Russians to seek peace and security through cooperation, it would be a united West, moving firmly toward the creation of a United States of Europe, and closely associated with the United States of America. The chief present aim of Soviet policy in Europe was to destroy the unity of the West, though this policy was cloaked in high-sounding slogans of peace and security. The Soviets had a justifiable security claim to protect themselves against Western aggression, in particular against the revival of German militarism; but the Soviet effort to force the United States out of Europe, and to neutralize Germany, was aggressive rather than defensive in character. Its aim was to create chaos rather than order in Europe, to keep the German problem unsolved rather than to solve it. It is most unlikely that German reunification, if achieved at the price of neutrality, could relegate the German problem to the dustbin of history. Nor is it likely that the Russians, following such a "solution" of the German problem, would declare themselves as feeling sufficiently secure to retreat from Europe.

The real solution of the German problem, serving the cause of peace as well as the security of both East and West, lies in integrating the Germans into a federated Europe. The emergency presented by the cold war had taught the West the wisdom of treating Germany in the spirit of European partnership. The rise of European unity, and within it the emergence of a democratic German state under the guidance of Chancellor Konrad Adenauer, were the fruits of this wisdom. Indeed, the cold war may prove to have been a blessing in disguise, inasmuch as it compelled the West to abandon the bankrupt methods of power politics and balance of power in trying to solve the German problem. The program of Second World War diplomacy to attempt by "East-West cooperation" to keep the world safe against the revival of German danger, a program which the Russians wrecked with their cold war against the West, could never really have solved the German problem. Nor would "East-West cooperation" for the neutralization of Germany achieve peace in Europe today. More likely, it would only stir up old rivalries and jealousies and throw Europe back into the anarchy of the nationalist past from which the current unity efforts are trying to extricate her.

However, if the federalization of Europe progresses to the point where the Russians can no longer hope to wreck it, and if that federalization clearly has peaceful intentions, the Russians may then come to realize that the solution of the German problem through European integration also serves their security interests; and in that case, the Russians may well come to regard this European solution of the German problem as a more attractive alternative than the costly military occupation of East Germany to which the German Communist puppet government owes its existence.

In the winter of 1958–59, the Russians launched a new offensive to force the Western Powers out of Berlin. The Soviet scheme to make West Berlin into a so-called "free city" was, to all appearances, part of a major Soviet strategy to undermine the Western position in Germany. The perilous crisis thus created in Central Europe was temporarily eased by a new attempt to discuss the East-West conflict at the conference table. The negotiations began on the foreign minister level in the spring of 1959. The second Geneva summit meeting, predicted for the summer, was delayed. However, a more spectacular event — the first of its kind — took place in the early autumn, with Premier Khrushchev's visit to the United States in a renewed mood of peaceful coexistence.

Whether this new round of East-West negotiations will ultimately lead to a European solution of the German problem will largely depend on the West's success in perfecting the ties of unity among the free nations both in Europe and within the Atlantic Community. The future of freedom is very much at stake in the East-West struggle over the control of Central Europe. Without a European solution of the German question the future of the newborn German democracy may be gravely imperilled. And, of course, on German reunification hinges also the future of European reunification. For the time being, it may well be true (as is often said) that the reunification of Germany in freedom is impossible — moreover, that powerful interests call for the continuance of Germany's division. But in the long run an unimaginative status quo policy may well spell ruin for Europe and the free world, no less than it did in the era between the two world wars. A European policy which relinquishes the objective of reunification may doom freedom to stagnation and ultimate failure.

Today it is Soviet Russia that obstructs the peace in Central Europe. But it was Hitler's war against the West, and against Russia, that brought the Russians into Central Europe. In fact, the Middle Zone problem of today is the outcome of two German wars and of two failures to make peace in that area.

The solution of the German question is the prerequisite in solving the problem of the Middle Zone. Moreover, an East-West agreement to settle the German question within the framework of European federation could also serve as a basis for an agreement to create a neutral regional federation of the Middle Zone nations. Such a federation may today seem remote and unattainable. Yet nothing less can lastingly remove these nations from the rivalry of the Great Powers and deliver them from the nationalist rivalries of their fratricidal past.

During the Second World War, Russia had condemned federal plans for Central and Eastern Europe by branding them as anti-Soviet schemes; but after the war, she opposed the federal plans even of Communists who were eager to be loyal to her. Yugoslavia's Tito and his fellow-dictator of Bulgaria, Georgi Dimitrov, hatched such plans in the Middle Zone for a separate federation of Communist nations allied to Russia. Soviet opposition was of course not the sole stumbling block to the success of these plans. Bulgaria and Yugoslavia could not agree on the form of a Balkan union; and elsewhere in the Middle Zone the chances for federal cooperation on a regional scale were no brighter.

Nevertheless, on a more limited scale, in an attempt to solve the nationality problems within the individual countries under Communist rule, the federalist principle was applied. Tito's Yugoslavia became a federal state founded on the so-called Marxist-Leninist principle of national equality. The Soviet Union too began to practise Marxist-Leninist nationality policy in the satellites after Communist domination had been firmly entrenched and ethnic rivalries could no longer serve the interests of the Soviet divide-and-rule policy. Thus in Czechoslovakia, following the Communist seizure of power, minority rights of the Hungarians were gradually restored. Quarrels also subsided between Czechs and Slovaks over the Slovak autonomy, guaranteed in the post-war

Czechoslovak federal constitution. The other satellites ensured the language rights of their national minorities in special articles of their new constitutions, all modelled after the Soviet federal constitution of 1936. A new mode of settling the Hungaro-Romanian controversy was introduced by the 1952 constitution of Romania, which established a so-called Hungarian Autonomous Region in Transylvania.

Simultaneously, treaties of friendship, cooperation and mutual assistance were signed among the satellites to complete this Soviet-sponsored drive for national reconciliation. The Soviet-controlled German Democratic Republic also was invited to take part in this satellite fraternization. The East Germans accepted the Oder-Neisse frontier vis-à-vis Poland, as well as the expulsion of the Germans from Poland and Czechoslovakia, as the final verdict of history. Similarly, the Hungarian Communist government assured its neighbors that the revisionist policy of the past was buried for ever and the territorial status quo accepted as final.

After the Second World War, the number of minority populations which needed protection against ethnic oppression was considerably smaller than before. Wartime migration and post-war persecution, expulsion and transfers, increased the ethnic homogeneity of the nation-states. Most radical was the change in the ethnic composition of Poland and Czechoslovakia. Before the war, the actual Polish and Czechoslovak majorities in the two countries were only about 69 percent. Poland now became 98 percent Polish, and Czechoslovakia 91 percent Czech and Slovak. The corresponding changes in the other states of the Middle Zone, although less revolutionary, were also significant. Romania increased her ethnic homogeneity from 72 to 85 percent. In Yugoslavia the Slav majority rose from 83 to 88 percent, while Hungary increased her ethnic homogeneity from 90 to 98 percent, and Bulgaria from 83 to 91 percent. However, even after this general increase of homogeneity, the ethnic minorities were not negligible. They represented about 8 percent of the area's total population. The largest portion are the Hungarians — now nearly 4 millions — who also are the largest ethnic minority in Europe as a whole. In the plain language of statistics, the Hungarians are only about 3 percent of Europe's total population but close to 18 percent of Europe's minority population.[11]

The price in human suffering paid for the ethnic homogeneity of the nation-states in the Middle Zone was enormous. Moreover, the intricate nationality problems of the Middle Zone, which before the Communists nobody had succeeded in solving, were far from being solved under the Communists. Neither the historical struggle between Slav and German, nor the conflicts among the Slavic nations of Yugoslavia (Serbs, Croats and Slovenes) and of Czechoslovakia (Czechs and Slovaks), nor the problem of the dismembered Hungarian nation which had been the focus of Danubian instability in the past, could be solved by Communist fiat. Whether or not friendship among the rival nations of yore was actually growing under Communist tyranny was debatable. At any rate, two views, both maintaining that reconciliation was making headway, gave opposing interpretations of the causes of growing friendship: the Communists attributed it to the Marxist-Leninist nationality policy, the anti-Communists ascribed it to the bitter experience of common servitude.

The national conflicts affecting the Middle Zone always were and still are of two kinds: one category consisting of the antagonism between Middle Zone nations and their two powerful neighbors, Russia and Germany; the other consisting of the disputes among the Middle Zone nations themselves.

Russia's relationship to the Middle Zone is of course the paramount issue today. Without the withdrawal of Russian military power from Europe no real peace is conceivable either in the Middle Zone or in the global conflict between East and West. Unfortunately, even if Russia withdrew within her present national frontiers, not all the conflicts between Russia and her western neighbors would be solved. Russia's immense territorial gains in the Second World War from the Baltic to the Carpathians would remain intact. But disputes over Russia's frontiers or over the status of entire nations annexed by Russia (as in the case of the three Baltic states) are of such a nature that no peaceful agreement, however desirable, could conceivably solve them; for only the disintegration of the U.S.S.R. itself (a very unlikely event), or a miracle of unheard-of wisdom and magnanimity, could change the boundary line between Russia and Europe.

Russia's relationship to her western neighbors is not, as the Russians claim, a matter of partnership among "Communist" or "Socialist" nations. The so-called East European problem of today is a matter of Soviet colonialism, Russian imperialism, Moscow's interference in the internal affairs of those nations which as a result of the Second World War came within the sphere of influence of Soviet military power. No nation in the Middle Zone, if free to choose, would ask the Russians for help to protect its so-called "socialist achievements." These achievements, as far as they served the cause of social justice, have been endorsed by an overwhelming majority of the people; to uphold them against domestic foes, the people need no outside help.

On the other hand, quite a number of nations in the Middle Zone would turn to Russia for protection if they felt Germany endangered their national security. To allay these fears, and to avoid a situation in which Russia could pose as the defender of nations threatened by German revenge, is certainly one of the great tests of statesmanship. If and when the time is ripe for East-West agreement on German reunification within the framework of a European federation, two issues in particular will call for simultaneous consideration: the Polish-German conflict over frontiers, and the Czech-German conflict over the expulsion of the Sudeten Germans. Unless both issues can be permanently settled, even fully independent Poland and Czechoslovakia may clamor for Russian protection.

There is a no less delicate situation regarding the conflicts among the Middle Zone nations themselves, conflicts which would most certainly come to the fore if Russia's military power were withdrawn from Europe. Here again only the West's supreme statesmanship could prevent Russia (or, for that matter Germany) from fishing in the muddy waters of national jealousies. If the Middle Zone nations were freed of Russia's domination, the intra-zone rivalries would be centered, as in the past, primarily in the Danube Valley. The conditions of peace among these nations (rather than the future of their social and economic institutions) should be very much a matter of international concern. These peoples — or at any rate their leaders — cannot compose their differences in a spirit of objectivity and fairness. They need the mediation of an impartial tribunal.

The Great Powers, who took a decisive part in the political settlement of this area, after both world wars supported exaggerated local nationalist aspirations, in accordance with their own power interests. If the Middle Zone could be removed from power rivalry by means of a European solution of the German problem, then the Great Powers might abandon power politics in the Danube Valley as well, and promote the cause of true peace among the nations there. In particular, the punitive peace which twice partitioned Hungary, in flagrant violation of the principle of ethnic equality, ought to be superseded by a peace of reconciliation to make the Danube Valley safe against cut-throat nationalist competition. And no other device but a Danubian federation could end these rivalries which, though petty in themselves, have aggravated for so long the insecurity of the European continent as a whole, through being intertwined with the rivalry of the Great Powers.

Essentially, the solution of the problem of Danubian Europe is no different in the twentieth century from what it was throughout the nineteenth century when, following the French Revolution, modern ideas of nationalism and democracy began in great force to penetrate the antiquated structure of the multinational Habsburg Empire. The great Czech historian František Palacký urged the Habsburgs in 1848 to federalize the Austrian Empire so as to forestall the great catastrophes (German and Russian domination of Central Europe included) which since then have all come true. He saw federalized Austria's mission as being to serve as "the bulwark and guardian of Europe against Asiatic elements of every kind." Of course, if a peaceful federalist solution of the present East-West conflict in Central Europe ever proved possible, no Danubian federation, or any kind of federation in the Middle Zone, could be anti-Russian in the sense of Palacký's "bulwark." Apart from the obsoleteness of a "bulwark" in the Atomic Age, Beneš's favorite idea of the role of a "bridge" between East and West would be a much more desirable one for the Middle Zone nations to play. But how can they ever play such an imposing role for the benefit of their own as well as the world's peace, if they fail, as they have failed in the past, in building the small bridges of peace among themselves? Indeed, "close and firm ties" among these nations are always needed, much as in Palacký's time, so that strife-torn Central Europe may enjoy freedom and welfare in "complete equality of rights."[12]

Since Palacký's time, the catalogue of failures to reconcile national rivalries has grown alarmingly. Meanwhile, they key to ending these rivalries has remained the same. As Oscar Jászi wrote, after his last visit to the Danubian countries in 1948: "Neither the hereditary conception of the Habsburg Empire, nor the principle of self-determination after the First World War, nor the homogeneous nation-states idea after the Second World War [can be the solution]. . . . Federalism is the only possible means of reconciling states and nations."[13] Or, as a writer in *The Times Literary Supplement* observed, in discussing one of the many books on the Habsburgs' failure — a topic still of lively interest on account of the failures of the Habsburgs' successors to remain free: "In

1918, after the First World War, the national states seemed to be the pattern for the future. Now we are not so sure. Even the old-established national states of western Europe are drawing together in terms of incipient federalism; how much less likely is it that the national states of eastern Europe will survive in undiminished sovereignty."[14]

The survival of these states in "undiminished sovereignty" is certainly most unlikely. The question is whether sovereignty is to be diminished by consent, so that freedom may be safeguarded through union; or whether it will be diminished by conquest, in which case freedom will be lost to the domination of alien powers. The peoples of the Middle Zone have no free choice between the two alternatives; nevertheless the part they may be called upon to play in the showdown between the Western and the Soviet types of federalism in Central Europe will not be negligible.

The two basic problems of the Middle Zone, the attainment of national freedom and of social justice, remain unsolved. If and when they are solved, the danger zone of Central Europe, which has triggered off two world wars in the twentieth century, may become a zone of peace and stability. For the time being, however, Central Europe continues to be a cockpit of conflict, a threat to the world's peace. The revolution of Central Europe which began with a vision of freedom over a hundred years ago is still unfinished. The struggle for a new order still goes on. Certainly the triumph of tyranny is not the last word of history.

Epilogue Two: Cold War Becomes Détente

The vantage point from which the preceding chapter, Epilogue One, was written was the late 1950s. Two decades later, Europe is still divided and the basic conflict between the democratic West and the Soviet dominated East remains unresolved. But the temper and tone of the conflict, if not its substance, has changed perceptibly.

In the late fifties, the Soviet offensive against Western rights in a divided Berlin kept the tensions of the cold war at a high pitch. In the early sixties, the unpredictable Khrushchev sprang two surprises on the West — in the summer of 1961 with the building of the Berlin Wall, then in Cuba with the rocket bases which were discovered in the fall of 1962. The Russian wall in Berlin stopped the flight of East Germans from communism: a total of about three and a half million of them in fifteen years. The wall was a shame, but it saved the life of Soviet Russia's German creation, the German Democratic Republic. Furthermore, the wall helped to stabilize the status quo in Europe and, as a living testimony to the kind of world we live in, the wall became an instrument of world peace. Meanwhile, the Cuban missile crisis brought the world to the brink of war more closely than any other crisis of the Atomic-Nuclear Age. Yet it was the Cuban crisis (resolved peacefully with the withdrawal of the Soviet nuclear warheads) that ushered in the improvement in East-West relations. The cold war changed into détente.

Some positive Soviet changes, labelled "liberalization" by the détentist vocabulary of the West, did play a role in improving East-West relations, but only marginally. The real base for détente was the balance of terror. Fear of a nuclear catastrophe prompted the American and Soviet superpowers to conclude the Nuclear Test Ban Treaty in July 1963, and negotiations for limiting the nuclear arms race have continued ever since. So overwhelming was the fear of nuclear war and the desire for peaceful coexistence that even major acts of violence on both sides — the American war in Vietnam and the Soviet invasion of Czechoslovakia — barely made a dent on East-West détente.

During the cold war, the conviction was widespread in the West that Soviet domination over Eastern Europe had to be resisted because it threatened the West. As the popularity of détente rose, this idea that the Russians might use Eastern Europe as a springboard for aggression started to sound like cold war propaganda. The revisionist interpretation of cold war origins also helped to minimize Soviet Russia's threatening image in Western minds. The revisionists blamed both sides, but particularly the United States, for the collapse of wartime Soviet-American cooperation. Packaged into a progressive ideology, the revisionist view of recent history appealed especially to the young, alienated from contemporary Western civilization.

Unlike in the West, people in Eastern Europe found it harder to accept the European status quo as final. They never believed that Soviet conquest was bad because it threatened the West. To them, Soviet domination was bad because it deprived them of their freedoms. Nevertheless, they too approved of détente as a way out of the cold war deadlock, hoping that lessened tensions between the Soviet and American superpowers might increase Eastern Europe's chances of shaking off Russian controls. The failure of the Czech bid for freedom in 1968 dashed many such hopes. Yet it did not obliterate the conviction that détente was preferable to cold war. On the other hand, the revisionist interpretation of cold war history, blaming the United States for its origins, found few followers among East Europeans. The idea that unfriendly Western acts toward the Soviet Union could have made the Russians behave the way they did sounded just too absurd to those who knew Soviet tyranny first hand.[1]

At the time East-West talks on peace in Europe resumed following Stalin's death in 1953, it was widely believed that a détente depended on solving two paramount issues: (1) German reunification and (2) the right to national self-determination of the Soviet satellites. Both problems, however, were bypassed during the course of events that marked the transition from cold war to détente.

The question of German reunification did come up for discussion in a series of East-West conferences, the last time in Geneva in 1959 at a meeting of foreign ministers of the Big Four. The Soviet satellites' right to self-determination, on the other hand, never made it even to the agenda of an East-West conference. The Russians categorically refused to talk about it. Thus, the demand of the satellites' right to freedom from

Soviet domination has been from the outset a matter of unilateral Western rhetoric. In the United States it has been something of a football in domestic politics, too, "kicked most vigorously at four-year intervals when presidential elections occur."[2] Both Republicans and Democrats have discovered that by standing up for the satellites' right to national self-determination they could gain votes from millions of Americans with roots in Eastern Europe.

On the international scene, the aftermath of the Hungarian Revolution of 1956 kept interest in the Soviet satellites alive for a while. The United Nations passed a dozen or so resolutions condemning the Soviet Union for the Hungarian atrocities. In the fall of 1958, the UN General Assembly appointed Sir Leslie Munro of New Zealand to be special representative on the "Question of Hungary." American, European, and United Nations protests, however, were all exercises in futility. They ceased even to be spontaneous outbursts of indignation against Soviet brutalities after a while and became mostly self-serving political theatrics. Nobody surpassed the United States in these sorts of protests; in 1959, a Congressional resolution called upon the President of the United States to proclaim a "Captive Nations Week" during which free people everywhere were invited to pray for the enslaved peoples. Since then, no session of Congress has ever shown the interest to stop these empty gestures.[3]

Desire for détente has muffled or stopped altogether any serious Western protests against Soviet oppression in Eastern Europe. In December 1962, the UN General Assembly approved for the last time the annual American resolution demanding Russian troop withdrawal from Hungary. The post of the UN Special Representative for the Question of Hungary was also abolished at the same time on American initiative. Western moral indignation lost to Russian military might and political intransigence. The Soviet status quo in Europe rapidly ceased to be an issue of East-West controversy. Accepted tacitly by the West even during the cold war, the status quo has been routinely recognized as a pragmatic prerequisite of détente.

Western recognition of the European status quo, a cherished target of Soviet diplomacy, was achieved with relative ease. The United States, as leader of the West, has often been criticized for conceding too much while receiving no comparable Soviet concessions in return. No public controversies, however, on the scale of the great Yalta debates of the forties and fifties have been stirred up by disagreement over détente in the sixties and seventies.

American détente policy toward Eastern Europe was formulated during the Kennedy and Johnson administrations. The ideological inspiration came from the academic community, its recognized source of wisdom being a *Foreign Affairs* article on East-West relations published in 1961. The authors were Zbigniew Brzezinski of Columbia University, a future presidential adviser on national security, and William E. Griffith of the Massachussetts Institute of Technology, a former political adviser for Radio Free Europe. More widely noticed than their academic article on détente was a follow-up on the political level: President Lyndon B. Johnson's "bridge building" speech, delivered on May 23, 1964, at the dedication ceremonies of the George C. Marshall Research Library at the Virginia Military Institute.[4]

In the cold war past, American presidents had rejected the European status quo because in the East it did not conform to the principle of national self-determination. In his Virginia speech, President Johnson struck a new tone of détente specifically with reference to this controversial East European situation. Although he mentioned the hope for German unification, he otherwise accepted the status quo as a starting point for East-West cooperation within the framework of peaceful coexistence. He proposed to build "bridges of increased trade, of ideas, of visitors, and of humanitarian aid" to Eastern Europe. He expressed the United States' readiness to engage peacefully with the Soviet satellites in economic and cultural cooperation — which, incidentally, was the sort of relationship the Western European countries had already been engaged in for some time. A few months later, on October 7, President Johnson delivered another speech on "peaceful engagement" at the National Conference of Editorial Writers in New York City. Again he mentioned German reunification, but tied it emphatically to East-West reconciliation. And, in order to reassure the Russians that there were no ulterior motives behind "bridge-building" to Eastern Europe, he spoke of healing Europe's division "with the consent of Eastern European countries and consent of the Soviet Union."

The American program of détente was spelled out. But bridge-building with Eastern Europe was slow. Always under domestic pressures serving narrow special interests, Congress was sluggish in responding to the subtleties of a détente relationship. It was obvious as ever that Eastern European issues were nowhere near to the priorities of American foreign policy. Only the security of Western Europe was of real interest to the United States. Tragedies in the Soviet satellites have always opened the hearts of Americans and evoked genuine sympathies to its victims. But as far as American foreign policy objectives went, Eastern Europe was cast either into a cold war role or into no role at all. And Eastern Europe's cold war role in its crudest form amounted only to that of cannon fodder: causing trouble for the Russians and easing Soviet pressure on the West.

A détente policy toward Eastern Europe required a sophistication which the United States was ill-prepared to apply. Die-hard cold war anti-Communists branded détente a betrayal. At the other end of the political spectrum, anti-communism came to be equated with "McCarthyism." Anti-communism was believed to be the cause of blunders that carried the country down the road to the catastrophe of Vietnam, the shame of Watergate and the disgrace of the Nixon resignation.[5] As a backlash to Vietnam, the suspicion was rising that perhaps Eastern Europe, too, was one of those places where no American interests were at stake, where cold-war involvement was just another offshoot of anti-Communist hysteria.

The new view of Eastern Europe's place (or rather, its lack of place) in American foreign policy thinking was well summed up by Henry A. Kissinger in an essay he wrote before he gained world fame as Washington's top diplomat: "During periods of détente, each ally makes its own approach to Eastern Europe or the U.S.S.R. . . . The major initiatives to improve relations between Western and Eastern Europe should originate in Europe with the United States in a reserve position."[6]

The United States was conducting the policy of détente from a position of reduced strength. The Vietnam War had sapped American energies and had spread isolationist sentiments. To compound the Western calamities, the sixties had also witnessed a weakening of unity among democracies as a whole. This was mainly caused by the fatal American involvement in Southeast Asia, but also by de Gaulle's ambition to restore France to her glory as a great power among nations.

Exaggerated as de Gaulle's fulminations against American influence in Europe had been, even more inflated was his romantic vision of "Europe from the Atlantic to the Urals." As a monument to his lack of realism stands his long visit to Moscow from June 20 to July 1, 1966. A joint declaration issued in Moscow asserted that "the problems of

Europe should be first of all discussed within European limits," and that cooperation between France and the Soviet Union would strengthen the role of Europe as "a seat of a civilization" in the interest of "progress and peace throughout the world."[7] For years, the Western democracies were told to rely on Atlantic partnership between Europe and America against Soviet imperialism. Now, all of a sudden de Gaulle appointed Soviet Russia as a fellow guardian of European civilization. The anti-American edge of the Moscow declaration was unmistakable, but de Gaulle's affair with Moscow was embarrassing "within European limits" as well. It came on the heels of the Franco-German friendship treaty of January 1963, hailed at the time of its signing as being the cornerstone of a new Europe.

De Gaulle himself must have felt embarrassed when two years after his Moscow visit the Soviets invaded Czechoslovakia. The destruction of the Czech experiment in Europeanizing Marxism-Leninism reinforced Soviet Russia's image in European eyes as the seat of a new barbarism rather than that of a guardian of their civilization. The Soviet Russians of course never sought to play the august role bestowed on them by de Gaulle's fantasies. They went along because de Gaulle was working on their behalf by weakening Western unity and the Atlantic alliance while blocking British membership in the Common Market and loosening France's ties with NATO.

It was left to Poland's Gomułka to remind de Gaulle of his lack of realism. On the occasion of his Polish visit in 1967, de Gaulle hailed Polish independence and proposed to his hosts an alliance. Gomułka squarely rejected the offer, recalling the melancholy end to Poland's pre-war alliance with France. However, unrealistic as de Gaulle's Eastern policy had been, it was beneficial in one respect: a self-confident French voice calling on the Europeans to be Europeans did strengthen the self-confidence of the Eastern Europeans; it emboldened their traditional desire to belong to the West.

The sense of European self-confidence was strengthened further by the unexpected role a modernized Roman Catholic Church began to play in détente diplomacy. The emergence of the papacy with a modern face was the work of Pope John XXIII and of his successor, Pope Paul VI. A realistic acceptance of communism superseded the superstitious fear of communism, and papal diplomacy mobilized its considerable international influence in support of détente. The excommunication of Marxists ended and Roman Catholics of Eastern Europe entered into pragmatic compromises with the Communist regimes. In due course, Communist officials from Eastern Europe were received in papal audiences on their visits to Rome. Among them were, in 1977, János Kádár of Hungary and Edward Gierek of Poland.

Even before the new papal trend, the solidly Catholic Poles had been engaged in formulating a policy of coexistence with communism. The chief strategist in maintaining a pragmatic compromise was the Primate of Poland, the politically astute Cardinal Stefan Wyszynski; one of his aides at one time was the Archbishop of Cracow, Cardinal Karol Wojtyła, who became Pope John Paul II in October 1978. No less than the election itself of a "Polish Pope," John Paul II's visit to his homeland in June 1979 made history. His ten days in Poland, the first papal journey to a Communist land, was a triumph watched with awe and exhilaration throughout the world. The papal visit also called global attention to the unusually strong position of the Church in a Communist country. This has been the achievement of a singularly capable Polish Catholic national leadership, knowing how to be both tough and conciliatory. But it has something to do with pragmatic Polish Marxist wisdom as well. The Polish Communists, eager to soothe social discontent and political frustration, have allowed the Polish masses to indulge in the opiate of religion.

In contrast to Poland, external guidance of a new pragmatic kind was much needed in two-thirds Catholic Hungary. There, coexistence with communism had raised thorny problems as nowhere else in the Soviet orbit, involving both the Roman center of the Catholic Church and the United States. Papal diplomacy aided normalization of state-church relations in Hungary mainly by negotiating the move into exile in 1971 of the militant anti-Communist churchman, Cardinal Mindszenty, sheltered by the American Embassy in Budapest ever since the Soviet suppression of the revolution in 1956. Another sensitive Hungarian issue was the fate of Hungary's Holy Crown, symbol of a millennium of Hungarian nationhood and of independence. Surrendered by Hungary's quislings to the Allied armies of the West in 1945, the crown was kept in American custody at Fort Knox. In the spirit of East-West détente, the U.S. government returned the crown to the People's Republic of Hungary in January 1978, with papal approval and in the face of conservative anti-Communist opposition.

It was not the Church which raised its voice against East-West détente, as might have been expected. It was the People's Republic of China.

Peking openly broke with Moscow over the American-Soviet Nuclear Test Ban Treaty of 1963. But even before East-West détente began to produce results in making the world safer from nuclear catastrophe, the Chinese had been accusing the Russians of betraying Marx and the world revolution. Deep historic conflicts had long undermined the initial friendship that existed between Mao Zedong's Communist China and Stalin's Soviet Russia. By the time the Western democracies had firmly assumed a détentist attitude toward the whole Communist world, Chinese communism had become a bitter enemy of Russian communism.

The erstwhile Bolshevik belief that national rivalry among Communist states was "by definition an impossibility"[8] was thus once again proven wrong. And the Sino-Soviet "new cold war"[9] in Asia only complicated Moscow's already tangled relationship with her European Communist neighbors. The Chinese accused Russia of "hegemonism" in Eastern Europe, whereas the Russians denounced China's aims as divisive" and unbecoming to Communists. The East Europeans, eager to shake off the fetters of Soviet captivity, stood only to gain from this Sino-Soviet conflict of views.

The 1960s added Maoism to the already existing Trotskyite and Titoist deviations from Soviet teachings on communism. The seventies have continued the multiplication of heresies with the articulation of a democratic form of communism in Western Europe, labelled felicitously Eurocommunism to distinguish it from totalitarian Russocommunism. The strongest single force, however, to split the Soviet-Russian model of monolithic communism has been nationalism.

Thus, while East-West détente has stabilized the territorial status quo in Europe, the status quo of communism has been constantly challenged within the so-called "Socialist" world. The national differentiation among the Communist states of Eastern Europe has become ever more conspicuous. And, with national differentiation, national differences, too, have become virulent. "Proletarian internationalism" was supposed to do away with national hostility. It did not. The confusion of loyalties in the Balkans, where Titoism started the nationalist disintegration of the Soviet bloc as far back as 1948, is a case in point of the Communist disarray.

Yugoslavia, internally plagued primarily by chronic ethnic tensions, has successfully maintained a non-aligned status in the danger zone between the two rival blocs of the superpowers. But Titoism as a form of national communism has been tied entirely to Tito's personal leadership. It offers no assurance for Yugoslavia's own continuing national independence nor does it serve as a universal model for other national Communist states. Thus, Albania, one of Yugoslavia's jealous neighbors, taking advantage of the Sino-Soviet cold war, found her ideological ally in far-away Asia. At odds with Moscow ever since Khrushchev's de-Stalinization speech in 1956 — and never at ease with Titoist Yugoslavia for fear of being dominated by her — Albania declared herself a follower of Chinese Maoism in the sixties. This Chinese orientation was of short duration. After Mao Zedong's death in 1976, the Albanian Communists, Stalinist as they still were, found the liberalizating tendencies of Mao's successors as distasteful as they did Khrushchev's similar preferences after Stalin's death. By 1978, national Communist Albania became an ideological loner, isolated from the outside world, Communist and non-Communist alike.

Albania's defection from the Chinese camp is no gain for the Soviets. Quite the contrary. Mao's successors have stepped up Communist China's interest in the non-aligned Communist countries of the Balkans, as demonstrated by Prime Minister Hua Guofeng's visits to Yugoslavia and Romania in August 1978. The Russians, on the other hand, retained one trusted friend in the national-Communist Balkans: Bulgaria. Their only European satellite which has caused them no serious trouble so far, Bulgaria has been loyally following the Soviet line ever since 1948, both in domestic and international affairs.

Several factors accounted for Bulgaria's loyalty to Soviet Russia. For one thing, geographic good fortune spared Bulgaria the traumatic experience of a prolonged Soviet occupation at the war's end. (Russia needed no westward-pointing "lines of communication" there.) Also, in the peace settlement, the Soviet Union helped Bulgaria win her territorial claim against Romania. Ancient territorial feuds with her other neighbors — in particular with Yugoslavia over Macedonia — further strengthened Bulgaria's reliance on the Soviet Union. The conservative spirit of the Bulgarian Communist leadership too made the Sophia regime largely immune to the temptation of so-called "separate roads to socialism." Indeed, unless Balkan rivalries miraculously disappear, whatever the coloration of future Bulgarian regimes, calculations of national interests may keep the country in Russia's camp for a long time to come.

The country in the Balkans that Russia trusted to the extent of withdrawing her troops from there, but then got disappointed with, was Romania. Soviet troops were withdrawn from Romania in June 1958, as a sign of trust as well as a reward for Romanian services rendered against the Hungarian revolution in 1956. The once-subservient Romanian Communists, however, soon turned into rebels. They rose against Khrushchev's plan in 1962 to invest the Comecon (the Soviet experiment in a common market) with a supranational authority. Led by Gheorghe Gheorghiu-Dej, the Romanians refused to accept a place in the "socialist division of labor" because it was designed to keep them an agricultural country. In a careful but uncompromisingly phrased statement of principles, Romania proclaimed her independence from Moscow in August 1964. To justify their rebellious step, the Romanian Communists invoked the sanctity of national sovereignty, the very principle Moscow herself had professed to respect unceasingly.

Romania thus went her own separate way as a Communist country. Under Nicolae Ceauşescu, the maverick Balkan politician who succeeded Gheorghiu-Dej in 1965, the country became for all practical purposes as independent of the Soviet Union as Tito's Yugoslavia has been since 1948. And Ceauşescu's success in entrenching his country's independence was the more remarkable since Romania, unlike Yugoslavia, bordered on the Soviet Union. If Romania's defection in the sixties seemed less dramatic than Yugoslavia's in the forties, it was due mainly to the different international climates: Tito broke away amid threats of the cold war; Ceauşescu did it in calmer times of détente.[10]

The international status of Ceauşescu's Romania resembled that of Tito's non-aligned Yugoslavia. In the winter of 1978–79, Ceauşescu underscored his independence from Moscow by boldly rejecting a Warsaw Pact bid for increased military expenditures and for much greater centralization under Soviet command. In domestic affairs, however, independent Romania did not emulate Tito's desovietized, less autocratic form of communism. Liberated from Moscow, Tito himself was in no hurry to embrace parliamentary democracy. But his domestic liberalization has shown at least some resemblance to Eurocommunism. Ceauşescu on the other hand has done nothing of that sort. Independent Romania has remained a purely repressive society of the Soviet Communist kind. No liberalization (the primary concern that preoccupied Communist Russia regarding her European neighbors) threatened to spill over into the Soviet Union from Ceauşescu's Romania. And this comforting consideration may be one of the principal reasons that the Russians have put up with Romanian rebelliousness.

The Ceauşescu regime has drawn its inspiration mainly from two articles of faith: nationalism and industrialization. Austerity was the price the Romanians had to pay for the regime's ambition to raise the country's rank to that of a developed nation. In compensation for the pains of forced industrialization Ceauşescu allowed his compatriots the joys of unbridled nationalism. The Romanians, to be sure, did not cease to grumble over economic privation, but the opiate of nationalism, dispensed so spiritedly by Ceauşescu, distracted their consumer discontent. The frenzy of nationalist agitation for a so-called "Romanian national unitary state"[11] was reminiscent of Romanian fascism. No Eastern European country has integrated the radicalism of nationalism with the ideology (or rather, phraseology) of communism as totally as Ceauşescu's Romania. And as always, the principal victims of Romanian nationalist intolerance have been the Transylvanian Hungarians. They have lost what they had gained in the Stalinist fifties, including regional autonomy patterned on the model of the Soviet federal union of nationalities. Familiar indignities of discrimination against ethnic minorities have multiplied; some new ones borrowed from Soviet practices have also been added, such as confinement of the regime's critics to psychiatric hospitals.[12]

Khrushchev, who with his unsuccessful Comecon reforms precipitated Romania's rebellion, was on the losing side, too. Romania's defection from Soviet control further undermined Khrushchev's already weakened position in the Kremlin oligarchy; he was replaced in the fall of 1964 by Leonid I. Brezhnev.

While Romania recovered her national independence, Romania's rival neighbor, Hungary, recovered her national prosperity after the ruins of her defeated 1956 revolution. The leader of this fortunate turn was the traitor of the 1956 revolution: János Kádár.

At first despised and hated, Kádár turned out to be one of the most curious successes in Hungarian political history. But neither the Russians nor Kádár could have succeeded so remarkably in pacifying Hungary had the Hungarians themselves not revealed a talent which they had seldom shown in the past — a sense of political realism. The slogan under which Kádár pacified and revitalized the society was a novelty in

Communist history as well. It said: "He who is not against us is with us!" Within its own pragmatic limits (determined by Russian tolerance, that is), the Kádár system has worked surprisingly well. Mixing socialist planning with a modified market economy, a system called "new economic mechanism" has raised the country's standard of living and has introduced a new model of socialist society within the Soviet orbit of power. Hungary started enjoying a measure of domestic freedom which was quite unusual under communism. This was "socialism with a bourgeois face," as one Western observer called it. Without class overtones and less provocatively, lest the Russians take umbrage, the Hungarians themselves simply called it "pragmatic socialism."[13] It was no fulfillment of the aims of the 1956 revolution (an independent Hungary, democratic and neutral), but it was a better compromise with the Russians than anybody could have hoped for in the desperate moment of defeat in 1956.

Along with the Hungarians, the Poles were fellow rebels against the Russians in 1956. However, neither Poland's revolt nor her post-revolt reforms went as far as Hungary's. Władysław Gomułka was popular after 1956, mainly because he saved Poland from the ruins of an all-out revolution of the Hungarian type. He failed, however, to live up to Polish expectations as a reformist. Maneuvering at first somewhere between reforming and conserving, he stopped trying after a while to change things altogether. The gist of the popular dissatisfaction was economic in nature. But disillusionment was also widespread due to Gomułka's general unresponsiveness to demands for liberalization. In the late sixties, riots broke out similar to those that ushered in the 1956 revolt. In the midst of anti-regime demonstrations at Christmas time in 1970, Gomułka fell and was replaced by Edward Gierek as party leader. In his formative years as a Communist, Gierek had lived in France and Belgium. Yet he seemed better attuned to Polish realities than the homegrown Gomułka. Gierek was the kind of European Communist the Poles could feel at ease with, even though his reforms so far have fallen short of ending popular dissatisfaction. The "Polish road to communism" in general may look promising to those who dislike the Soviet model, but Gierek has still to prove that there is a way to satisfy the Poles without upsetting the Russians.[14]

Poland has been less satisfied with either Gomułka or Gierek than Hungary has become with Kádár. The Polish achievements, however, are by no means inferior to those of Hungary's in finding so-called "separate roads" to communism — or, rather, away from it. The Poles in fact are ahead of everyone else in Eastern Europe in maintaining a national life of their own behind the Communist facade. A private national life, different from the official one, has evolved in Poland on a scale which has no parallel elsewhere. It owes its success to an informal alliance of patriotic workers and peasants, progressive intellectuals and the ubiquitous Church. This "Other Poland" is highly visible, and the Communists evidently have no choice but to tolerate it. Another private success, but devoid of the Polish example's patriotism, is Hungary's "second economy" — a capitalist triumph for all practical purposes. The Communist party is trying to curb it, but would not destroy it, recognizing its advantages for both the economy and the peace of the society in general.

The Poles have shown greater boldness than the Hungarians in probing the limits of the delicate domestic compromises. Poland's size alone must account for that. The largest country in the Soviet satellite orbit, with a rapidly growing population, Poland today looms almost like an eastern counterpart of France on the map of Europe. It is no easy task for either the Polish Communists or the Soviet Union to keep her under tight control. The Hungarians are the third largest ethnic group of the region (only the Poles and Romanians surpass them in numbers). As a country, however, Hungary is small, close to the bottom among the Soviet bloc states (only Bulgaria is smaller). Political boundaries forcibly imposed by jealous neighbors keep Hungarian ethnic territory mutilated, reducing well over one-quarter of Hungarians in the Danube region to a repressed minority status under the supremacy of rival rulers. A sense of smallness and fresh memories of national catastrophes counsel caution; bitter experiences have taught the Hungarians to be realistic about their attainable goals.

Whatever the differences between Polish and Hungarian attitudes today, both these nations of rebellion-prone reputation have been equally successful since 1956 in keeping their relations with the Soviet Union reasonably free of trouble. Unexpectedly, the number one troublemaker among the Soviet satellites since the late 1960s has been Czechoslovakia.

Czechoslovakia's awakening from Stalinism was slow, but when it happened it made history. After several years of fermentation, the historic "Prague Spring" occurred in 1968. It began in January, when Alexander Dubček succeeded the Stalinist Antonín Novotný as party leader. It was a rebirth of democracy in a country which had known democracy before. The new democratic era lasted less than eight months and took its name from Dubček, the Slovak-born, Soviet trained Communist. But the true force of Czechoslovakia's democratic resurrection was the Czech spirit of democracy. Deeply embedded in European civilization, shining brightest earlier in the century, Czech democracy was sorely tried under the twin nightmares of Nazi and Soviet tyranny. During the Prague Spring its former glory was temporarily restored.

The Dubček era started as a reform movement within the Communist party. Dubček readily allied himself with the rising democratic reformist forces both within and outside the party, but he himself was not a convinced democrat. As a devout Communist, all he wished for was that the popular reforms he presided over as party secretary should make the party and the Soviet Union loved and respected. With the removal of the Stalinist controls, however, the long repressed democratic spirit of the society burst into the open, turning the reform movement into a revolution.[15]

It was a time of great ideas and confused action, as revolutions more often than not are. Unbridled freedom of speech was its most attractive and most memorable expression. It produced a deluge of inspired words, including the famous "socialism with a human face," proudly disassociating itself from the inhumanities of the Stalinist past. The plan was to achieve a "Czechoslovak road to socialism," to create a "new model of socialist democracy." The new model was described at great length in the Action Program of April 5, 1968, a document of several thousand words, propagating a mixture of ideas, old and new, but not easy to follow as a guideline for action.[16]

The triumph of liberty after years of tyranny was an exhilarating experience. It was like Hungary in 1956. In both instances, Communists started to talk and behave like Western democrats. They were truly "Eurocommunists," as they would be called in the seventies.[17] But, apart from that, there was no similarity between 1956 in Budapest and 1968 in Prague. There was no Russian occupation in Czechoslovakia, and the Communist party never lost control of events, as was the case in Hungary. The unique aim of the Czech revolution was the reform of the Communist party and, furthermore, of communism itself into a democratic institution. This the Russians would not tolerate. They declared themselves against democratic communism in the Eurocommunist sense — and they did it with the full force of their military might.

The Russians were not alone in taking a dim view of the Czechoslovak experiment in democratic communism. The East German and Polish leaders, Czechoslovakia's two northern neighbors, voiced their alarm even before the Russians did. The decision to intervene against Prague of course was Moscow's. The Czechs themselves were well aware of the mounting perils threatening their revolution. The most moving proclamation of the revolution, oscillating between hope and fear, was the "2,000 Words to Workers, Scientists, Artists, and Everyone," written in late June. Its ominous last words were: "The spring has now ended and will never return. By winter we will know everything."[18] The Russians did not wait until winter. They invaded Czechoslovakia on August 21, putting an end to the revolution.

The Russians took no great risks by resorting to force. The precedent of Hungary in 1956, the United States' involvement in Vietnam, and the pacifist mood of détente were assurances enough that they had nothing to fear from the West. Czechoslovakia herself was not prepared to fight. Even while provoking Moscow's ire, the Czechoslovak Communists kept reassuring Moscow of their loyalty. The Russians, however, trusted their tanks more than their Czech friends. Militarily, the invasion posed no problems. The surprise that did paralyze the Russians was political. They found no Kádár of 1956 among the Czech Communists. There was no repetition of President Hácha's 1939 surrender to the Nazis either. After the Soviet invasion, President Ludvík Svoboda humiliated the victorious Russians by refusing to appoint a government of traitors. The revolutionary leadership, having been arrested and deported to Moscow, had to be released and restored in Prague. It took the Russians eight months to ease out Dubček as party leader and replace him with another Slovak, Gustav Husák.

A Slovak at the helm during the revolution seemed to cement the not so solid brotherhood of Czechs and Slovaks. A Slovak as a henchman of the Russians after the defeat of the revolution did no good to Czech-Slovak relations. Proclamation of Slovak national equality with the Czechs took place as scheduled on the fiftieth anniversary of the founding of the Republic. But the Slovaks alone had cause for celebration. The new federal constitution that went into effect in October 1968 fulfilled a national dream; it was cheered by Slovaks both at home and abroad. The dream of reviving democracy, however, lay in ruins. The Slovaks could console themselves with their newly won status of national equality. The Czechs had only their defeat to mourn.[19]

The Hungarian citizens of the Slovak Socialist Republic of freshly federated Czechoslovakia were in an unmitigatedly mournful mood too. During the revolution, the Hungarians felt free to say what was on their minds. They openly demanded autonomy in accordance with the principle of national equality espoused by the revolution. Now, they were face to face with a triumphant Slovak nationalism untempered by democratic tolerance. And, once the Slovaks had brought Slovakia under their exclusive control, the Czechs, themselves battered under Russian occupation, began to feel sympathetic toward the Hungarians suffering under Slovak repression. Such was the melancholy ending of Czech-Hungarian hostility, for so long a leading force in fanning the flame of nationalist rivalry in the Danube Valley.[20]

To cushion the world's anticipated, critical reaction to their invasion, the Russians dragged their remaining four satellites with them on their punitive expedition against Czechoslovakia, with the intention of making it look like a collective enterprise of the Warsaw Treaty nations. The unreformed East German leadership, still Stalinist in spirit, was in fact a most eager accomplice of the Russians against the Czechs. The frightened conservative leaders of Poland and Bulgaria, too, were in accord with the Soviet decision to stop the Dubček liberals. Even liberalized Hungary went along, but out of fear rather than conviction. The Hungarians were at the time busily implementing their "new economic mechanism," which in many ways was similar to the economic plans of the reformist Czech Communists. Hungarian reformists wanted no conflict with Moscow.

To add insult to injury, the Russians called their armed intervention in Czechoslovakia an act of duty of one socialist country saving another. The democratic West ridiculed this Soviet hypocrisy, calling it derisively the Brezhnev doctrine. The label stuck, and this annoyed the Russians no less than did the continuing Czech passive resistance. Meanwhile, among Communists and fellow-travelers the world over, the Brezhnev doctrine triggered a new wave of defection from Moscow; and Communists who were already at odds with Moscow felt their negative view of Soviet communism once again confirmed.

There was a bitter irony, too, in Czechoslovakia's tragedy. Although born under Western and democratic auspices in 1918, the modern Czech nation had always been an enthusiastic supporter of both pro-Russian and pro-Soviet political orientations. The shock of the Soviet Russian invasion in 1968 and the pain of its aftermath changed all that. Once a Russophile Slav nation in the heart of Europe, the Czechs since 1968 have swelled the ranks of Russia's opponents. Jiří Pelikán, a bitterly disillusioned Czech Communist exile, described this post-revolutionary attitude as "socialist opposition." He appealed for an alliance with democratic Eurocommunism and hoped for a united front of all socialist opposition in Eastern Europe.[21]

The Soviet invasion of Czechoslovakia did not interrupt the process of East-West détente as the Soviet suppression of the Hungarian revolution had in 1956. The storm of Western indignation blew over very quickly. Détente in fact picked up momentum toward the end of the 1960s by West Germany's entry into the arena of Eastern European diplomacy.

Before Adenauer's retirement in 1963, it was an axiom of German diplomacy that détente with the Russians could come only after German reunification. Adenauer's successors, on the other hand, endorsed the new Western thesis, first formulated by de Gaulle, that if reunification were to be at all possible it had to follow détente rather than precede it. Chancellors Erhard and Kiesinger had already deviated from Adenauer's rigidity, especially by lifting the so-called Hallstein doctrine which forbade dealings with countries who recognized Eastern Germany (the Soviet Union excepted). But the dramatic change came with Chancellor Willy Brandt's *Ostpolitik,* which opened a new chapter in détente history.

A series of West German diplomatic moves changed both Germany's and the Western world's relations to Eastern Europe and the Soviet Union. It started in 1970 with the affirmation of existing Eastern boundaries: with the Soviet Union in the Moscow Treaty, and with Poland in the Warsaw Treaty. (Both treaties were ratified in 1972.) Stabilization of the status of West Berlin followed in 1971 with agreements among the four occupying powers as well as East and West Germany. Then came the so-called Traffic Treaty in 1972 between the two Germanys and, to complete the series, the Prague Treaty in 1973 with Czechoslovakia (ratified in 1974) which declared Munich null and void. In October 1973, both West and East Germany were admitted to the United Nations. A sort of general German settlement had thus been effected. The former allies who defeated Hitler were still unable to agree among themselves on a formal peace treaty with Germany. Even so, formal recognition of German territorial losses in the Second World War normalized Germany's relations with her Slavic neighbors. Mutual diplomatic recognition between the two Germanys further normalized German relations with all Soviet bloc nations. And agreement on the status of Berlin brought one of the most explosive issues in the East-West global conflict under control, even though it did not bring down the Berlin Wall between the two Germanys. Relations between the two Germanys in fact were still far from normal.

East Germany regarded the division of Germany into two states and two nations to be final. To emphasize this fact, the Constitution of the German Democratic Republic was amended in 1974, cancelling the "responsibility of showing the entire German nation the road to a future of peace and socialism" through "unification on the basis of democracy and socialism." At the same time, an addition to the Constitution declared that the right of the German Democratic Republic to "social, economic, state and national self-determination" had been accomplished, and thus the victory of the socialist order became "irrevocable and final," and East Germany henceforth was "irrevocably and forever" linked with the Soviet Union. In contrast to this East German position, West Germany saw no cause for changing its Constitution. The Basic Law of 1949, the "Bonn Constitution," continued to call upon the entire German people "to accomplish, by free self-determination, the unity and freedom of Germany." And Chancellor Brandt defined the status of the two Germanys as "one nation, two states," while the West German press, commenting on the revision of the East German Constitution, noted with sarcasm that East Germany was the first Soviet bloc country to support "complete integration in the Soviet system."[22]

Thus, Bonn's *Ostpolitik* brought greater improvement to the relations between Germans and non-Germans than to those between the two Germanys. The Slavs' fear of Germans in Eastern Europe had practically disappeared, despite Russian propaganda efforts to keep alive the image of a West German "Fascist" threat to peace and security. It looked as though the German Communists would be among the last Europeans to be afraid of the German danger and the *Drang nach Osten*.

The crowning success of East-West détente diplomacy was the "Conference on Security and Co-operation in Europe," concluded in Helsinki on August 1, 1975, with thirty-five states participating, including the Vatican, the Soviet Union, the United States and Canada. But whose success was really crowned at Helsinki?

The idea itself of a European conference had been formulated by Khrushchev almost twenty years before its triumph in Helsinki. The Soviet idea was to bring the West around to ratifying the territorial and political status quo of post-war Europe. The Western democracies went along with the Soviet initiative as part of a global design of American foreign policy, described by Secretary of State Kissinger as a "new structure of world peace." The Helsinki Declaration (also known as the "Final Act" or "Accord") was the fruit of a series of conferences that spread over a period of two years. On the Western side, Americans and Europeans made equally significant contributions, with the Europeans taking the lead in the area which came to be known as the "third basket," or human rights.

There was nothing specifically new in the Helsinki Declaration that was not already spelled out in the UN Charter, the Universal Declaration on Human Rights, or in the domestic constitutions and laws of both East and West. The participating states reaffirmed respect for each other's sovereign equality and individuality, "including in particular the right of every state to juridical equality, to territorial integrity and to freedom and political independence," as well as respect for "each other's right to freely choose and develop its political, social, economic and cultural systems as well as its right to determine its laws and regulations," and also "the right to belong to or not to belong to international organizations," including "the right to neutrality." They agreed that frontiers in Europe were "inviolable" and could be changed only "in accordance with international law, by peaceful means and by agreement." In general, they committed themselves to settling their disputes only by "peaceful means." They ruled out the "military occupation" of each other and pledged the principle of "equal rights and self-determination of peoples," adding for good measure that "all peoples always have the right, in full freedom, to determine, when and as they wish, their internal and external political status, without external interference, and to pursue as they wish their political, economic, social and cultural developments."

The Helsinki Declaration recognized the "universal significance of human rights and fundamental freedoms" as an "essential factor for the peace," listing the "freedom of thought, conscience, religion or belief, for all without distinction as to race, sex, language or religion." The right of "national minorities" to equality was spelled out separately, eliciting lively praise at the conference from Hungary, the only nation left in

Europe whose members in great numbers were exposed to forcible assimilation as minorities. And, finally, there were sections on "confidence building measures," such as notifying each other of major military maneuvers, on "cooperation in the field of economics, of science and technology, and of the environment," and also "in humanitarian and other fields," including "freer movement and contacts." But all this plethora of pledges for peace in Europe was to be implemented with "due regard to security requirements," which, if security were interpreted the customary Soviet way, could have invalidated all the Helsinki promises from "A" to "Z."

Abounding in the phraseology of liberal political philosophy, the text of the Helsinki Declaration, if taken at face value, was a Western success. On the other hand, by going to Helsinki, the Western democracies had also lent their support to the Russian pretense that the Soviets were practising believers in all the lofty principles endorsed by the conference. Soviet delegate Leonid Brezhnev in fact addressed the assembled European nations as a judge scolding their miserable historical record: "It was here in Europe that aggressors time and again adorned themselves with notorious laurels, later only to be cursed by the peoples. It was here in Europe that claims to world domination raised to the level of political doctrine ended in the collapse of states whose resources had been made to serve criminal and misanthropic purposes." And Brezhnev further made it clear that Russia was guided by nobody's standards but her own: "No one should try to dictate to other peoples . . . the manner in which they ought to manage their internal affairs."[24]

Whether Helsinki benefited tyranny or freedom depended in the long run neither on the high-sounding words of the Declaration nor on Brezhnev's hectoring comments. Helsinki had created another Yalta situation. What mattered was the follow-up: whether the lofty phrases would be interpreted according to Western or Soviet standards. For, like Yalta, Helsinki meant two different things to the two sides. To the Soviets Helsinki meant the final sanctioning of the status quo. To the victims of Soviet tyranny, it meant a new beginning to correct the status quo.

Secretary of State Kissinger took an optimistic Western view of the follow-up. Speaking in defense of the Helsinki accord, he said before the Southern Commodity Producers Conference in Birmingham, Alabama: "It is not we who were on the defensive at Helsinki; it is not we who were being challenged by all the delegations to live up to the principles being signed. At Helsinki, for the first time in the post-war period, human rights and fundamental freedoms became recognized subjects of East-West discourse and negotiation. The conference put forward our standards of humane conduct, which have been — and still are — a beacon of hope to millions. The winds of change are blowing from the West; the ideals of liberty and the challenges of technical innovation come from the West." He also assured his Alabama audience: "This Administration shall never forget the moral difference between freedom and tyranny."[25] This particular assurance was contradicted a year later by President Gerald R. Ford in his election debate with Jimmy Carter when he said that the Eastern European states were not dominated by the Soviet Union. Some people believed moreover that President Ford's "gaff" was not "a trivial mistake," but rather "the authentic voice of the unconscious Western desire to believe that the satellite states of the Soviet Union were free, and that therefore there is no need to feel either responsibility or anxiety."[26]

During Secretary of State Kissinger's tenure, the United States certainly did not distinguish itself by holding high the ideals of liberty and human rights. It was in fact a close Kissinger aide who caused the greatest uproar with a remark on Eastern Europe; Helmut Sonnenfeldt, an Eastern European expert in the State Department, deplored that "no development of a more viable, organized structure" had taken place between the Soviet Union and the Eastern European countries, and he advised "to strive for an evolution that makes the relationship between the Eastern Europeans and the Soviet Union an organic one."[27] One should not, however, single out Nixon, Ford, Kissinger, or Sonnenfeldt for showing a lack of interest in Eastern Europe under Soviet domination. The democratic world at large had long before lost the interest of an earlier generation, once animated by Wilsonian idealism, toward the oppressed peoples of Europe. Western curiosity had been switched to the new nations of the Third World and, in the particular case of the United States (home of the largest Jewish population in the world), to the new state of Israel. Only in times of great tragedies has sympathy been collectively aroused for the "East" European members of Western civilization. And East-West détente in particular dimmed the Western awareness of Eastern Europe's humiliation under Soviet domination, while the focus of American interest in the Communist world came to be centered mainly on the emigration of Jews from Soviet Russia to Israel.

The American preoccupation with emigration became truly extravagant. The Trade Act of 1974, Section 402, tied the most-favored-nation treatment to free emigration as an assurance of "continued dedication of the United States to fundamental human rights." Communist governments of Eastern Europe, too, eager to qualify for most-favored-nation status, had to prove their respect for free emigration, although their citizens were more eager to exercise their human rights at home. Only under President Carter did the United States return to a more comprehensive interpretation of fundamental human rights.

Ever since Helsinki, the human rights issue has stirred up resistance movements both in Eastern Europe and the Soviet Union — modest in scope but quite remarkable as a phenomenon of opposition considering the risks involved under the police-state conditions of these societies. The defenders of Helsinki seemed to be right; détente was good for freedom.

The most significant human-rights event in Eastern Europe was the "Charter 77" movement in Czechoslovakia, so called after a manifesto issued in late 1976. It was signed by hundreds of Czechs and Slovaks from all walks of life, but mostly by Czech intellectuals who initiated it. The Czech Chartists invoked not only Czechoslovak laws but international agreements as well, such as the International Covenant on Civil and Political Rights, the International Covenant on Economic, Social and Cultural Rights, the UN Universal Declaration on Human Rights and, of course, the Helsinki Declaration. They charged that most of the fundamental human rights existed "only on paper" in Czechoslovakia. The Chartists were promptly branded as traitors by the Prague government. A new wave of terror hit the Czech intellectual community, core of the "socialist opposition," particularly hard. The Czech Chartist movement rapidly assumed international dimensions. Declarations of sympathy were heard from all over Eastern Europe, and Prague's repressive policies were censured by the West, including the Eurocommunists of Italy, Spain and France.

By a happy coincidence, President Carter (tutored in foreign affairs by his Polish-born national security adviser, Zbigniew Brzezinski) embraced the human rights issue as a central theme of his policy. Dissidents everywhere who lived under tyrannical regimes hailed Carter's Washington Spring of 1977. The President's human rights campaign, however, was received with less enthusiasm in the free world. A human rights scare, so to speak, gripped supporters of détente, afraid lest the Carter policy might antagonize the Russians, ruin improved East-West relations, and thus damage the very cause it was intended to serve. Western détentists were worried about the upcoming Belgrade follow-up conference to Helsinki when angry voices against Carter were raised in Moscow as well as in the satellite capitals. Negative reactions started pouring in from other parts of the world, too. Injecting the issue of human rights into international relations was criticized as an interference in the domestic affairs of sovereign states. Even believers in human rights began to doubt the effectiveness of the Carter campaign.

Under pressure from friend and foe, both at home and abroad, President Carter toned down his human rights propaganda. To reassure the Russians, as well as the rest of the world scared by human rights, he delivered two foreign policy speeches in the spring and early summer of 1977. In his commencement address at the University of Notre Dame, President Carter listed human rights at the top of his "cardinal policy premises," but he also stressed his desire to improve relations with both Soviet Russia and Communist China, declaring: "Being confident of our future we are now free of that inordinate fear of communism which once led us to embrace any dictator who joined us in our fear." For good measure, in a speech before the Southern Legislative Conference in Charleston, South Carolina, he addressed himself specifically to American-Soviet relations. Eager to dispel Soviet suspicion that his campaign was aimed against Russia, the President denied any "hidden meanings" and emphasized that his universal concern for human rights was "not designed to heat up the arms race or bring back the cold war."

Carter's critics seemed to be satisfied. The human rights scare quieted down, the Belgrade review conference of the Helsinki accords ran its course in the fall and winter of 1977–78 without any major crisis despite East-West deadlock over the human rights issue. A minor crisis flared up again in early summer of 1978 over the trials of Soviet dissidents. But the most important item on the détente agenda, the Soviet-American talks for another strategic arms agreement (SALT II), went on and the world learned to live with periodic American reminders to respect human rights. Meanwhile the upsurge of dissident hopes throughout Eastern Europe in the wake of Washington's spring call for human rights had ended in 1977 in a "silent fall."[29] The Soviet dissidents were decimated by stepped-up police measures which included a new method of getting rid of political opponents by deportation and emigration. Western détentists termed this "liberalization." In any manner of speaking, it certainly was an improvement over the old Soviet method of murder, or the slow death by torture in forced labor camps.

Détente confronted the democracies with the dilemma of how to advocate freedom and coexist peacefully with tyranny at the same time. Believers in the primacy of *Realpolitik* thought that the best way to avoid such dilemmas was to avoid situations that raised such dilemmas. The pessimists on the other hand felt that tyranny had won another battle. Only the optimists continued to hope against hope that the raising of the human rights issue in itself had brought freedom one step closer to triumph over tyranny.

The 1980s began inauspiciously for détente. In the wake of the Soviet New Year's aggression against Afghanistan in 1980, détente was in danger of slipping back into cold war or worse — or into something in between that was neither détente nor cold war and for which no name has yet been invented. However, one conclusion could already be safely drawn from the new East-West crisis: Western democracy and Soviet communism were as far from reconciling their fundamental differences as they have ever been since their Grand Alliance of the war against Hitler collapsed and Moscow has spread its tyrannical power over the eastern half of the divided European continent.

The end of tyranny was not in sight in Central Europe — or Eastern Europe, as Central Europe has come to be known in the West since the Second World War. Referring to this unlucky half of Europe, Hugh Seton-Watson wrote: ". . . about eighty million Europeans are subjected to national humiliation, and this makes Europe one of the most explosive parts of the world."[30] But there was also some cause for optimism in this sick situation.

Over thirty years ago, in 1948, when the Communist coup in Czechoslovakia made the Soviet conquest in Europe complete, the Czechs were the Russians' best friends. The Russians did not need even the backing of the Red Army to bring Czechoslovakia under their control.[31] Today, Czechoslovakia is the heart of socialist resistance against Eastern Europe's Soviet domination. And the Czech situation is symbolic of the bankruptcy of Soviet Russia's policy in general toward her European neighbors.

Thirty years ago it looked as if the people's democracies set up by Soviet conquest in Europe would go the Mongolian way. The Mongolian precedent in fact had most likely served as a model for Soviet intentions in Eastern Europe. Outer Mongolia, Soviet Russia's Asian satellite, was the first of the so-called people's republics; and the Mongols were said to be "extremely proud" of it.[32] Eastern Europe, however, did not go the Mongolian way. Unlike what was said about the Mongolians of Asia, few people in the Communist people's republics of Europe were proud of becoming Russian satellites. As allies of the West, the Soviet Russians were welcome in Europe as liberators from Nazi tyranny. As political teachers, they were rejected. Socialism had become a way of life with Eastern Europeans. But the Soviet form of socialism — and the Russian ways in general — were found to be repugnant. Some Easternization through forcible association with Soviet Russia did take place in the region formerly known as Central Europe. But it was mostly limited to Communist party trappings aping Soviet totalitarianism. Beyond that, the Russians in Europe were singularly unsuccessful in reaching the people over whom they had wielded so much power for so many years.

Russian influence in Eastern Europe rested exclusively on military might. Even Communist loyalty to Moscow was safe, as a rule, only where Soviet troops were present. There were no Soviet troops in the Balkans; the four Communist states there — Yugoslavia, Romania, Bulgaria, Albania — were independent and all of them, with the exception of Bulgaria, steered away from Soviet Russia. And even the loyalty of the Bulgarian Communists was motivated primarily by Bulgaria's territorial feud with neighboring Yugoslavia. Bulgarian reliance on Russian help in fact has dated back to Tsarist times and it has paid repeatedly handsome territorial dividends, compensating for less pleasant Russian historical memories.

There were Soviet troops in the four Communist states of Central Europe — Poland, the German Democratic Republic, Czechoslovakia and Hungary. The Soviet troops were ostensibly there as allies, but in fact as props of the Communist regimes and guarantees against defection from the Soviet bloc. These four states of Central Europe were not independent. Yet some of them enjoyed greater internal freedom than some of the independent Communist states in the Balkans — a paradox and a reminder that Eastern Europe's "liberation" was not a matter of Russian withdrawal alone. Hungary was the Central European country with the greatest internal freedom of any Communist state in the Soviet sphere (as of 1980 in any case). Poland, with a peasantry barely touched by forcible collectivization and with religious freedom almost on a

Western scale, was a unique case too. The country worst off was Czechoslovakia. She was under virtual Russian occupation, while the German Democratic Republic as a separate German nation was a Soviet invention, most likely to last as long as the Russian rule in Central Europe.

Soviet military mastery over the entire Communist orbit of Europe is indisputable. The limits of Soviet tolerance for independence in Eastern Europe, as well as Soviet freedom of action to enforce their will there, have been tested. Precedents, however, are not necessarily a clue to predicting the future. The East-West balance of power may change to Russia's advantage or to Europe's advantage, depending on internal as well as on external developments. American-Soviet, American-European, American-Chinese, and Sino-Soviet relations may greatly affect Europe's destiny. But the evolution inside Europe, both East and West, is the most decisive factor in shaping Europe's future.

Since the mid-1970s, Western democratic self-confidence has been on the rise in Europe. Democracy was restored in Greece, Portugal and Spain. Eurocommunism has made its appearance, professing its loyalty to Western democratic principles. With prospects of Communist participation in Western governments also rising, Eurocommunism's democratic trustworthiness soon turned into a hotly debated issue. But democratic behavior in government is not the sole question mark about Eurocommunism. Another uncertainty is Eurocommunist loyalty to the idea of a new Europe as articulated by postwar federalist believers in democratic internationalism. French Eurocommunists in particular made no bones about their opposition to surrendering any bit of national sovereignty to a European Union.[33] Defense of national sovereignty of course is no Communist speciality, but certainly it is one of several suspicious paradoxes in Communist history. Theoretically, communism is an international movement uniting the proletariat of the world. However: "Communism in practice has turned out to be a form of idolatry of the National State," in the words of Richard Löwenthal, one of Europe's most astute experts on Communist affairs.[34] And the reasons are obvious. The Communists favor internationalism on their own terms only, while national sovereignty serves to protect their monopoly of power in countries they rule. Not a long time ago, absolute national sovereignty was seen by Oscar Jászi as a "vicious feudal dogma."[35] Today, national sovereignty is a shield protecting totalitarian ruling minorities of all sorts, including those of the Communist variety.

Distrust of Eurocommunism is widespread, among capitalists as well as socialists, among conservatives as well as progressives. Many agree with Jean-François Revel that nothing in the Communist record has made it possible to believe that they do not have as their goal the monopoly of power.[36] On the other hand, a progressive political coalition with the Eurocommunists, working according to the Western rules of parliamentarianism, would be democracy's greatest triumph over Soviet tyrannical communism since the Bolshevik victory in 1917. A democratic Eurocommunist success in the West could also precipitate a democratic upheaval in Communist Eastern Europe that would be difficult, if not impossible, for the Russians to suppress by Hungarian or Czechoslovakian-style invasions.[37]

It is impossible to predict the prospects of new stages in the age-old conflict between Russia and Europe. It is difficult to unravel even a relatively minor enigma, such as the future of Yugoslavia after Tito, judged to be the next most critical Eastern European issue, involving both Russia and the West. In the spring of 1980, the Yugoslav dictatorship appeared confident to be able to keep the lid over internal forces of discord in the wake of Tito's death. But the question is whether the Soviet Union would resist the temptation to exploit the predictable post-Tito difficulties. The 1971 "Zagreb Spring" of liberal-minded Croat Communists, ruthlessly repressed by Belgrade's "centralist coup" of December 1971, revealed anew the gravity of the simmering Serb-Croat antagonism.[38] There are other unsettled nationality problems, too. The Soviet Union may be tempted to take advantage of ethnic rivalries in and around Yugoslavia, with the strong hand and unique authority of Tito gone.

For that matter, national rivalries everywhere in the Middle Zone have changed little, if at all, in spite of the many common tragedies that could have been averted by united effort. We know how much harm the smaller nations, squeezed into a narrow and dangerous zone between the powers of the East and the West, have done to themselves by their regional discords. We can only guess how much good they would do if they could unite. A neutral, democratic, socialist, independent Central Europe between East and West is a dream living in many hearts and minds. Even under the present mixed and uncertain state of freedom and independence, the nations in the Communist eastern half of Europe would do a lot better if they would accept each other as equals and learn the art of cooperation.

It would be a mistake to belittle the threat of an aggressive Soviet

Russian power hovering over Europe. But to underestimate the potential strength of the Europeans would be no less a mistake. The strength of the Europeans to meet the Soviet Russian challenge depends primarily on how united they can become. Progress in Western Europe toward an international democratic community, however disappointingly slow, has been far more successful since the Second World War than the advance toward unity in the Communist eastern half of Europe. It would be easy to blame the Russians for that. Unfortunately, beyond the empty slogans of "proletarian internationalism," the Eastern Europeans have shown no real change of heart from the narrow-minded nationalism of the past to a truly effective democratic internationalism which would end their petty rivalries. It is hard to contradict the widespread fatalistic Western judgment (rooted evidently in memories of the late thirties) relegating the Middle Europeans to a perpetual oppression of one sort or another. This line of Western thinking sees no chance for the peoples of the Middle Zone to overcome their dismal fate. For, as Max Beloff once expressed it: "Either Germany and Russia will join hands to partition them or they must rely on one or the other. Their only real hope is that Russia will evolve in such a way as to make the tutelage less oppressive."[39]

We should hope of course that the Soviet Union becomes less oppressive. Yet our real hope is that the Europeans themselves will come to their senses and unite their forces against foreign tutelage of whichever sort. It is within their collective power whether they will stagnate in a sense of crisis and live in fear of foreign domination or whether they will live as free people, self-confident and unafraid, having placed their trust in the collective strength of a democratic European Union.

Notes

All page references are to the American edition of the work cited. Where a British edition is known to exist the publisher's name is given in brackets.

Preface to the New Edition

1. Cf. Hugh Seton-Watson, "Is There an East Central Europe," in Sylva Sinanian, Istvan Deak, Peter D. Ludz, *Eastern Europe in the 1970s* (New York and London: Praeger, 1972), 3–12.

2. Cf. Endre Arató, *Kelet-Európa története a 19. század első felében* (Budapest: Akadémiai Kiadó, 1971). The author manipulates the history of Central and Eastern Europe in such a manner that Communist rule and Soviet-Russian hegemony over the eastern half of Europe appears already in the first half of the nineteenth century as a preordained sequence of history. See my review of Arató's book, *Slavic Review,* XXXII (1973), 415–16.

3. D. C. Fleming, *The Cold War and Its Origins 1950–1960,* II (New York: Doubleday, 1961), 1042.

4. Neville Chamberlain's words in a broadcast, September 27, 1938, on the eve of Munich, as quoted in A.J.P. Taylor, *English History 1914–1945* (Oxford: Oxford University Press, 1965), 431.

From the Preface to the First Edition

1. On the meaning of modern tyranny, see Oscar Jászi and John D. Lewis, *Against the Tyrant: The Traditions and Theory of Tyrannicide* (Glencoe, Ill.: The Free Press, 1957), VII. The authors, it seems to me, rightly point out that "modern dictatorships followed the historic models of tyrannical government" and that "in the thoroughness and machine-made efficiency of suppression and indoctrination they far surpassed the classic examples of tyranny, which had operated without modern devices for mass persuasion and intimidation." Also, the authors call attention to the opinion of the distinguished French historian Élie Halévy, who in 1936 (in his "L'Ére des tyrannies," *Bulletin de la Société française de philosophie*) suggested that the new phenomena "could be best characterized by the word *tyranny* — a word which came from Greek experience of a similar era — rather than by the Roman word *dictatorship,* which originally applied to a temporary, constitutional expedient."

2. How nationalism sacrificed liberty to the demands of nationality in Central and Eastern Europe has been analyzed most penetratingly by Hans Kohn.

See, for example, his essay, *Nationalism: Its Meaning and History* (Princeton, N. J.: D. Van Nostrand, 1955), 46, 81–82. [Allen &Unwin]

Introduction

1. For detailed ethnic and religious statistics on the countries in question, see Hugh Seton-Watson, *Eastern Europe Between the Wars: 1918–1941* (London: Cambridge University Press, 1945), App. 1, 430–33.

2. David Hunter Miller, *My Diary at the Conference of Paris,* XIII (London: privately printed, 1925), 96; see also David Lloyd George, *Memoirs of the Peace Conference,* II (New Haven: Yale University Press, 1939), 608.

3. Winston S. Churchill, *The Second World War: Triumph and Tragedy* (Boston: Houghton Mifflin, 1953), 750. [Cassell]

4. Sir Duff Cooper's letter in the *Daily Telegraph* (London), April 18, 1950. See also Wickham Steed's letter in *The Times Literary Supplement,* September 24, 1954.

5. See Oscar Jászi, *The Dissolution of the Habsburg Monarchy* (Chicago: The University of Chicago Press, 1929), 6ff. For more recent appraisals of the question of dissolution, see Arthur J. May, *The Passing of the Hapsburg Monarchy* (Philadelphia: University of Pennsylvania Press, 1966); Robert A. Kann, *The Habsburg Empire* (New York: Praeger, 1957); Z.A.B. Zeman, *The Break-up of the Habsburg Empire* (London: Oxford University Press, 1961).

1 The Lost Peace

1. Winston S. Churchill, *The Second World War: The Gathering Storm* (Boston: Houghton Mifflin, 1948), 38, 42–43. [Cassell]

2. L. B. Namier, *Europe in Decay: A Study in Disintegration* (London: Macmillan, 1950), 153.

3. Jacques Bainville, *Les conséquences politiques de la paix* (Paris: Nouvelle Libraire Nationale, 1920), 172–73.

4. *Papers and Documents Relating to the Foreign Relations of Hungary,* II (published as a manuscript by the Royal Hungarian Ministry for Foreign Affairs, Budapest, n.d.), 225–41 *passim.*

5. Edward Hallett Carr, *German-Soviet Relations Between the Two World Wars* (Baltimore: Johns Hopkins University Press, 1951), 61. [Oxford University Press]

6. However, as Professor Craig pointed out, Rathenau's policy basically sought understanding with the West. Rathenau was persuaded to sign the Rapallo Treaty by Baron Maltzen, the head of the Eastern Division of the German Foreign Ministry, an enthusiast for Soviet-German ties. Rathenau's cool reception by the Western Allies also contributed to his "surrender." Cf. Gordon A. Craig, *From Bismarck to Adenauer: Aspects of German Statescraft* (Baltimore: Johns Hopkins University Press, 1958), 68–69.

7. I. Deutscher, *Stalin: A Political Biography* (New York and London: Oxford University Press, 1949), 390.

8. On this subject, see Hans W. Gatzke, *Stresemann and the Rearmament of Germany* (Baltimore: Johns Hopkins University Press, 1954).

9. Deutscher, *Stalin*, 409.

10. Ibid., 410. The Communist International took a no less critical view of the "imperialist" Trianon Treaty which dismembered Hungary. In the spirit of "proletarian" justice, the Fifth Congress of the Comintern in 1924 advocated independence for the Slovaks, a special régime of autonomy for Transylvania, and a frontier revision by which Hungarian-speaking areas of Slovakia, Romania and Yugoslavia were to be added to the Hungarian state. See Walter Kolarz, *Russia and Her Colonies* (New York: Praeger, 1952), 305. [G. Philip]

2 Federalist Failures

1. José Ortega y Gasset, *The Revolt of the Masses* (New York: Norton, 1932), 200. [Allen & Unwin]

2. Robert Schuman, "France and Europe," *Foreign Affairs*, XXXI, 3 (April, 1953), 349–50.

3. Oscar Jászi, *Revolution and Counter-Revolution in Hungary* (London: King & Son, 1924), IX.

4. Ibid., 38.

5. Cf. C. A. Macartney, *National States and National Minorities* (London: Oxford University Press, 1934), 276–77.

6. Oscar Jászi, "The Significance of Thomas G. Masaryk for the Future," reprinted from *Journal of Central European Affairs*, X, 1 (April, 1950), 6–7.

7. Thomas Garrigue Masaryk, *The Making of a State: Memories and Observations, 1914–1918* (New York: Frederick A. Stokes, 1928), 364–65 [Allen & Unwin]; see also Feliks Gross, *Crossroads of Two Continents: A Democratic Federation of East-Central Europe* (New York: Columbia University Press, 1945), 13–14. [Oxford University Press]

8. Cf. David Mitrany, *Marx Against the Peasant* (Chapel Hill: University of North Carolina Press, 1951), 138, 250. [Weidenfeld & Nicolson]

9. Cf. Josef Hanc, *Tornado Across Eastern Europe* (New York: Greystone Press, 1942), 113. [Museum Press]

10. Nikolaus von Horthy, *Ein Leben für Ungarn* (Bonn: Athenäum, 1953), 168.

11. Count Stephen Bethlen, *The Treaty of Trianon and European Peace* (London: Longmans, 1934), 176.

12. Harry Nichols Howard, "The Little Entente and the Balkan Entente," in *Czechoslovakia*, ed. Robert J. Kerner (Berkeley and Los Angeles: University of California Press, 1949), 384.

3 The Nazi Challenge

1. Quoted in Hubert Ripka, *East and West* (London: Lincoln-Prager, 1944), 41.

2. I. Deutscher, *Stalin: A Political Biography* (New York and London: Oxford University Press, 1949), 423.

3. E. H. Carr, *International Relations Between the Two World Wars* (London: Macmillan, 1948), 220.

4. Hans Kohn, *The Twentieth Century: A Midway Account of the Western World* (New York: Macmillan, 1949), 211. [Gollancz]

4 Czechs and Hungarians

1. A. J. P. Taylor, "Czechoslovakia and Europe: The Foreign Policy of Dr. Beneš," in *Edward Beneš: Essays and Reflections Presented on the Occasion of his Sixtieth Birthday,* ed. Jan Opočenský (London: Allen & Unwin, 1945), 163–64.

2. Cf. Oscar Jászi, *Revolution and Counter-Revolution in Hungary* (London: King & Son, 1924), 37, 55–57, 97–98. Also *Memoirs of Michael Karolyi: Faith Without Illusion* (London: Jonathan Cape, 1956), 155.

3. Stephen D. Kertesz, *Diplomacy in a Whirlpool: Hungary Between Nazi Germany and Soviet Russia* (Notre Dame: University of Notre Dame Press, 1953), 20.

4. Edward Táborský, "Beneš and the Soviets," *Foreign Affairs,* XXVII, 2 (January 1949), 304; see below, Chapter 15, "Beneš and the Russians."

5. Rustem Vámbéry, *The Hungarian Problem* (New York: The Nation, 1942), 19.

6. Cf. Count Stephen Bethlen, "Szent István napján," *Pesti Napló,* August 20, 1937; idem, *The Treaty of Trianon and European Peace* (London: Longmans, 1934).

7. S. Harrison Thomson, *Czechoslovakia in European History* (Princeton: Princeton University Press, 1953; revised edition of the 1943 first edition), 5. [Oxford University Press]

8. Eduard Beneš, *Reč k Slovákom o našej národnej prítomnosti a budúcnosti* (Bratislava, 1934); idem, *Reden an die Deutschen in der Č.S.R.* (Aussig, 1935).

5 Appeasement of Hitler

1. Cf. Henry L. Roberts, "Diplomacy of Colonel Beck," in *The Diplomats,* ed. Gordon A. Craig and Felix Gilbert (Princeton: Princeton University Press, 1953), 612 [Oxford University Press]; see also Zygmunt J. Gasiorowski, "Did Pilsudski Attempt to Initiate a Preventive War in 1933?" *The Journal of Modern History,* XXVII, 2 (June 1955), 151.

2. Cf. Karl Renner, "Austria: Key for War and Peace," *Foreign Affairs,* XXVI, 4 (July 1948), 596–97.

3. Sir Lewis Namier, *In the Nazi Era* (London: Macmillan, 1952), 120.

4. Winston S. Churchill, *The Second World War: The Gathering Storm* (Boston: Houghton Mifflin, 1948), 221, 242. [Cassell]

5. Ibid., 254–55; cf. Lord Halifax, *Fullness of Days* (New York: Dodd, Mead & Co., 1957), 196.

6. Churchill, *The Gathering Storm,* 293.

7. Cf. John W. Wheeler-Bennett, *Munich: Prologue to Tragedy* (New York: Duell, Sloan & Pearce, 1948), 32. [Macmillan]

6 *Munich: Hopes and Lessons*

1. Winston S. Churchill, *The Second World War: The Gathering Storm* (Boston: Houghton Mifflin, 1948), 319, 310–12 *passim.* [Cassell]

2. Ibid., 302.

3. Edward Táborský, "Beneš and the Soviets," *Foreign Affairs,* XXVII, 2 (January 1949), 306.

4. *Documents on British Foreign Policy, 1918–1939,* Third Series, I, 1938; II, 1938; ed. E. L. Woodward, Rohan Buttler, Margaret Lambert (London: H. M. Stationery Office, 1949).

5. Cf. Sir Lewis Namier, *In the Nazi Era* (London: Macmillan, 1952), 163.

6. Cf. Edward Táborský, "The Triumph and Disaster of Edward Beneš," *Foreign Affairs,* XXXVI, 14 (July 1958), 673. The author, Beneš's wartime secretary, described Beneš's state of mind between October 1938 and March 1939 in these terms: ". . . he assumed that Hitler would leave the crippled and helpless torso of Czechoslovakia alone and turn to his next victim. . . . Hitler's destruction of what was left of Czechoslovakia in March 1939 came therefore as a terrible shock."

7. R. W. Seton-Watson, *From Munich to Danzig* (London: Methuen, 1939), 116, 118.

8. Churchill, *The Gathering Storm,* 322.

9. A.J.P. Taylor, "Czechoslovakia and Europe: The Foreign Policy of Dr. Beneš," in *Edward Beneš: Essays and Reflections Presented on the Occasion of his Sixtieth Birthday,* ed. Jan Opočenský (London: Allen & Unwin, 1944), 161.

10. C. A. Macartney, *Problems of the Danube Basin* (Cambridge: The University Press, 1944), 103.

11. Oscar Halecki, *Borderlands of Western Civilization: A History of East Central Europe* (New York: The Ronald Press Company, 1952), 435.

7 *From Munich to Moscow*

1. Gyula Szekfű, *Forradalom után* (Budapest: Cserépfalvi, 1947), 69.

2. Cf. L. B. Namier, *Europe in Decay* (London: Macmillan, 1950), 250–58 *passim.*

3. *Falsifiers of History: An Historical Document on the Origins of World War II* (New York: Committee for Promotion of Peace, [1948]), 37.

4. Cf. Eduard Beneš, *Paměti: Od Mníchova k nové válce a k novému vítězství* (Prague: Orbis, 1948), 65ff., 295; idem, *Nová slovanská politika* (Prague: 1948), 44, 52. For further details on this subject, see below, Chapter 9,

"Federalist Interlude," and Chapter 15, "Beneš and the Russians." All quotations from Beneš's *Paměti* (Memoirs) are the author's own translations; an English edition of the Beneš memoirs, by Godfrey Lias, is now available — *Memoirs of Dr. Eduard Beneš: From Munich to New War and New Victory* (Boston: Houghton Mifflin, [1955]) [Allen & Unwin]; see Stephen Borsody, "Beneš, Memoirs," *Political Science Quarterly,* LXXI, 1 (March 1956), 143–46.

5. Beneš, *Paměti,* 203–04; 114–22 *passim.*

6. Ibid., 203–04.

7. Ibid., 208.

8. Ibid., 226.

9. Ibid., 302–33 *passim.*

10. Michael Károlyi's "Introduction" to G. Pálóczy-Horváth, *In Darkest Hungary* (London: Gollancz, 1945), 18.

11. Beneš, *Paměti,* 462.

12. Cf. C. A. Macartney, *A History of Hungary: 1929–1945,* I (New York: Praeger, [1957]), 83.

13. Walter Kolarz, *Myths and Realities in Eastern Europe* (London: Lindsay Drummond, 1946), 138. Another Sudeten German of unimpeachable democratic loyalty, the Socialist politician Wenzel Jaksch, offered a very different interpretation which appeared, however, less convincing. The overwhelming majority of Czechoslovakia's multinational population, according to Jaksch, was loyal to the state, while the main cause of Czechoslovakia's capitulation was the defeatism of President Beneš and Premier Hodža. Cf. Wenzel Jaksch, *Europas Weg nach Potsdam: Schuld und Schicksal im Donauraum* (Stuttgart: Deutsche Verlags-Anstalt, 1958), 317–19, 321, 324–25.

14. Eduard Beneš, *Šest let exilu a druhé světové války: Řeči, projevy a dokumenty z r. 1938–45* (Prague: Orbis, 1946), 59.

8 German Hegemony

1. Cf. *Nazi-Soviet Relations, 1939–1941* (Washington, D.C.: U.S. Department of State, 1948), 163.

2. Sumner Welles, *The Time for Decision* (New York: Harper, 1944), 78, 79, 141. [Hamish Hamilton]

3. *Nazi-Soviet Relations,* 255ff.

4. Hugh Seton-Watson, *The East European Revolution* (New York: Praeger, 1951), 66. [Methuen]

5. *Nazi-Soviet Relations,* 316ff.

6. *Falsifiers of History* (New York: Committee for Promotion of Peace [1948]), 51, 59.

9 Federalist Interlude

1. Cf. Piotr S. Wandycz, *Czechoslovak-Polish Confederation and the Great*

Powers: 1940–43 (Bloomington: Indiana University Publications in the Slavic and East European Series, 1956), 105; István Borsody, *Beneš* (Budapest: Athenaeum, [1943]), 201. See also above, Chapter 7, "From Munich to Moscow," and below, Chapter 15, "Beneš and the Russians." For the wartime federal plans, see Feliks Gross, *Crossroads of Two Continents: A Democratic Federation of East-Central Europe* (New York: Columbia University Press, 1945). [Oxford University Press]

2. Winston S. Churchill, *The Second World War: The Gathering Storm* (Boston: Houghton Mifflin, 1948), 10, 17. [Cassell]

3. Joseph Stalin, *Problems of Leninism* (Moscow: Foreign Languages Publishing House, 1940), 337–38.

4. Winston S. Churchill, *The Second World War: The Grand Alliance* (Boston: Houghton Mifflin, 1949), 629. [Cassell]

5. S. Harrison Thomson, *Czechoslovakia in European History* (Princeton: Princeton University Press, 1953), 426. [Oxford University Press]

6. Robert E. Sherwood, *Roosevelt and Hopkins* (New York: Harper, 1948), 714. [Eyre & Spottiswoode]

7. Eduard Beneš, *Paměti: Od Mníchova k nové válce a k novému vítězství* (Prague: Orbis, 1948), 213ff.

8. Ibid., 330. Italics added

9. Ibid., 285. Beneš's italics.

10. For further details on this subject, see below, Chapter 15, "Beneš and the Russians."

11. Oscar Jászi, "Postwar Pacification in Europe," in *Federation: The Coming Structure of World Government,* ed. Howard O. Eaton (Norman: University of Oklahoma Press, 1944), 147–48, 153; cf. Eduard Beneš, "The Organization of Post-War Europe," *Foreign Affairs,* XX, 2 (January 1942), 237–38.

12. Winston S. Churchill, *The Second World War: The Hinge of Fate* (Boston: Houghton Mifflin, 1950). [Cassell]

13. Sumner Welles, *Seven Decisions That Shaped History* (New York: Harper, 1950), 184. [Hamish Hamilton]

14. Churchill, *The Hinge of Fate,* 802–07 *passim.*

15. *The Memoirs of Cordell Hull* (New York: Macmillan, 1948), 1463. [Hodder & Stoughton]

16. Ibid., 1298–99 *passim.*

17. Ibid., 1234.

18. See below, Chapter 15, "Beneš and the Russians."

19. *The Memoirs of Cordell Hull,* 1642.

20. Winston S. Churchill, *The Second World War: Triumph and Tragedy* (Boston: Houghton Mifflin, 1953), 158. [Cassell]

21. Winston S. Churchill, *The Second World War: Closing the Ring* (Boston: Houghton Mifflin, 1951), 360, 400–03 *passim.* [Cassell]

10 Partition of Europe

1. Robert E. Sherwood, *Roosevelt and Hopkins* (New York: Harper, 1948), 748. [Eyre & Spottiswoode]

2. Chester Wilmot, *The Struggle for Europe* (New York: Harper, 1952), 634. [Collins]

3. Winston S. Churchill, *The Second World War: Triumph and Tragedy* (Boston: Houghton Mifflin, 1953), 158. [Cassell]

4. *The Memoirs of Cordell Hull* (New York: Macmillan, 1948), 1163. [Hodder & Stoughton]

5. Ibid., 1465.

6. Edward Hallett Carr, *Conditions of Peace* (New York: Macmillan, 1942), 210–11. [Macmillan]

7. *The Secret Treaties and Understandings,* ed. F. Seymour Cocks (London: Union of Democratic Control, 1918), 68.

8. Norman Angell, "Why We Lost the Peace," *The New Leader* (April 14, 1952), 16–18.

9. *The Memoirs of Cordell Hull,* 1166–67 *passim.*

10. Ibid., 1170–72 *passim.*

11. Sumner Welles, *Where Are We Heading* (New York: Harper, 1946), 151. [Hamish Hamilton]

12. *The Memoirs of Cordell Hull,* 1460.

13. David J. Dallin, *The Big Three: The United States, Britain, Russia* (New Haven: Yale University Press, 1945), 129, 131. [Allen & Unwin]

14. See Hans Kohn, *Pan-Slavism: Its History and Ideology* (Notre Dame: University of Notre Dame Press, 1953), chap. 3: "Pan-Slavism and the World Wars 1905–1950."

15. General Gundorov's report to the Belgrade Slav Congress, in *Slovanský Sjezd v Bělehradě r. 1946* (Prague: Orbis, 1947), 122.

16. Kohn, *Pan-Slavism,* 234.

17. Milan Hodža, Memorandum to the U.S. State Department, "Europe at the Crossroads," in the *Bulletin* of the International Peasant Union (January-February 1954), 14–18. For Hodža's views on federation, see his wartime book, *Federation in Central Europe: Reflections and Reminiscences* (London: Jarrolds, 1942).

18. Hubert Ripka, *East and West* (London: Lincoln-Prager), 57, 59–60.

19. A.J.P. Taylor, *The Course of German History* (New York: Coward-McCann, 1946), 9. [Hamish Hamilton]

11 Churchill's Bargain

1. *The Memoirs of Cordell Hull* (New York: Macmillan, 1948), 1436. [Hodder & Stoughton]

2. Nicholas Kállay, *Hungarian Premier: A Personal Account of a Nation's Struggle in the Second World War* (New York: Columbia University Press, 1954), 381–82. [Oxford University Press]

3. Winston S. Churchill, *The Second World War: Triumph and Tragedy* (Boston: Houghton Mifflin, 1953), 73, 74, 78. [Cassell]

4. Ibid., 148.

5. Ibid., 227.

6. Ibid., 73–81 *passim*; see also *The Memoirs of Cordell Hull,* 1452–59 *passim.*

7. Churchill, *Triumph and Tragedy,* 89.

8. C. A. Macartney, *A History of Hungary: 1929–1945,* I (New York: Praeger, [1957]), 3.

9. Churchill, *Triumph and Tragedy,* 208.

10. Ibid., 227.

11. Ibid., 240–41.

12. Edward R. Stettinius, Jr., *Roosevelt and the Russians: The Yalta Conference* (New York: Doubleday, 1949), 23.

12 Yalta: Hopes and Lessons

1. Winston S. Churchill, *The Second World War: Triumph and Tragedy* (Boston: Houghton Mifflin, 1953), 278–79. [Cassell]

2. Ibid., 337, 341.

3. Edward R. Stettinius, Jr., *Roosevelt and the Russians: The Yalta Conference* (New York: Doubleday, 1949), 68.

4. Ibid., 36.

5. Churchill, *Triumph and Tragedy,* 365.

6. Ibid., 420.

7. Ibid., 353; see also Philip E. Mosley, "Hopes and Failures: American Policy Toward East Central Europe, 1941–1947," in *The Fate of East Central Europe,* ed. Stephen D. Kertesz (Notre Dame: University of Notre Dame Press, 1956), 54ff.

8. See below, Chapter 13, "Stalin's Triumph."

9. See below, Chapter 15, "Beneš and the Russians."

10. Henry Steele Commager, "Concessions to Reality — Was Yalta a Calamity? A Debate," *New York Times Magazine* (August 3, 1952), 48.

11. Karl Mundt, speaking on the NBC television program "The American Forum," on March 27, 1955.

12. Elliot Roosevelt, *As He Saw It* (New York: Duell, Sloan & Pearce, 1946), XVIII.

13. Rexford G. Tugwell, *The Democratic Roosevelt: A Biography of Franklin D. Roosevelt* (New York: Doubleday, 1957), 679.

14. Chester Wilmot, *The Struggle for Europe* (New York: Harper, 1952), 640. [Collins]

15. Arthur Schlesinger, Jr., "Wilmot's War, or 'Churchill was Right,'" *The Reporter* (April 29, 1952), 37.

16. Winston S. Churchill, *The Second World War: Closing the Ring* (Boston: Houghton Mifflin, 1951), 344. [Cassell]

17. Ibid., 346.

18. Ibid., 368; concerning Churchill's "volatile" views on Russia, see Herbert Feis, *Churchill, Roosevelt, Stalin* (Princeton: Princeton University Press, 1957), 468–69. [Oxford University Press]

19. Churchill, *Triumph and Tragedy,* 148; see above, Chapter 11, "Churchill's Bargain."

20. See below, Chapter 13, "Stalin's Triumph."

21. Churchill, *Triumph and Tragedy,* 233.

22. Stettinius, *Roosevelt and the Russians,* 300–01.

23. George F. Kennan, *American Diplomacy: 1900–1950* (Chicago: The University of Chicago Press, 1951), 85.

24. Hanson W. Baldwin, *Great Mistakes of the War* (New York: Harper, 1949), 10. [Alvin Redman]

25. Hajo Holborn, "American Foreign Policy and European Integration," *World Politics,* VI, 1 (October 1953), 5–6; idem, *The Political Collapse of Europe* (New York: Knopf, 1951), 176.

26. Paul-Henri Spaak, "Creating a New Europe — 'It Must Be Done,'" *New York Times Magazine* (April 20, 1952), 12.

27. Hugh Seton-Watson, *The East European Revolution* (New York: Praeger, 1951), 166. [Methuen]

28. Wallace Carroll, *Persuade or Perish* (Boston: Houghton Mifflin, 1948), 373.

13 Stalin's Triumph

1. I. Deutscher, *Stalin: A Political Biography* (New York and London: Oxford University Press, 1949), 536–37.

2. Hugh Seton-Watson, *The East European Revolution* (New York: Praeger, 1951), 169–71 [Methuen]; idem, *From Lenin to Malenkov: The History of World Communism* (New York: Praeger, 1953), 248–49.

3. H. R. Trevor-Roper, "The Politburo Tries a New Tack," *New York Times Magazine* (October 19, 1947), 67.

4. Philip E. Mosely, *Face to Face with Russia* (New York: Foreign Policy Association, Headline Series, No. 70, 1948), 23.

5. Edward R. Stettinius, Jr., *Roosevelt and the Russians: The Yalta Conference* (New York: Doubleday, 1949), 232.

6. On Beneš's dealings with the Soviets, motivated by "self-righteous and narrow-minded nationalism," see the documented article by Vojtech Mastny, "The Beneš-Stalin-Molotov Conversations in December 1943: New Documents," *Jahrbücher für Geschichte Osteuropas,* XX, 3 (1972), 367–402.

7. King Peter II of Yugoslavia, *A King's Heritage* (New York: Putnam, 1954), 272. [Cassell]

8. Winston S. Churchill, *The Second World War: Triumph and Tragedy* (Boston: Houghton Mifflin, 1953), 420–21, 422. [Cassell]

9. Ibid., 423.

10. Ibid., 425.

11. Ibid., 446–54 *passim.*

12. Robert E. Sherwood, *Roosevelt and Hopkins* (New York: Harper, 1948), 900, 905–06. [Eyre & Spottiswoode]

13. Edward J. Rozek, *Allied Wartime Diplomacy: A Pattern in Poland* (New York: Wiley, 1958), 387, 390. Cf. Churchill, *Triumph and Tragedy,* 583.

14. Churchill, *Triumph and Tragedy,* 503.

15. Ibid., 426, 432, 456–57 *passim,* 501–03 *passim,* 573.

16. Ibid., 571, 573, 601, 603.

17. Ibid., 569–70.

18. Ibid., 672.

19. Ibid., 455.

14 From Potsdam to Prague

1. James F. Byrnes, *Speaking Frankly* (New York: Harper, 1947), 68, 71. [Heinemann]

2. Winston S. Churchill, *The Second World War: Triumph and Tragedy* (Boston: Houghton Mifflin, 1953), 636, 665. [Cassell]

3. Ibid., 654.

4. Cf. Byrnes, *Speaking Frankly,* 100–01, 105.

5. Sumner Welles, *Seven Decisions That Shaped History* (New York: Harper, 1950), 208. [Hamish Hamilton]

6. Hugh Seton-Watson, *The East European Revolution* (New York: Praeger, 1951), 170. [Methuen]

7. Ibid., 183–84.

8. John C. Campbell, "The European Territorial Settlement," *Foreign Affairs,* XXVI, 1 (October 1947), 213–14.

9. See the opinion of Zbyněk Zeman, *The Masaryks: The Making of Czechoslovakia* (New York: Harper & Row, 1976), 213: "There was no need for assassins to disturb the peace of the ancient cavernous palace in which Masaryk spent his last night. He knew, as well as his adversaries did, that his life was at an end. . . ." This refutation of the assassination theory, like my own, did not disturb the myth makers. They felt fortified by the investigation ordered of the circumstances of Masaryk's death by the Dubček regime but stopped by the Russians following their invasion of Czechoslovakia in 1968. The suicide version was corroborated by a British government paper made public in January 1979. It described Masaryk on the eve of his death, in a report by the British Ambassador to Prague, as a broken man, despondent, bitter over the bankruptcy of Czechoslovakia's Soviet orientation.

10. Seton-Watson, *The East European Revolution,* 190.

11. Hubert Ripka, *Czechoslovakia Enslaved: The Story of the Communist Coup d'État* (London: Gollancz, 1950), 11.

12. Cf. Hamilton Fish Armstrong, *Tito and Goliath* (New York: Macmillan, 1951), 53–56, 173. [Gollancz]

13. Quoted in Otto Friedman, *The Break-up of Czech Democracy* (London: Gollancz, 1950), 97.

14. Ripka, *Czechoslovakia Enslaved,* 10–11.

15 Beneš and the Russians

1. Eduard Beneš, *Paměti: Od Mníchova k nové válce a k novému vítězství* (Prague: Orbis, 1948), 213ff.

2. See above, Chapter 9, "Federalist Failures."

3. Beneš, *Paměti,* 357.

4. Ibid., 303.

5. Otto Friedman, *The Break-up of Czech Democracy* (London: Gollancz, 1950), 22.

6. Cf. Eduard Beneš, *Nová slovanská politika* (Prague: Orbis, 1946).

7. Friedman, *The Break-up of Czech Democracy,* 24.

8. Beneš, *Paměti,* 362ff.

9. Hans Kohn, *The Twentieth Century: A Midway Account of the Western World* (New York: Macmillan, 1949), 212. [Gollanz]

10. Edward Táborský, "Beneš and the Soviets," *Foreign Affairs,* XXVII, 2 (January 1949), 311.

11. Beneš, *Paměti,* 395–96.

12. Táborský, "Beneš and the Soviets," 310.

13. R. W. Seton-Watson, *Masaryk in England* (Cambridge: Cambridge University Press, 1943), 133; and T. G. Masaryk, *Nová Evropa: Stanovisko slovanské* (Prague: 1920), 143.

14. Ibid., 144.

15. Cf. *Documents on the Expulsion of the Sudeten Germans* (Munich: University Press, 1953); *Hungary and the Conference of Paris,* II and IV (Budapest: Hungarian Ministry of Foreign Affairs, 1947); *The Deportation of the Hungarians of Slovakia* (Budapest: Hungarian Society of Foreign Affairs, 1947); Istvan D. Kertesz, "Minority Population Exchanges: Czechoslovakia and Hungary," *American Perspective* (June 1948), 138–44. For a pro-Slav interpretation of the eviction of the Germans, see Elizabeth Wiskemann, *Germany's Eastern Neighbours: Problems Relating to the Oder-Neisse Line and the Czech Frontier Regions* (London: Oxford University Press, 1956).

16. F. A. Voigt, "'Orderly and Humane,'" *Nineteenth Century and After,* DCCCXXV (November 1945), 200–01.

17. Oscar Jászi, "Danubia: Old and New," reprinted from *Proceedings of the American Philosophical Society,* XCIII, 1 (April 1949), 14.

18. Oscar Jászi, "The Significance of Thomas G. Masaryk for the Future,"

reprinted from *Journal of Central European Affairs,* X, 1 (April 1950), 7. Furthermore it should be noted that pre-World War I Hungary's sins against the national minorities were of a very different kind (and much less grave) than those of post-World War II Czechoslovakia. Hungary tried to become a homogeneous nation-state by means of assimilation, while Czechoslovakia chose to attain the same end by expelling the minorities. In view of these differences, the double standard in judging the Czech and Hungarian sins of nationalism, as noted by Jászi, becomes even more striking.

19. Cf. Táborský, "Beneš and the Soviets," 306, 314.

20. Friedman, *The Break-up of Czech Democracy,* 103; cf. also Vaclav E. Mares, "Could the Czechs Have Remained Free?," *Current History* (September 1952), 154.

21. Czech exiles, attempting to vindicate Beneš's Russian policy, have considerably played up Beneš's doubts about Stalin. See for instance Edward Táborský, "The Triumph and Disaster of Eduard Beneš," *Foreign Affairs,* XXXVI, 4 (July 1958), 675, 681.

22. Cf. R. W. Seton-Watson, *Masaryk in England,* 126–27.

Epilogue One: The Unfinished Struggle for Independence

1. Milovan Djilas, *The New Class: An Analysis of the Communist System* (New York: Praeger, 1957), 35, 38, 70. [Thames & Hudson]

2. Apologetic explanations of Czech passivity were offered by Czech exiles. According to one such interpretation, the Czechs, as people with democratic traditions, "may rationalize themselves into any compromise and away from the barricades." Furthermore, the Czechs "know the West," therefore they knew that they cannot expect help from the West. See Ivo Duchacek, "A 'Loyal' Satellite: The Case of Czechoslovakia," *Annals of the American Academy of Political and Social Science,* CCCXVII (May 1958), 116–17.

3. *Imre Nagy on Communism: In Defense of the New Course* (New York: Praeger, 1957), 63, 244. [Thames & Hudson]

4. See above, Chapter 14, "From Potsdam to Prague."

5. *Imre Nagy on Communism,* 40, 64.

6. For an interpretation giving full justice to the democratic aspirations of the Hungarian Revolution see François Fejtő, *Behind the Rape of Hungary* (New York: McKay, 1957); Bill Lomax, *Hungary 1956* (New York: St. Martin's Press, 1976). [Allison & Busby]

7. In contrast with its impotence in the field of action, the United Nations did splendid research work in providing information on the Hungarian Revolution. See *Report of the Special Committee on the Problem of Hungary,* General Assembly — Official Records: Eleventh Session — Supplement No. 18 (A-3592) (New York: Columbia University Press, 1957).

8. Max Beloff's letter to the *New York Times,* November 18, 1958.

9. Cf. Raymond Aron, "Second Thoughts on Suez," *The New Leader* (January 28, 1957), 19.

10. "East Wind, West Wind," *The Economist* (November 30, 1957), 752. More recently, George F. Kennan somewhat revised his disengagement views, envisaging as an immediate task "the definition of Germany's supra-national obligations within the European community as an integral part of any initial agreement on German unification and disengagement of Europe." It is possible, he wrote, that "such problems as the formulation of a general European security pact, the future scope of the institutions of the European community, and probably even the bitter question of Germany's eastern border, may have to be faced simultaneously with the first steps towards a general disengagement." This view — unlike the idea of disengagement itself — found, unfortunately, no echo in Western public opinion, although the integration of Germany into the European community (the "European" or "federalistic" solution, as I call it below) may well be the key to solving the East-West conflict by peaceful means. See George F. Kennan, "Disengagement Revisited," *Foreign Affairs,* XXXVII, 2 (January 1959), 197–98. Also, for a forceful endorsement of European federation, as a solution of the German problem as well as the East-West conflict, see Eugene V. Rostow, "Negotiating a Berlin Settlement: A 'European' Approach to Germany," *The New Republic,* CXL, 8 (February 23, 1959), 16–18.

11. The Iron Curtain had blotted out the West's perception of the problem of Hungary's dismemberment, which in the inter-war period was one of the great issues of European politics. By contrast, national minority problems of much lesser magnitude — those of Cyprus or Tyrol, for instance — commanded world attention: to say nothing of German national reunification, which was permanently on the agenda of international politics. For detailed ethnic statistics of post-World War II Central and Eastern Europe, see "Satellite Demography," *News from Behind the Iron Curtain,* IV, 2 (February 1955), 27ff; and III (March 1958), 25ff; also István Révay, "Hungarian Minorities Under Communist Rule," in *Facts About Hungary,* comp. Imre Kovács (New York: Hungarian Committee, 1958), 240–41.

12. Cf. Palacký's letter to the Frankfurt Parliament of 1848, as quoted in Hans Kohn, *Pan-Slavism: Its History and Ideology* (Notre Dame: University of Notre Dame Press, 1953), 67.

13. Oscar Jászi, "Danubia: Old and New," reprinted from *Proceedings of the American Philosophical Society,* XCIII, 1 (April 1949), 26–27.

14. "The Failure of the Habsburg Monarchy," *The Times Literary Supplement* (April 27, 1951). A review of Robert A. Kann's book *The Multinational Empire.*

Epilogue Two: Cold War Becomes Détente

1. With reference to Eastern Europe, all revisionists share a common point of view as summed up by Charles S. Maier: ". . . there was no legitimacy for any American concern with affairs in that distant region. However ugly the results in Eastern Europe, they should not really have worried Washington. Russia should

have been willingly accorded unchallenged primacy because of her massive wartime sacrifices, her need for territorial security, and the long history of the area's reactionary politics and bitter anti-bolshevism. Only when Moscow's deserved primacy was contested did Stalin embark upon a search for exclusive control." Charles S. Maier, "Revisionism and the Interpretation of Cold War Origins," *Perspectives in American History,* IV (1970), 317.

2. John C. Campbell, *American Policy Toward Communist Eastern Europe* (Minneapolis: The University of Minnesota Press, 1965), 3.

3. For an outspokenly critical evaluation of American policy toward the Soviet satellites, see Bennett Kovrig, *The Myth of Liberation: East-Central Europe in U.S. Diplomacy and Politics Since 1941* (Baltimore and London: The Johns Hopkins University Press, 1973).

4. Zbigniew Brzezinski and William E. Griffith, "Peaceful Engagement in Eastern Europe," *Foreign Affairs,* XXXIX, 4 (July 1961), 642–54. Cf. Kovrig, *The Myth of Liberation,* 238–39, 252–53. As a result of détente, the Brzezinski-Griffith article envisaged the emergence ultimately of a "neutral belt of states" in the Middle Zone which, "like the Finnish, would enjoy genuine popular freedom of choice in internal policy while not being hostile to the Soviet Union and not belonging to Western military alliance." The Johnson speech was less visionary; it appealed in fact to the "powerful forces of national pride" of the East Europeans, forces which were not likely to generate among East Europeans the kind of cooperation needed for the creation of a neutral belt of states. Before his joint article with Griffith, Brzezinski had published another discussion related to the same subject in the April 1961 issue of *Foreign Affairs,* "The Challenge of Change in the Soviet Bloc."

5. For a point of view, relating the anti-Communist cold war attitude toward Eastern Europe to the Vietnam War and Watergate, see Daniel Yergen, *Shattered Peace: The Origins of the Cold War and the National Security State* (Boston: Houghton Mifflin, 1977). Characteristically, unlike the much praised Yergen book, another recent work by a highly qualified expert, treating cold war origins in their own historical settings, has passed almost unnoticed: Vojtech Mastny, *Russia's Road to the Cold War* (New York: Columbia University Press, 1979).

6. Henry A. Kissinger, "Political Multipolarity: The Changed Nature of Alliances," *American Foreign Policy* (New York: W. W. Norton, 1969), 73, 76.

7. Official text of a Soviet-French declaration, issued in English by Tass, the Soviet press agency, *The New York Times,* July 1, 1966.

8. Nikolai I. Bukharin's phrase, as quoted in Hamilton Fish Armstrong, *Peace and Counterpeace* (New York and London: Harper & Row, 1971), 419.

9. Cf. Edward Crankshaw, *The New Cold War: Moscow vs. Peking* (Penguin Books, 1963).

10. For an interpretation of the Romanian "break-through" as a move toward "Communist neutralism," see Ghita Ionescu, *The Break-up of the Soviet Empire in Eastern Europe* (Penguin Books, 1965), 133ff.

11. Cf. Constantin C. Guirescu, *The Making of the Romanian National Unitary State* (Bucharest: Meridiane Publishing House, 1975).

12. Awareness abroad of the Hungarians' plight under Romanian rule owes a great deal to the publicity a Communist protest has received in the world press; see Károly Király, "An Ethnic-Hungarian Communist in Rumania Complains to His Party About Bias," *The New York Times*, February 1, 1978. Cf. George Schöpflin, *The Hungarians of Rumania* (London: Minority Right Group Report No. 37, August 1978); "Ethnic Discrimination and Persecution: Hungarian Prisoners of Conscience in Romania," in *Romania* (New York: An Amnesty International USA Publication, 1978), 39–42.

13. Ivan Volgyes, "Limited Liberalization in Hungary," *Current History*, LXX, 414 (March 1976), 107; Manuel Lucbert, "Hungary's Consumer Economy: A Model of Pragmatic Socialism?" (Translated from *Le Monde*, December 15, 16, 1978), *Manchester Guardian Weekly* (December 17, 1978), 10. Favorable prospects of democratization in Hungary were anticipated by Zbigniew Brzezinski, "Eastern Europe: Tendencies and Prospects," in *The People's Democracies after Prague*, ed. Jerzy Lukaszewski (Bruges: De Tempel, 1970), 307.

14. Cf. Peter Osnos, "The Polish Road to Communism," *Foreign Affairs*, LVI, 1 (October 1977), 209, 216–20.

15. On whether the Prague Spring should be called a "revolution," see H. Gordon Skilling, *Czechoslovakia's Interrupted Revolution* (Princeton: Princeton University Press, 1976), 827–36. On Dubček's role: William Shawcross, *Dubček* (New York: Simon and Schuster, 1970), 100, 143, 165.

16. Robin Alison Remington, ed., *Winter in Prague: Documents on Czechoslovak Communism in Crisis* (Cambridge, Mass. and London: The MIT Press, 1969), 88–136.

17. Cf. Stephen Borsody, "Imre Nagy and Eurocommunism," in *The Hungarian Revolution of 1956 in Retrospect*, eds. Béla K. Király and Paul Jónás (Boulder, Colo.: East European Monographs, 1978), 127–34.

18. Remington, *Winter in Prague*, 97.

19. The difference between the Czech and Slovak situations in post-invasion Czechoslovakia was poignantly described by one of the leading Czech reform-Communists, Jiří Hájek: "The Slovaks do not have a national cause to feel that their hopes were frustrated as the Czechs do." Quoted in Vladimir V. Kusin, *From Dubček to Charter 77* (New York: St. Martin's Press, 1978), 310. [Peter Chiene] For a Slovak separatist reaction abroad, see Joseph A. Mikus, *Slovakia and the Slovaks* (Washington: Three Continent Press, 1977), 57–58.

20. Kálmán Janics, "Czechoslovakia's Magyar Minority," *Canadian Review of Studies in Nationalism*, III, 1 (February 1975), 34–44. On the Hungarian minorities in general, Stephen Borsody, "Hungary at the U.N.: The Red Badge of Courage," *The New York Times*, March 15, 1977.

21. Jiří Pelikán, *Socialist Opposition in Eastern Europe: The Czechoslovak Example* (New York: St. Martin's Press, 1976). [Palach, 1975] On the "strategy"

of opposition in Poland, Czechoslovakia and Hungary, see chapters by Jiří Pelikán, "Réforme ou révolution," and by Adam Michnik, "Le nouvel évolutionnisme," in *1956: Varsovie-Budapest. La deuxième révolution d'Octobre,* eds. Pierre Kende and Krzysztof Pomian (Paris: Éditions du Seuil, 1978), 201–229.

22. *Frankfurter Rundschau,* October 7, 1974, as quoted in *German Press Review* (Washington, D.C.), October 16, 1974.

23. Official English version of the Helsinki Declaration, *The New York Times,* July 30, 1975.

24. Unofficial translation of Leonid Brezhnev's speech before the Helsinki conference, July 31, 1975, as reported by Reuters, in *The New York Times,* August 1, 1975.

25. Speech by Secretary of State Kissinger on August 14, 1975, as released by the State Department, *The New York Times,* August 15, 1975.

26. Maurice Cranston, "The Meaning of Détente," *Survey* (London), XXII, 3/4 (1976), 41.

27. Official State Department summary of remarks made in December 1975 by Helmut Sonnenfeldt at a London meeting of American ambassadors in Europe, *The New York Times,* April 6, 1976.

28. Text of "Charter 77," based on a translation in the *New Leader,* January 31, 1977.

29. Malcolm W. Brown, "Silent Fall," *The New York Times Magazine,* October 23, 1977.

30. Hugh Seton-Watson, *The "Sick Heart" of Modern Europe: The Problem of the Danubian Lands* (Seattle and London: The University of Washington Press, 1975), 74.

31. Czech Communist exiles after Czechoslovakia's Soviet invasion in 1968 testified that the Communist takeover in February 1948 had actually been a Soviet takeover. A special Soviet security group took control of the Czechoslovak Ministry of Interior and within a few months every member of the government and party leadership became dependent on these "advisers." Eugen Loebel, "The Lessons of 'The Confession,'" *The New York Times,* February 20, 1971.

32. Owen Latimore, "Notes on Mongolia at 50," *The New York Times,* November 25, 1974.

33. Jean Kanapa, "A 'New Policy' of the French Communists," *Foreign Affairs,* LV, 2 (October 1976), 292.

34. Richard Löwenthal, "Can Communism Offer an Alternative World Order?," *Encounter* (April 1977), 25.

35. Oscar Jászi, "Dismembered Hungary and Peace in Central Europe," *Foreign Affairs,* II, 2 (December 1923), 250.

36. Jean-François Revel, "The Myths of Eurocommunism," *Foreign Affairs,* LVI, 2 (January 1978), 305. For a comprehensive discussion of Western European Communist attitudes toward European integration, see François Fejtő,

L'héritage de Lénine (Paris: Le Livre de Poche, 1977), Chapter VIII, "L'eurocommunisme: mythe ou réalité?"

37. According to Leonard Schapiro, Western Eurocommunism "can give succour to popular centres of resistance" in Eastern Europe, "but the ability of non-party groups to act upon their feelings is limited." Also, according to Schapiro, a united "Socialist" Europe would be an "overwhelming threat" to the Soviets; however, a united anti-Soviet Communist-Socialist Europe is a "remote possibility," "highly unlikely." Quoted in Roy Godson and Stephen Haseler, *'Eurocommunism': Implications for East and West* (New York: St. Martin's Press, 1978), 103–04, 122–24. For a less guarded evaluation of Western Eurocommunism's positive impact on Eastern Europe, see Charles Gati, "The 'Europeanization' of Communism?" *Foreign Affairs,* LV, 3 (April 1977), 544, 547; Edward Crankshaw, "Europe's Reds: Trouble for Moscow," *The New York Times Magazine,* February 12, 1978. Raymond Aron, too, encouraged positive speculations in this matter; see his *Plaidoyer pour L'Europe décadente* (Paris: Éditions Robert Laffont, 1977), 114.

38. Since the "centralist coup of December 1971," a decentralization and a genuine federalist reorganization to save Yugoslavia was repeatedly urged by Cyril A. Zebot: Letters, *The New York Times,* September 26, 1972; May 1, 1973; October 14, 1976; June 26, 1977; October 2, 1977; *Washington Post,* May 30, 1977. Tito's way of vindicating his coup was to argue that "Croat chauvinism" threatened to reopen a fratricidal civil war, leading eventually to the break-up of Yugoslavia. The Croat Communists thus accused rejected Tito's charges. According to democratic Yugoslav political exiles, what the Croats really wanted was "to reconstruct Yugoslavia on a confederative basis believing that only by granting the legitimate national and economic demands not only of the Croats but of the Macedonians, Albanians and other nations of Yugoslavia as well could a firm and lasting voluntary union be established. . . ." Letter by Bogdan Raditsa and Matthew Mestrovic, *The New York Times,* December 24, 1971. A reorganization of Yugoslavia's "fourteen historical provinces" on the Swiss Confederation principle was championed by Ante R. K. Jeric, former Chief of the Economic Information Service of Tito's first Commissariat for Trade and Industry, now in exile: Letter, *The New York Times,* January 5, 1972.

39. Max Beloff, reviewing my book, "The Triumph of Tyranny," *The Listener,* (March 10, 1960), 463.

Index